MW01618217

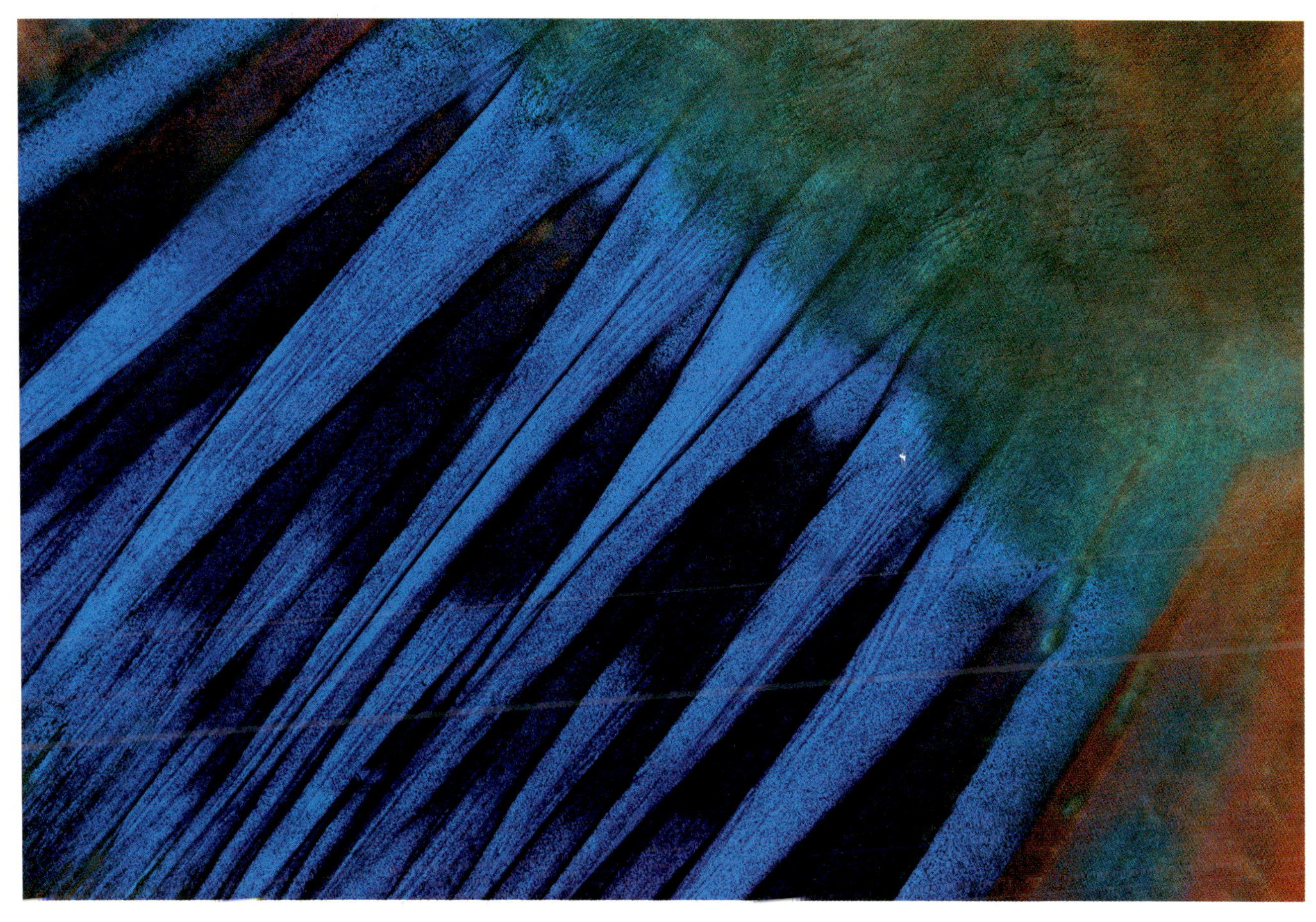

Wildlife Photographer of the Year Portfolio 16

Wildlife Photographer of the Year
Portfolio 16

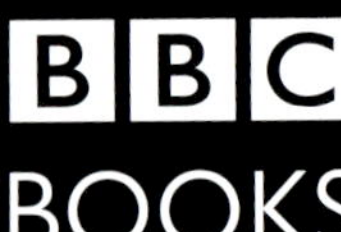

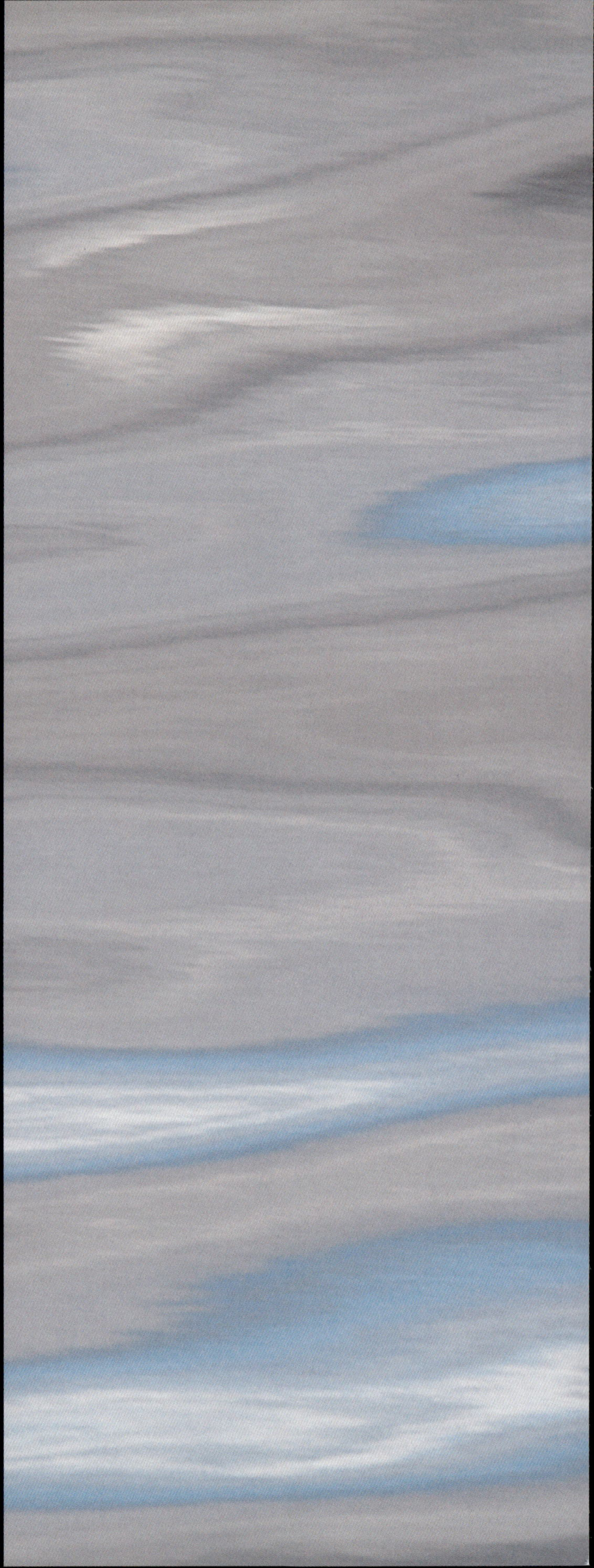

BOOKS

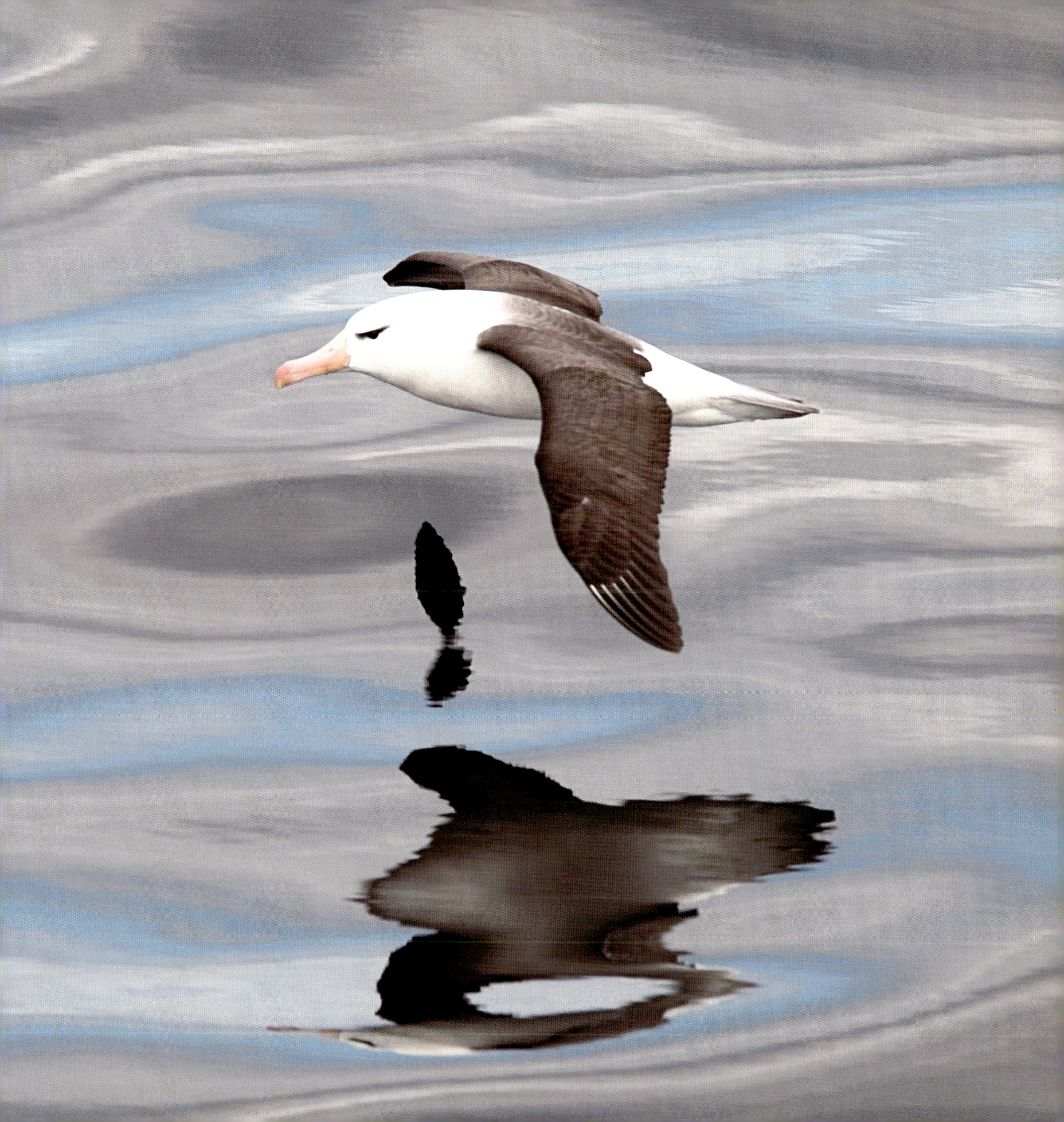

Commissioning Editor
Shirley Patton
Managing Editor
Rosamund Kidman Cox
Designer
Simon Bishop
Caption writer
Rachel Ashton
Production Controller
David Brimble
Competition Manager
Deborah Sage
Competition Officer
Gemma Webster

Published in 2006 by BBC Books, an imprint of Ebury Publishing, which is a division of the Random House Group

The Random House Group Limited Reg. No. 954009

Addresses for companies within the Random House Group can be found at www.randomhouse.co.uk

A CIP catalogue record for this book is available from the British Library

Colour separations by Butler & Tanner Origination
Printed and bound in Great Britain by Butler & Tanner Limited

ISBN 0563493844
ISBN 13 = 9780563493846

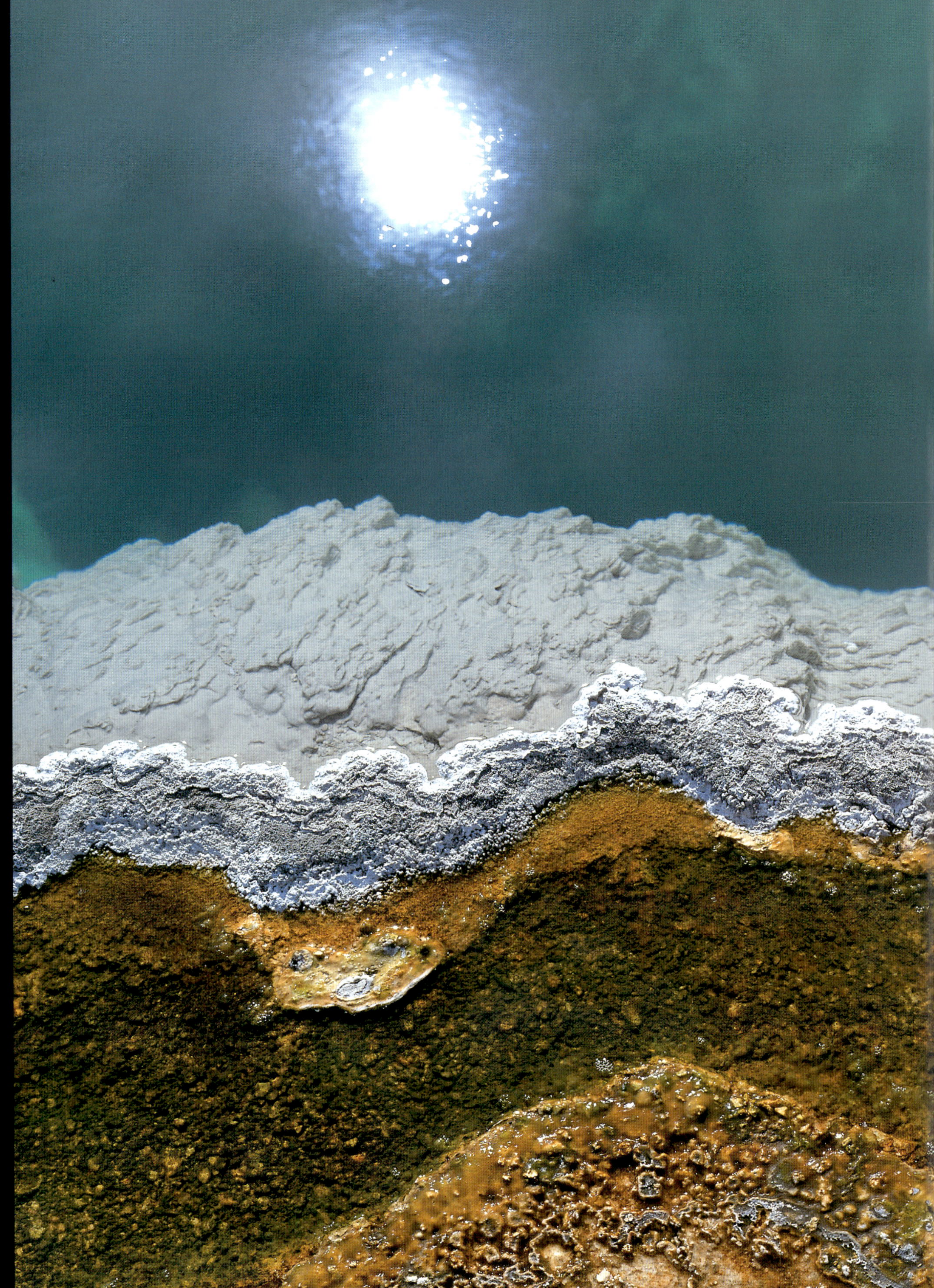

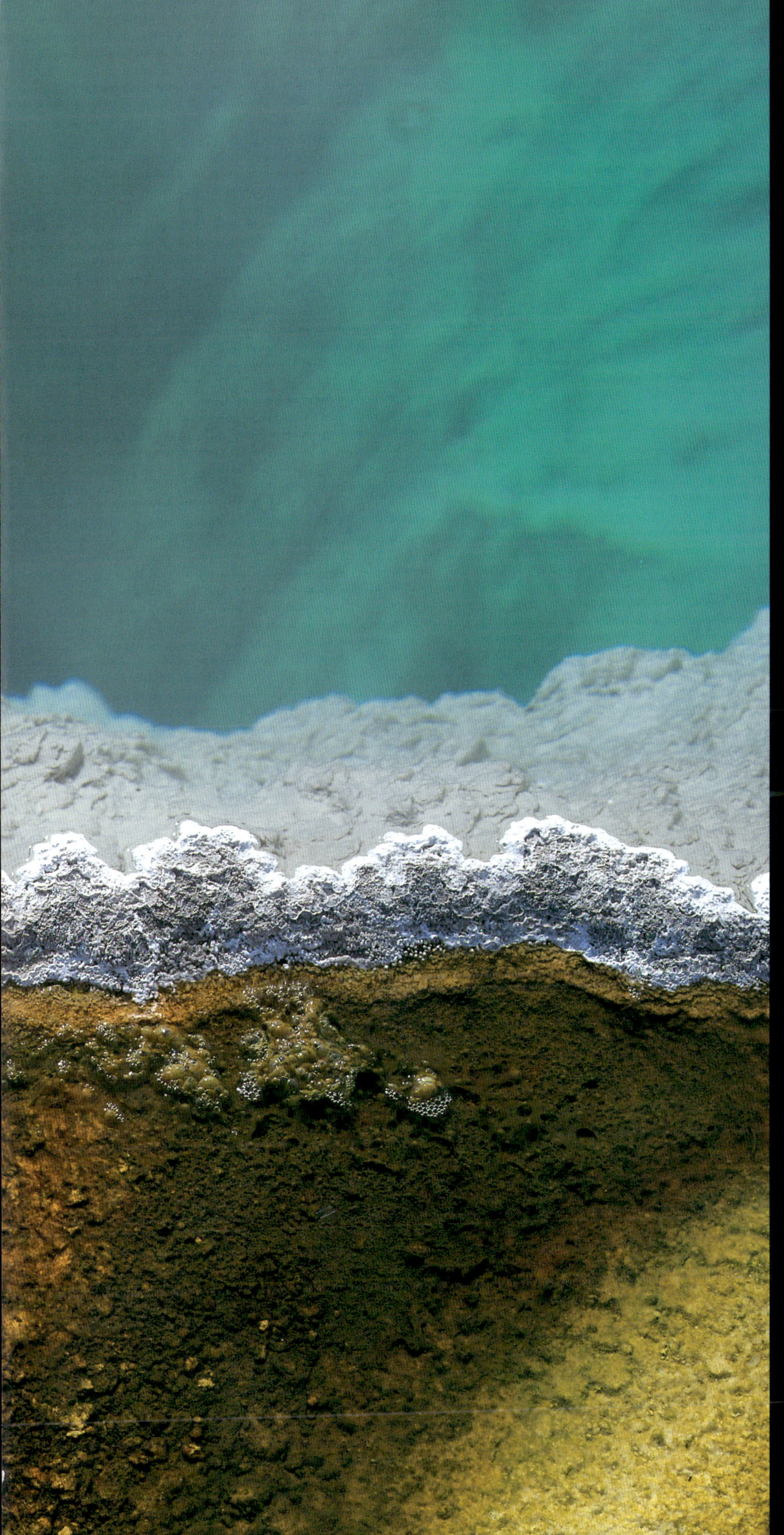

Contents

7 Foreword

8 The Competition

14 The Shell Wildlife Photographer of the Year Award

16 Animal Behaviour – Mammals

20 Animal Behaviour – Birds

32 Behaviour – All Other Animals

38 Animals in Their Environment

52 The Underwater World

62 Animal Portraits

74 In Praise of Plants

80 Urban and Garden Wildlife

86 Creative Visions of Nature

98 Wild Places

108 The World in Our Hands

114 Gerald Durrell Award for Endangered Wildlife

122 Eric Hosking Award

130 Young Wildlife Photographers

156 Index of Photographers

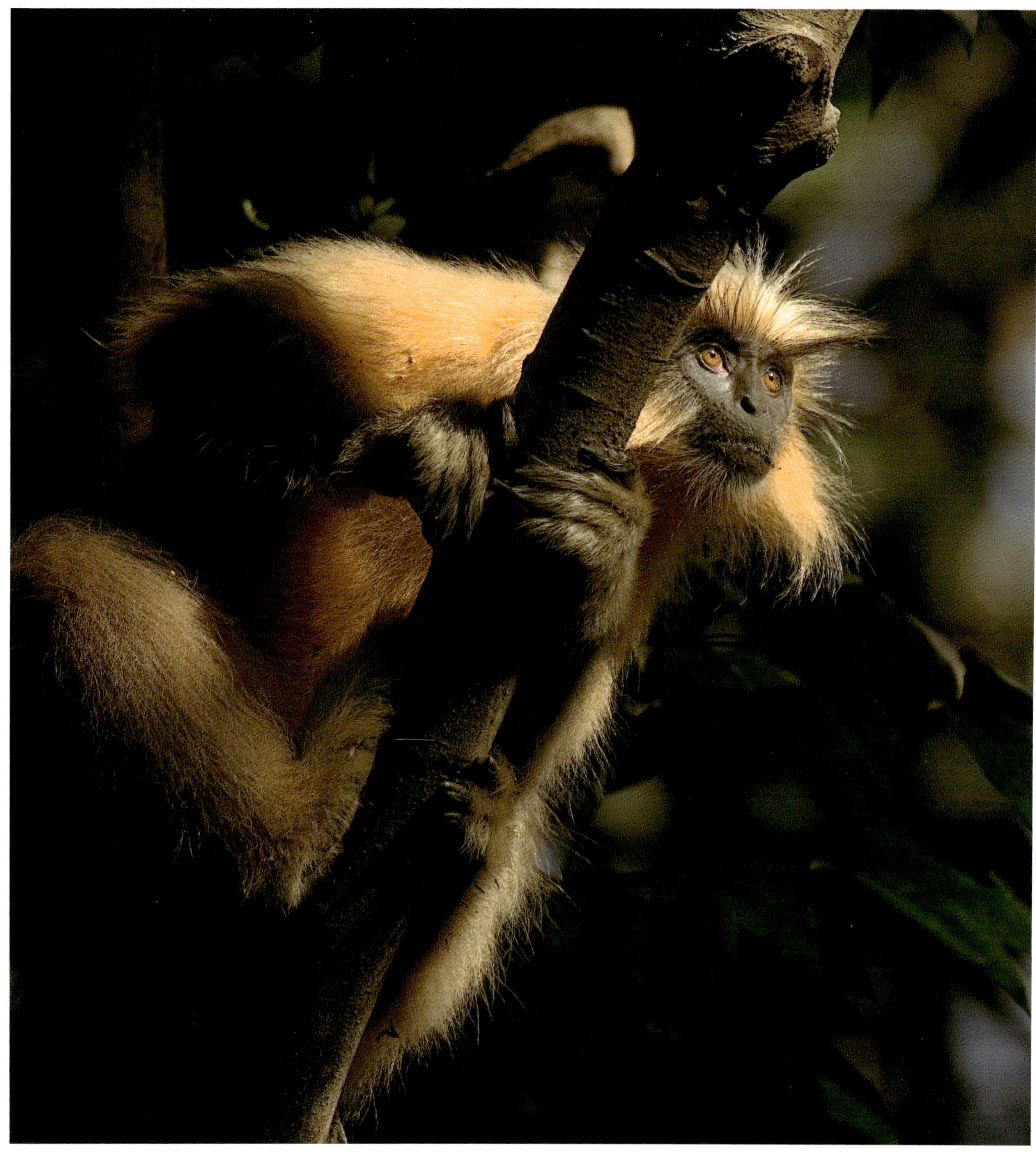

Foreword

A book that celebrates the beauty of the natural world through the work of talented photographers invites reflection on aesthetics. Recent times have, though, brought us painful proof of a rapidly changing planet. Faced with an imminent extinction wave, climate change and civil conflict over diminishing resources, we must reflect instead on the relevance of nature photography.

Can images influence the fate of our planet's natural wonders? The answer is a resounding yes. From the creation of the first national parks in the US to the recent establishment of an entirely new protected area system in Gabon, photography has played a pivotal role in showcasing the beauty and uniqueness of wild places, the frailty and irreplaceability of endangered species and the wonder of indigenous cultures.

In fact, images have always been used as powerful campaign symbols and pictorial calls to action. A photograph created by the late Peter Dombrovskis as an anguished cry for the imminent loss of the mighty Franklin-Gordon River in Tasmania, Australia, became the lightning rod that inspired an entire nation to oppose a project that would have dammed one of our planet's most beautiful wild rivers.

The image worked because it was infused with a sense of purpose. It was crafted with emotion, with urgency, with tears; it was meant to show those who could not see with their own eyes the beauty, the wildness, the incomparable value of what was to be lost.

Photographs are powerful tools to mould perceptions, to call on our principles, to inspire. As photographers, we have a choice to give our work a higher purpose and to invest it with a fundamental value that goes far beyond the mere beauty of an image.

One may argue that many, if not most, beautiful images are achieved in the absence of purpose. I submit to you, however, the idea that photographs born out of concern for the tragic loss of our natural world carry an intrinsic emotional and spiritual weight that is projected onto those who view them.

The magnificent images in this collection will no doubt capture the world's attention. They will find their place in hundreds of publications and will be enjoyed by a million people on computer screens. As they travel, they will become ambassadors for a world that is changing fast. I invite photographers around the world to make it their mission not just to capture beautiful moments but also to produce work that infects others with purpose.

Cristina Goettsch Mittermeier
Executive Director
International League of
Conservation Photographers

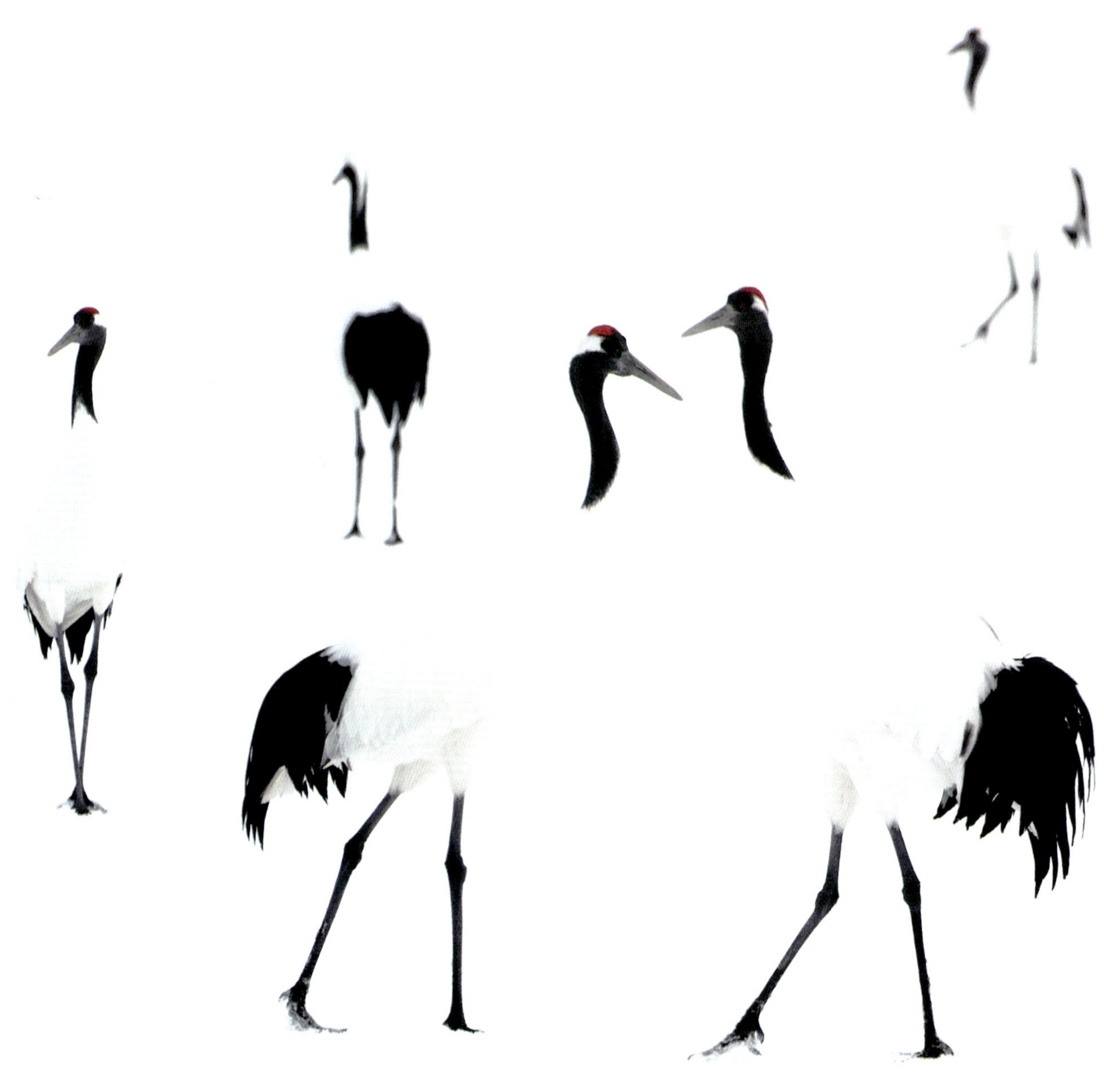

Judges

Laura Barwick
picture researcher

Mark Carwardine
zoologist, writer and photographer

Tim Flach
art and commercial photographer

Rosamund Kidman Cox
editor and writer

Paul Lund
photographer, Natural History Museum

Emilie Marsh
picture editor, Getty Images

Andy Mclane
senior creative partner at Tequila London

Manuel Presti
Wildlife Photographer of the Year 2005

Colin Prior
travel and landscape photographer and author

Rob Sheppard
group editorial director, *Outdoor Photographer*, *PCPhoto*, *Digital Photo Pro* magazines

Wanda Sowry
picture researcher, *BBC Wildlife Magazine*

Sophie Stafford
editor, *BBC Wildlife Magazine*

Staffan Widstrand
photographer and writer

Norbert Wu
underwater photographer and film-maker

The Competition

All the pictures in this book are prize-winning or commended images from one year of the Shell Wildlife Photographer of the Year Competition, which is an international showcase for the very best photography featuring natural subjects. The competition is owned by two UK institutions that pride themselves on revealing and championing the diversity of life on Earth – the Natural History Museum and *BBC Wildlife Magazine*.

Being placed in this competition is something that wildlife photographers, worldwide, aspire to. Professionals win many of the prizes, but amateurs succeed, too. And that's because achieving the perfect picture is down to a mixture of vision, camera literacy, knowledge of nature and luck. And such a mixture doesn't always require an armoury of equipment and global travel, as the pictures by young photographers so often emphasise.

The origins of the competition go back as far as 1964, when the magazine was called *Animals* and there were just three categories and about 600 entries. But even then it was the leading event of its kind for nature photographers. It grew in stature over the years, and in 1984, *BBC Wildlife Magazine* and the Natural History Museum joined forces to create the competition as it is today, with the categories and awards you see in this book.

Now there are between 15,000 and 20,000 entries, a major exhibition at the Natural History Museum and exhibitions touring through the year, not only in the UK but also worldwide, from the US, the Caribbean and South Africa, through Europe and across to China, Japan and Australia. The winning and commended pictures appear in *BBC Wildlife Magazine* and publications worldwide. As a result, the photographs are now seen by millions of people.

The aims of the competition are

- to be the world's most respected forum for wildlife photographic art, showcasing the very best photographic images of nature to a worldwide audience;
- to inspire a new generation of photographic artists to produce visionary and expressive interpretations of nature;
- to use its collection of inspirational photographs to make people worldwide wonder at the splendour, drama and variety of life on Earth;
- to raise the status of wildlife photography into that of mainstream art.

The judges, who change from year to year and represent artists and professionals from other media as well as photography, put aesthetic criteria above all others. But at the same time, they place great emphasis on photographs taken in wild and free conditions, considering that the welfare of the subject is paramount. They are also always looking for pictures with that extra something – creative flair that takes a picture beyond just a representation of nature.

Organisers

The competition is owned by the Natural History Museum, London, and *BBC Wildlife Magazine*, and is sponsored by Shell.

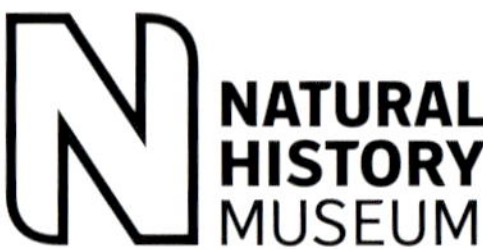

Home to a world-class natural history collection, a leading scientific research institution with ground-breaking projects in 68 countries, and one of London's most beautiful landmarks, the Natural History Museum is also highly regarded for its pioneering approach to exhibitions, welcoming more than three million visitors of all ages and levels of interest.

Shell Wildlife Photographer of the Year is one of the museum's most successful and long-running special exhibitions, and we are proud to have helped make it the most prestigious competition of its kind in the world.

The annual exhibition of award-winning photographs attracts a large audience, which comes not only to admire the striking images, but also to gain an insight into important global concerns such as conservation and biodiversity – issues at the heart of the museum's work.

Through studying the museum's collections, scientists can better understand the enormous variety of life on Earth and the functioning of the global ecosystem. Many of our exhibitions, including Shell Wildlife Photographer of the Year, celebrate the beauty and importance of the natural world and encourage visitors to see the environment around them with new eyes.

Further information

Visit www.nhm.ac.uk for further information about activities. You can also call +44 (0)20 7942 5000, email information@nhm.ac.uk
or write to: Information Enquiries,
The Natural History Museum,
Cromwell Road, London SW7 5BD.

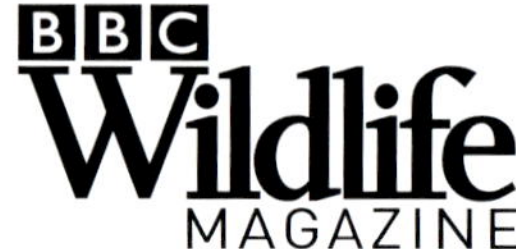

BBC Wildlife Magazine is a celebration of the natural world. It aims to inspire readers with the wonder and beauty of wildlife, and enable them to understand, experience and enjoy nature more.

Every issue is packed with breathtaking images by the world's finest wildlife photographers and informative features on animal behaviour written by top experts. It also includes the latest environmental news from around the world, new insights into British wildlife, biological discoveries, wildlife gardening and practical travel ideas.

BBC Wildlife publishes all the winning images from the Shell Wildlife Photographer of the Year Competition in a special glossy showguide free with the November issue, and works closely with the competition's award-winning photographers to showcase their finest work throughout the year.

It also helps readers to improve their wildlife photography with a unique series of masterclasses led by past winners of the competition and Mark Carwardine, chairman of the judges 2005/6.

BBC Wildlife is essential reading for anyone with a passion for nature and wildlife photography.

Further information

Visit www.bbcwildlifemagazine.com for more information about *BBC Wildlife*, back issues, special offers and reader photos.
You can also email
wildlifemagazine@bbcmagazinesbristol.com
call +44 (0)117 314 8363 or write to *BBC Wildlife*,
14th Floor, Tower House, Fairfax Street, Bristol BS1 3BN.

Subscriptions To get 25% off the shop price of *BBC Wildlife*, call +44 (0)870 444 7013 or email wildlife@galleon.co.uk and quote WPOY06.

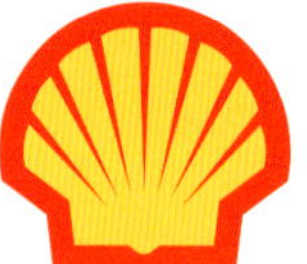

Shell is proud to support the world's largest and longest-running wildlife photography competition.

The Shell Wildlife Photographer of the Year Competition opens our eyes to nature's amazing variety and highlights the importance of supporting global biodiversity.

This is an area of considerable importance to Shell and one to which we are keenly committed through the promotion of knowledge and the support of biodiversity conservation. This responsibility is reflected in our partnerships with, for example, the Smithsonian Institution, the World Conservation Union (IUCN) and the Earthwatch Institute.

We hope you enjoy this book and the wonderful display of biodiversity within it.

James Smith
Chairman
Shell UK

Further information

Please visit www.shell.com/biodiversity

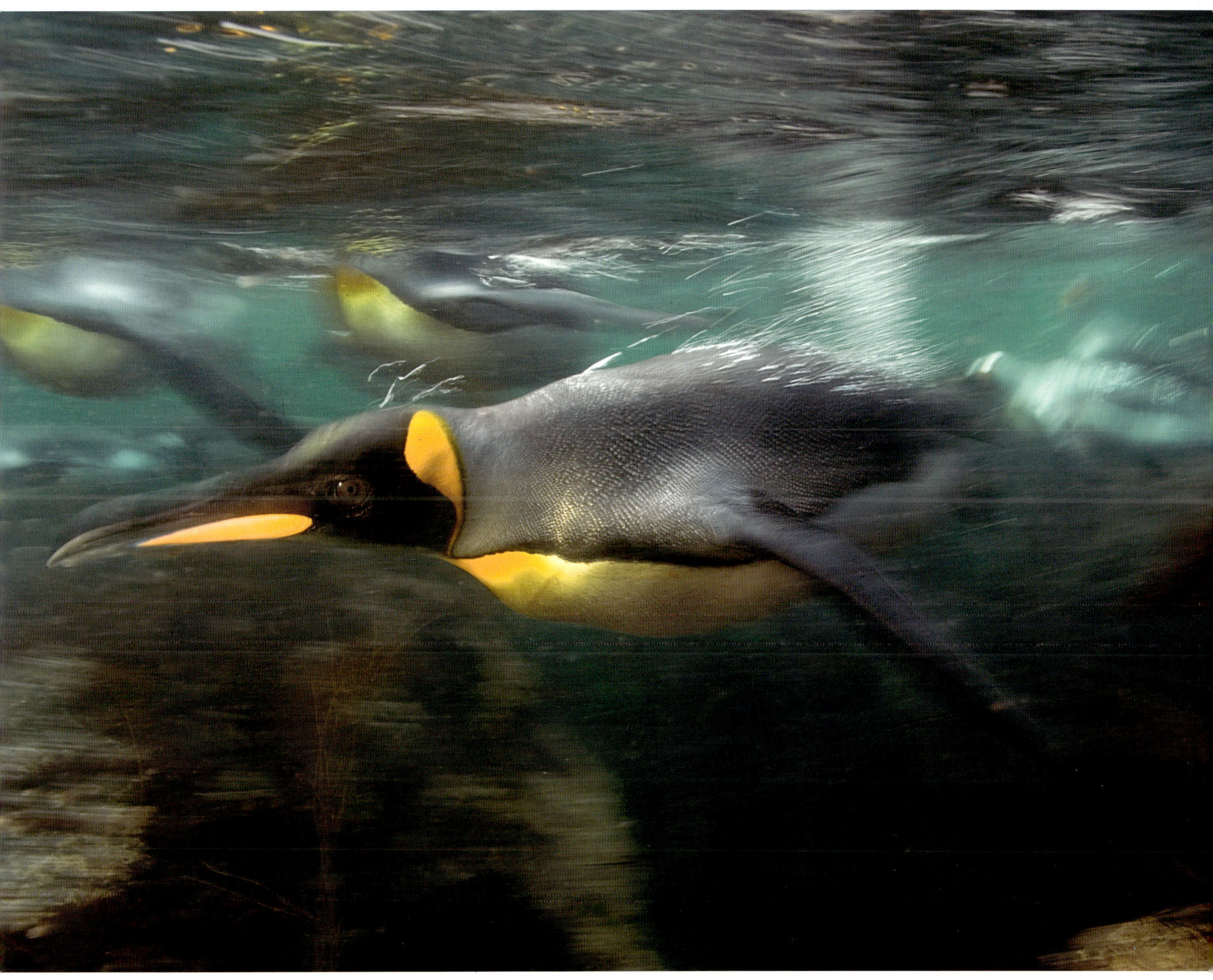

The Shell Wildlife Photographer of the Year Award

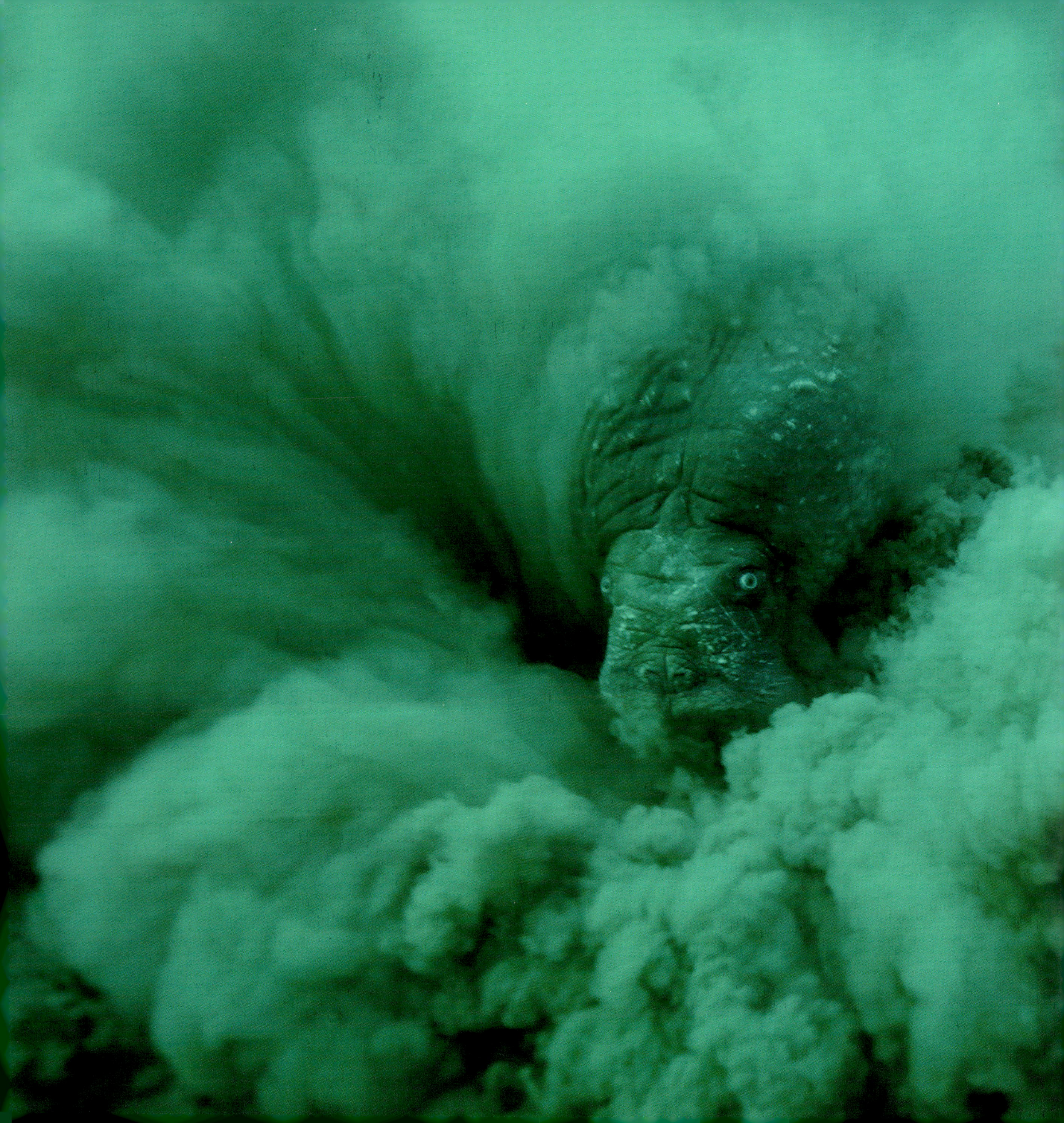

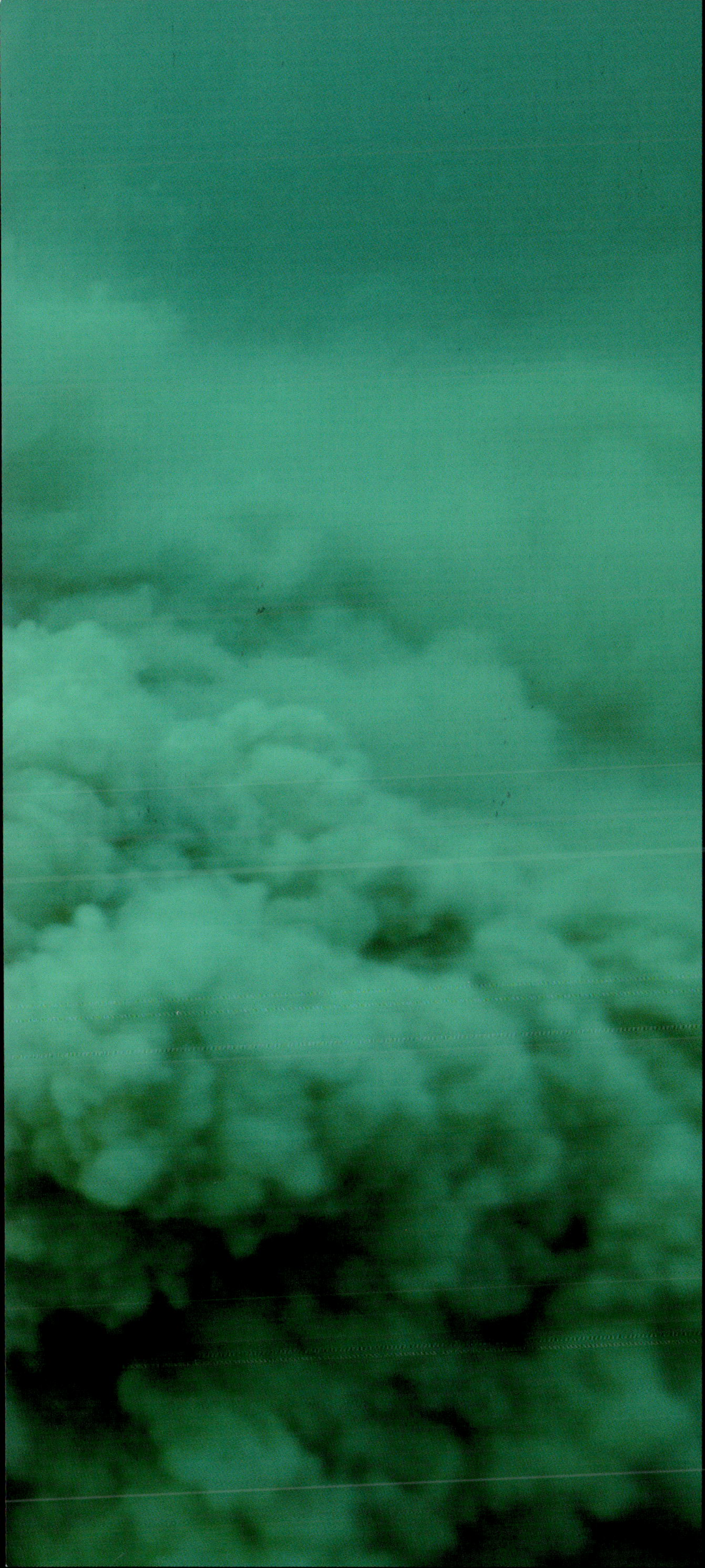

The Shell Wildlife Photographer of the Year Award goes to the photographer whose picture is voted as being the most striking and memorable of all the competition's entries.

Göran Ehlmé

SWEDEN

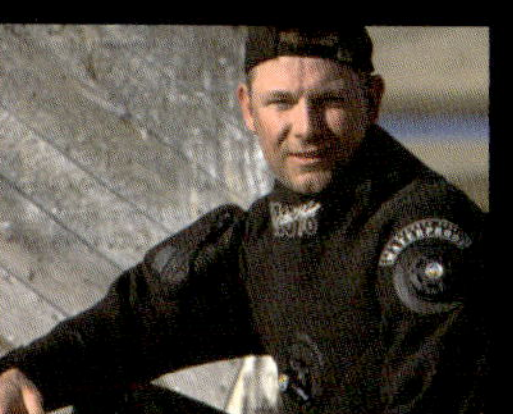

Göran has been diving since 1979 and shooting stills under water since 1984, specializing in freezing conditions and polar species, in particular, walruses, killer whales and leopard seals. Part of his income comes from designing high-quality neoprene drysuits and wetsuits, which he markets through his own company. But he also dives professionally – mainly in the Arctic and Antarctic – for at least two months every year, taking stills and filming. Over the past ten years, he has worked as an underwater cameraman, shooting in the polar regions for a variety of films on killer whales, walruses, narwhals, leopard seals, penguins and polar bears, for productions from *Planet Earth* to *March of the Penguins*. He isn't averse to working in warm waters, though, and has spent four seasons diving in the Azores with sperm whales.

BEAST OF THE SEDIMENT

Like most bottom-feeders, a walrus has messy table manners. Gorging on bivalve shells, it uses its facial bristles to brush away the sediment and then may root, pig-like, with its snout or beat a flipper (most walruses are right-flippered) to whip up the sediment – as is happening here. Swimming with this huge beast off northeast Greenland, Göran took more than 400 images with his new digital camera rather than being limited to 36 before needing to surface to change film (the walrus, though, had to surface for air every 4-5 minutes). Hours later, after shooting from every angle, 'the moment came,' says Göran. 'The walrus looked round as it was about to surface, and we made eye contact.' It took Göran years of studying walrus behaviour to consider diving with them. 'At first I was very nervous,' he says, 'but now I know how to approach them safely and respectfully.'

Animal Behaviour Mammals

The pictures in this category must show action and have interest value as well as aesthetic appeal.

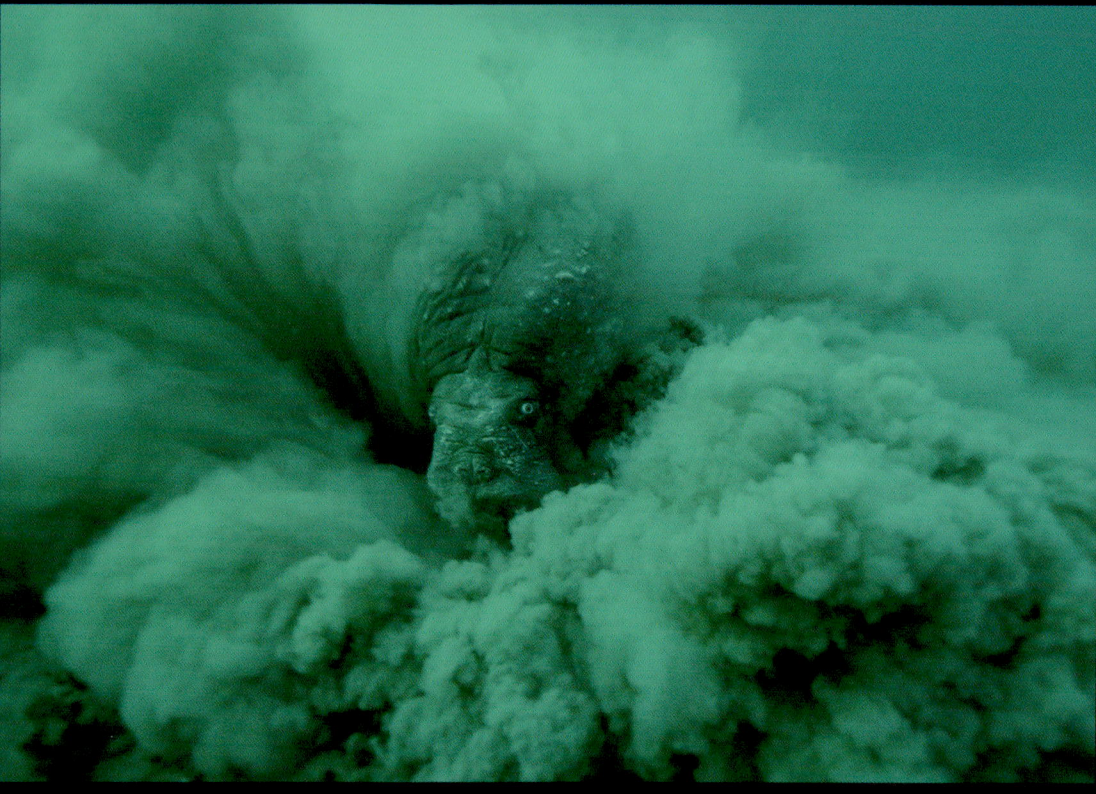

Beast of the sediment

WINNER

Göran Ehlmé

SWEDEN

Nikon D2x with 12-24mm lens; 1/50 sec at f4; 400 ISO; Seacam housing with wide-angle port.

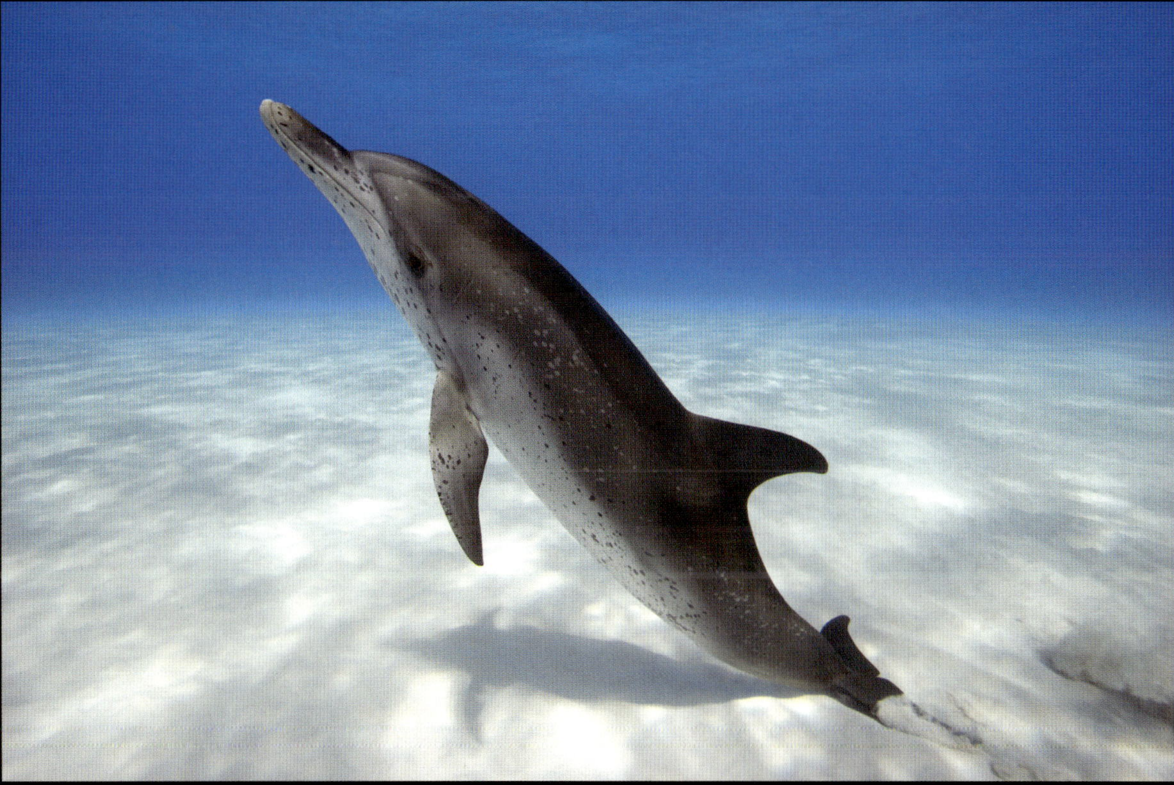

Dolphin in its element

John Johnson

USA

The Bahamas has attracted John for three years in a row to its clear waters and its Atlantic spotted dolphins. One day, when he held his breath and dropped to the sandy bottom to watch a group of dolphins, this playful individual swam by to look at him. As it did so, it arched its back and dragged its tail to swirl the sand ever so slightly before heading up to the surface. 'Though I try not to anthropomorphize my experiences with animals,' says John, 'I can't help wondering what the dolphins must think when they encounter people in the middle of their ocean like that.'

Canon 20D with 10-22mm f3.5-4.5 EF-S lens; 1/200 sec at f8.

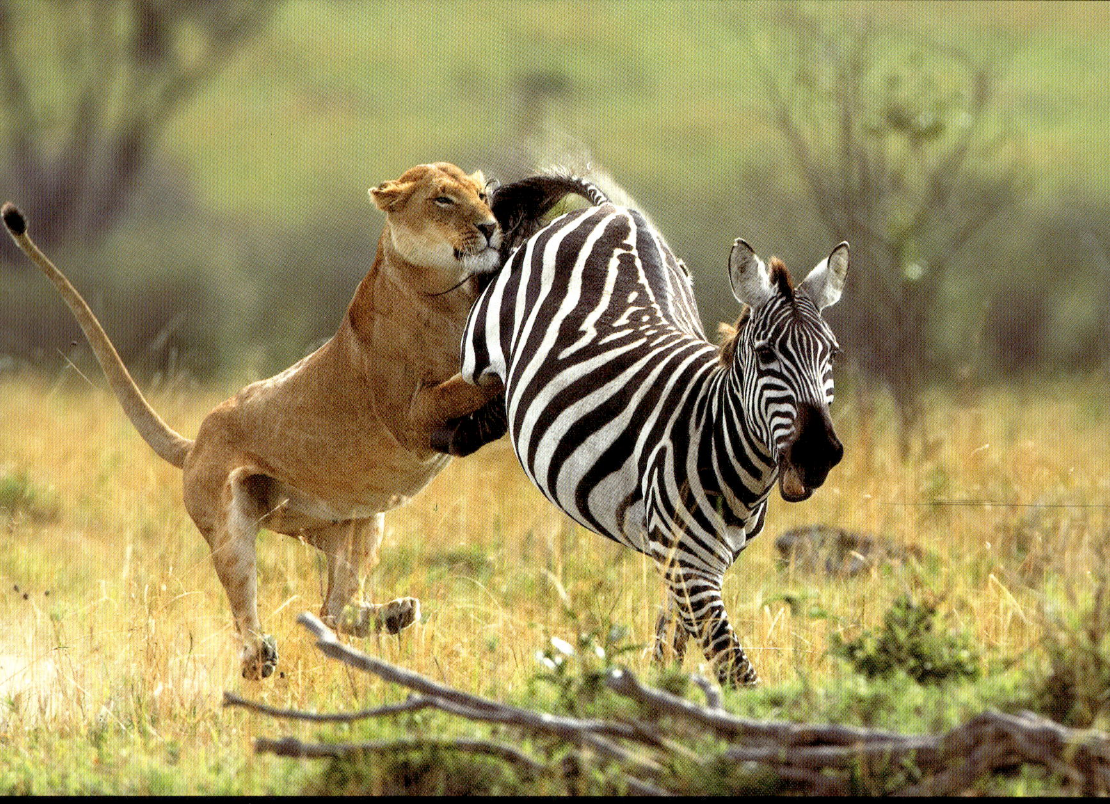

Fatal trip

Joe McDonald

USA

While watching zebras in Kenya's Masai Mara Game Reserve, Joe noticed a lone female standing just 100 metres (330 feet) or so from three lionesses, with a wound on her flank that appeared to be from a lion attack. She remained immobile for three hours and then, with an apparent death wish, walked closer to the lionesses. They did nothing. But when the zebra began to rub its wound against a tree, a lioness charged. The zebra galloped off but suddenly did an unexpected 180-degree turn straight towards Joe. 'I got this shot just before my camera memory became full,' he says. Seconds later the zebra was down.

Canon EOS 1D Mark II with 600mm f4 AF lens; 1/1250 sec at f6.3; 250 ISO.

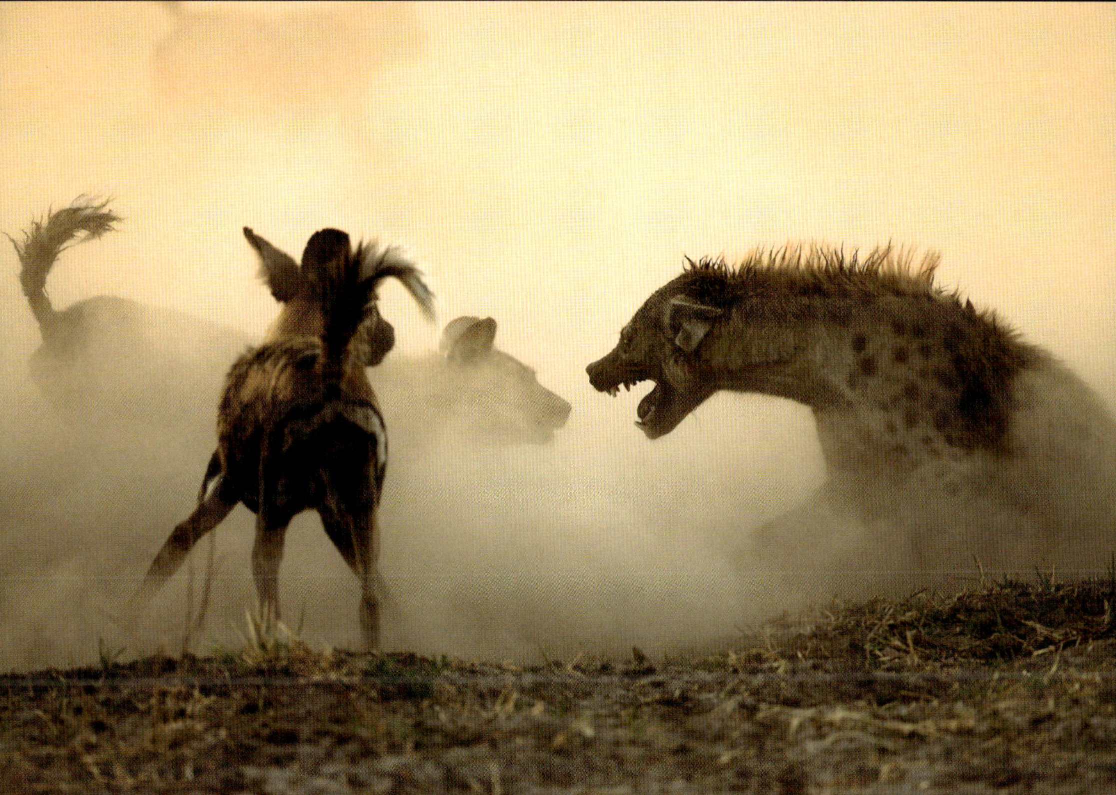

Hyena at bay

Christophe Courteau

FRANCE

Christophe discovered four spotted hyenas eating an elephant's foot beside a lagoon in Botswana. So did a pack of 20 or so African wild dogs. Without hesitating, the dogs charged the hyenas, which fled – except one. 'All hell broke lose,' says Christophe, 'but the action was in the grass, and I found myself wishing they would all move to a nearby dusty patch.' And as though following director's orders, they did, the swirling dust and backlighting improving the drama no end. The hyena avoided the snapping jaws by facing the dogs full on but, finally, after more than 15 minutes, she fled, her persecutors quickly giving up the chase.

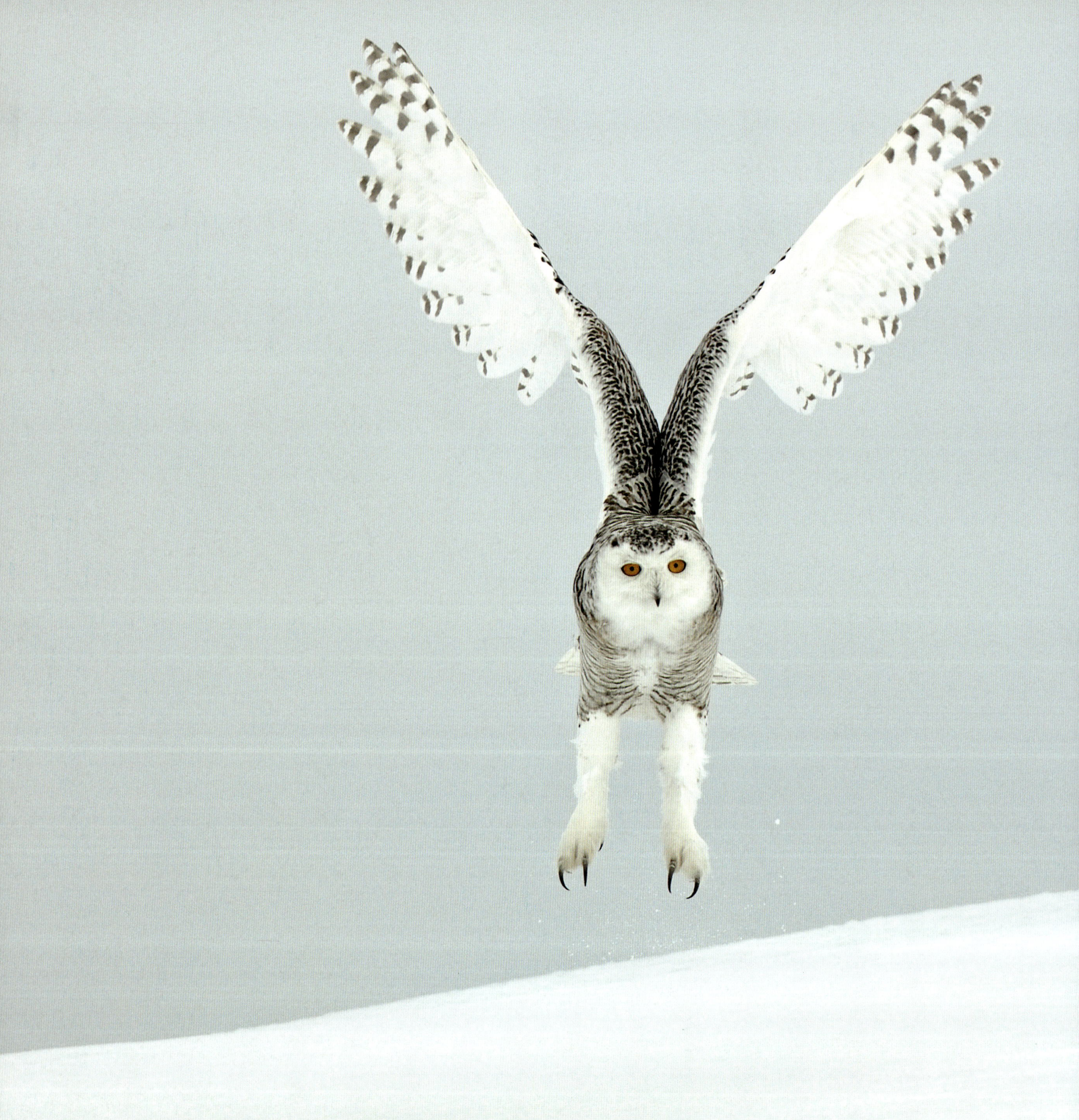

Animal Behaviour Birds

As with all the behaviour categories, the pictures must show action and have interest value as well as aesthetic appeal.

Snowy landing

WINNER

Vincent Munier

FRANCE

A snowy owl comes in to land – beautiful in its symmetry. Vincent has always been captivated by snowy owls, and in north Quebec, Canada, he fulfilled his dream of spending time with them. 'I have usually had to photograph European birds from hides,' says Vincent, 'so it was a surprise to find that the owls were unperturbed by my presence and I could move freely in the open.' This year-old youngster became a favourite. 'Sitting in the snow from dawn till dusk, I got to know its character.' The soft grey-blue sky provided the ideal backdrop to show off 'the sheer perfection of the bird'.

Nikon D200 with 300mm f2.8 AFS lens; 1/4000 sec at f4.5; 200 ISO; tripod.

Flamingo dance

RUNNER-UP

Todd Gustafson

USA

With around 4 million lesser flamingos to choose from, Todd's problem was 'where to stop and how to compose a picture that wasn't just a mass of pink'. Arriving at Lake Nakuru, Kenya, just before dawn, he chose a spot where the rising sun would hit the lake's edge. The collective noun for flamingos is a 'stand', and this is the stand that eventually caught Todd's eye. Males group together, arching their necks and ruffling feathers to impress a single female. Others may join the dance, and the circling and swirling stand can swell to the hundreds. As the sun rose, this stand huddled in anticipation at the edge of the dance floor, illuminated by a beautiful soft light, their chilli-pepper-like bills perfectly poised. 'I found that the lower down I got, the better the birds looked against the clear grey sky,' says Todd. 'By the time I took the shot, I was flat on the ground among the flamingo droppings.'

Canon EOS 1D Mark II with 600mm IS lens; 1/1250 sec at f5.6; 100 ISO; Todd-Pod with a Wimberly head.

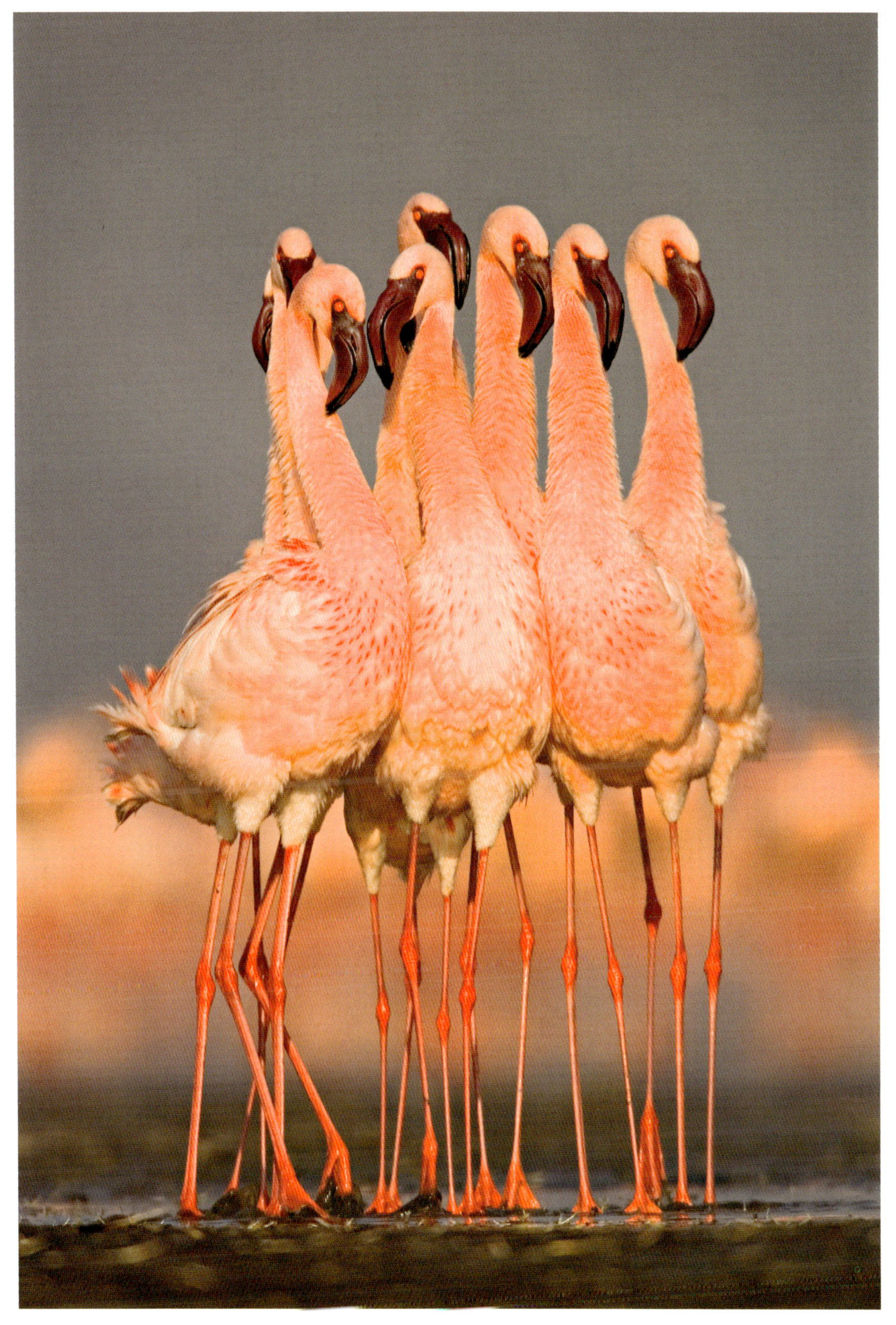

Rockhopper rush-hour

SPECIALLY COMMENDED

Solvin Zankl

GERMANY

Safety in numbers is the best option for penguins – prey of leopard seals and killer whales, which lurk around landing or departure areas near breeding colonies. Here, a big group of rockhoppers returns from foraging at sea, and the birds hurry across the beach before hopping up onto the rocks and climbing up to their nests. Solvin spent a month on Saunders Island in the Falkland Islands and got to know the birds' behaviour well. His first attempts to photograph the rush-hour were made in bright sunlight, which resulted in distracting stark shadows on the white sand. 'I had to wait for the right mix of low tide, indirect sunlight and, of course, a big enough group of penguins,' says Solvin. 'When these ones made a dash for the beach, my finger was ready on the release.'

Nikon D2x with 400mm f1-2.8D lens; 1/320 sec at f6.7; 1.4x converter.

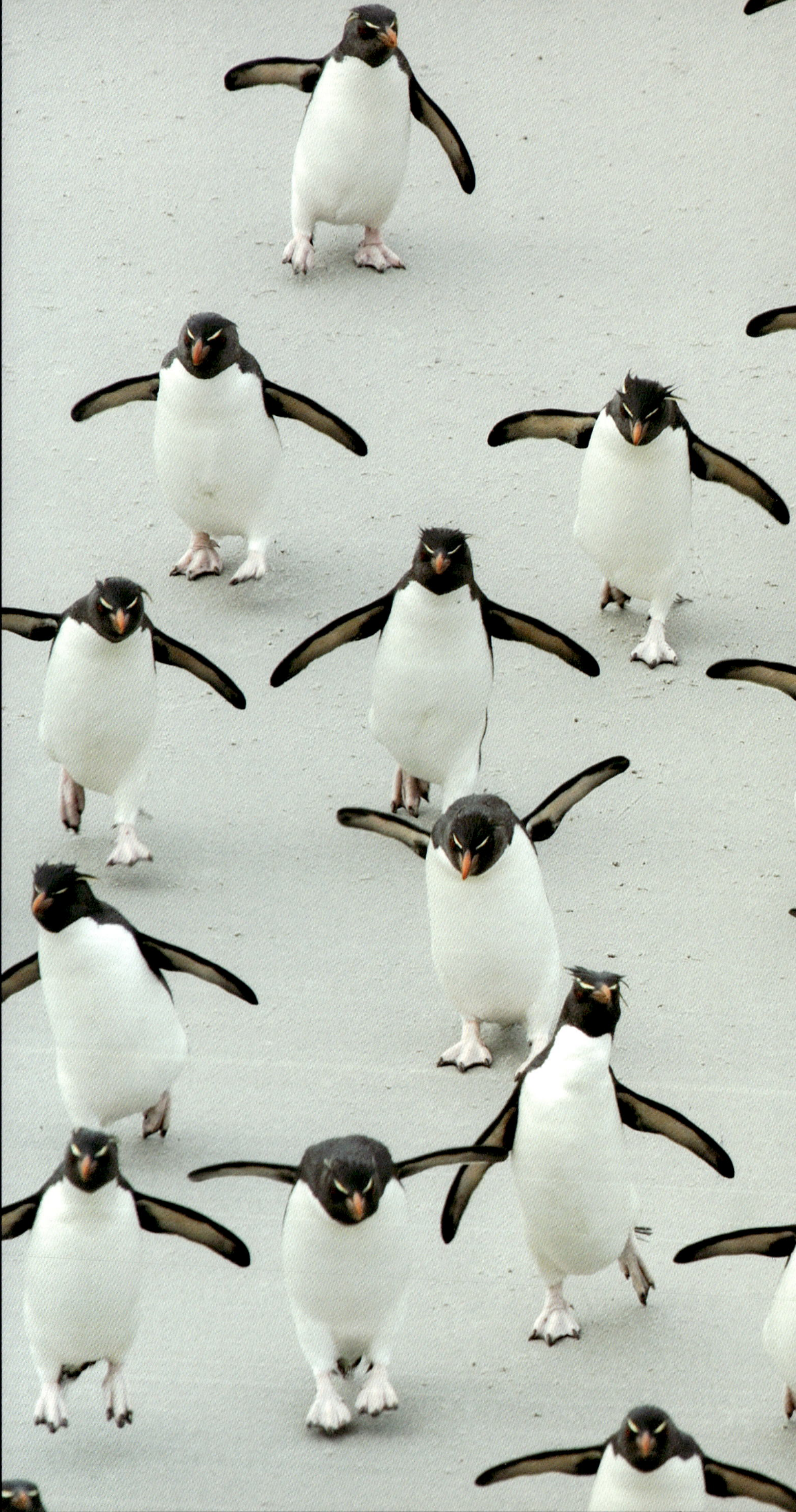

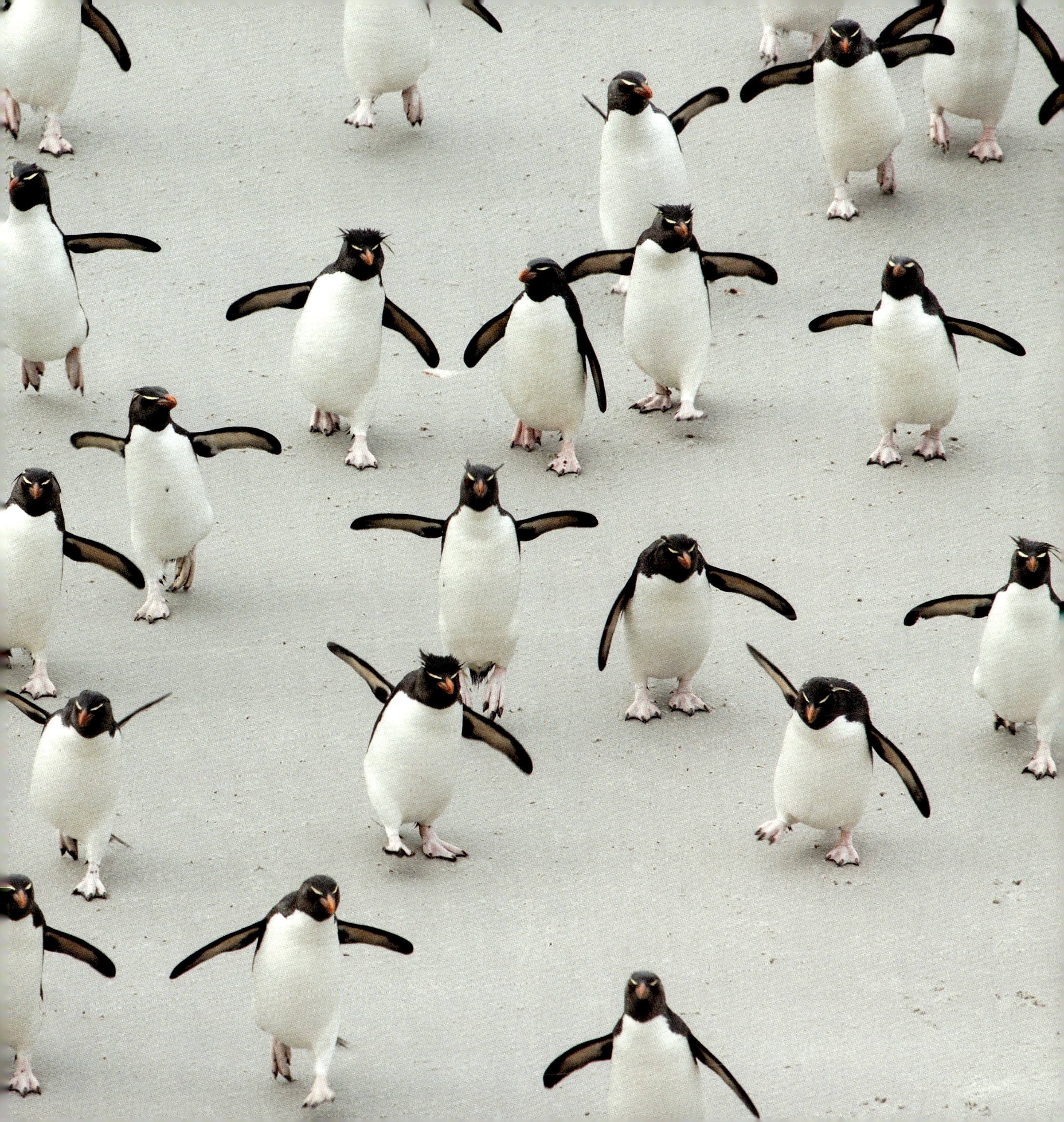

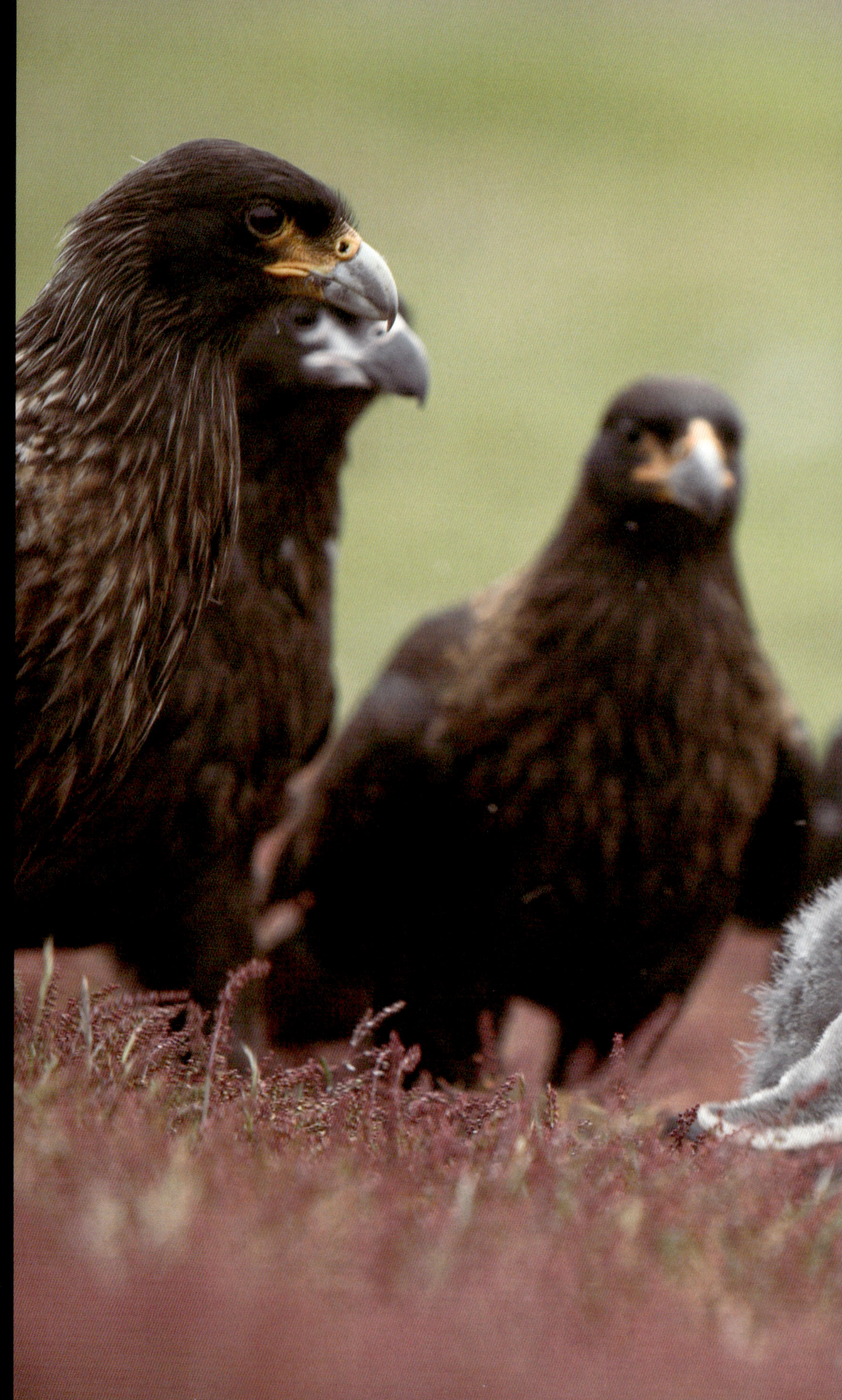

Caracaras in for the kill

SPECIALLY COMMENDED

Andy Rouse

UK

When penguin parents go to sea, the fledglings stay together for warmth and safety, often in protective association with adults. Straying too far from the edge of the crèche is dangerous. This gentoo fledgling, in the Falkland Islands, took a step too far and was immediately singled out by striated caracaras keeping watch for such a moment. These falcons are scavengers and opportunists. In this case, several caracaras worked as a pack, isolating the chick. 'It tried to fight back but, of course, didn't stand a chance,' says Andy. 'The image shows the power between predator and prey. The expressions of the caracaras say it all.' Caracaras have their own problems, though, and are now classified by the International Union for the Conservation of Nature (IUCN) as being in need of protection.

Canon EOS-1Ds Mark II with 300mm f2.8L IS lens; 1/125 sec at f5.6; 160 ISO.

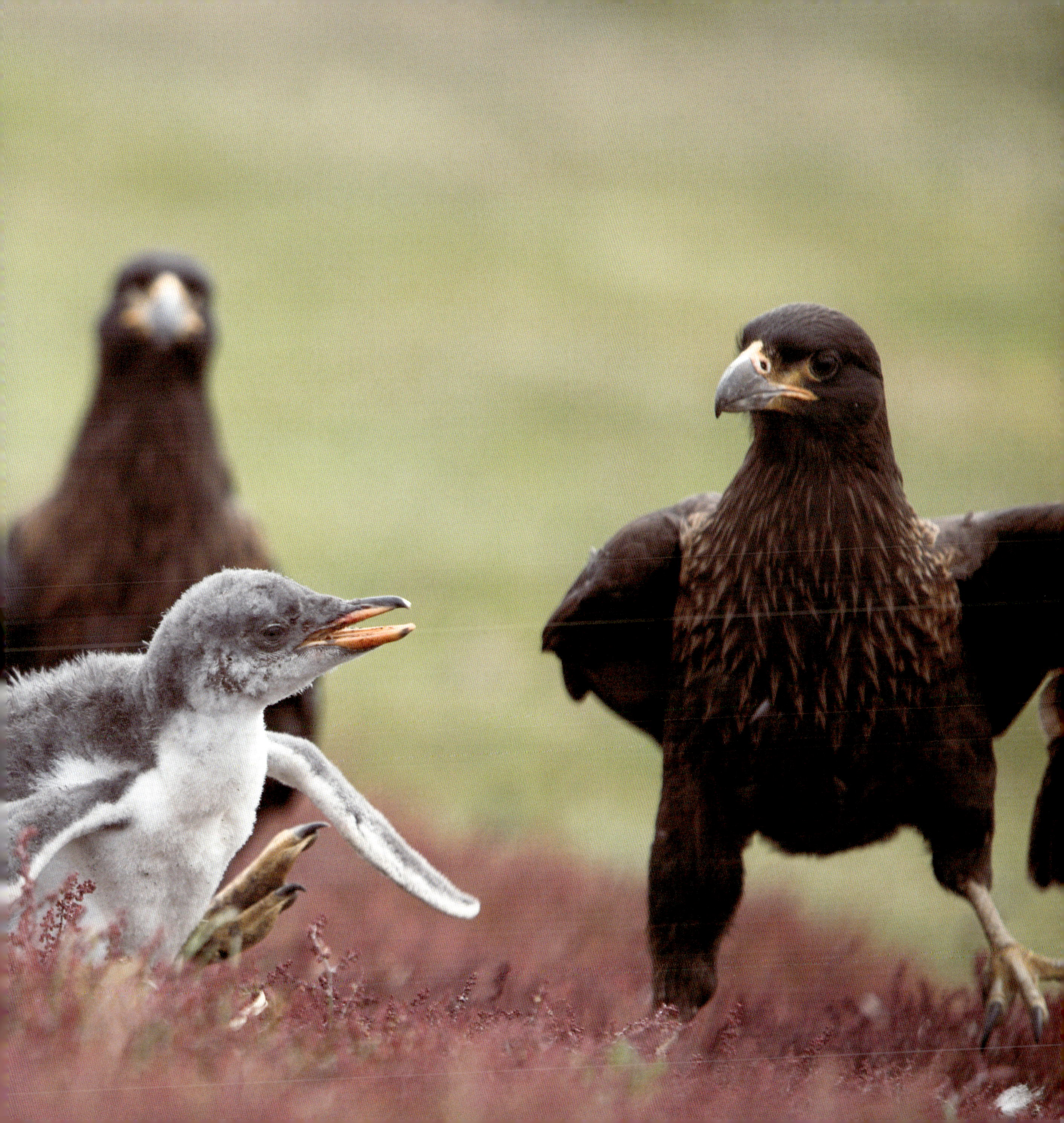

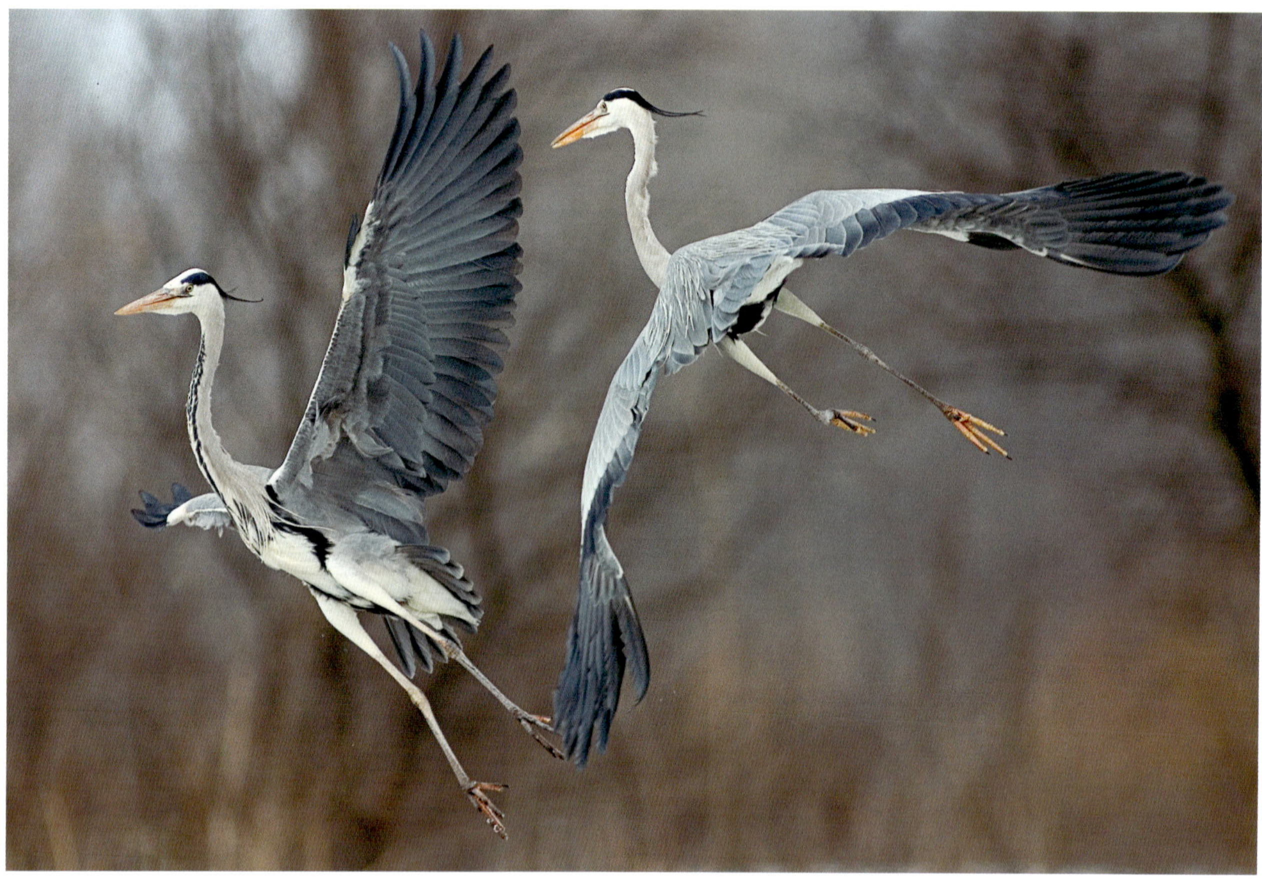

Sparring herons

SPECIALLY COMMENDED

Bence Máté

HUNGARY

When a cold snap freezes the lakes near Bence's home in Pusztaszer, grey herons gather where a waterfall prevents an area freezing over. Only a few can fish at a time, and so weaker ones must wait for the stronger ones to feed and leave. Inevitably, squabbles break out. Bence is usually on hand to record the drama, wrapped in a sleeping bag – last year, when this picture was taken, the temperature was -10°C (14°F). 'Grey herons maintain their elegance even when arguing,' says Bence, 'their plumage accentuated by the dull, flat light.'

Canon EOS 300D with Nikon MF 300mm f2.8 lens and Canon EOS-Nikon converter, Nikon TC-14B teleconverter; 1/2000 sec at f4; hide.

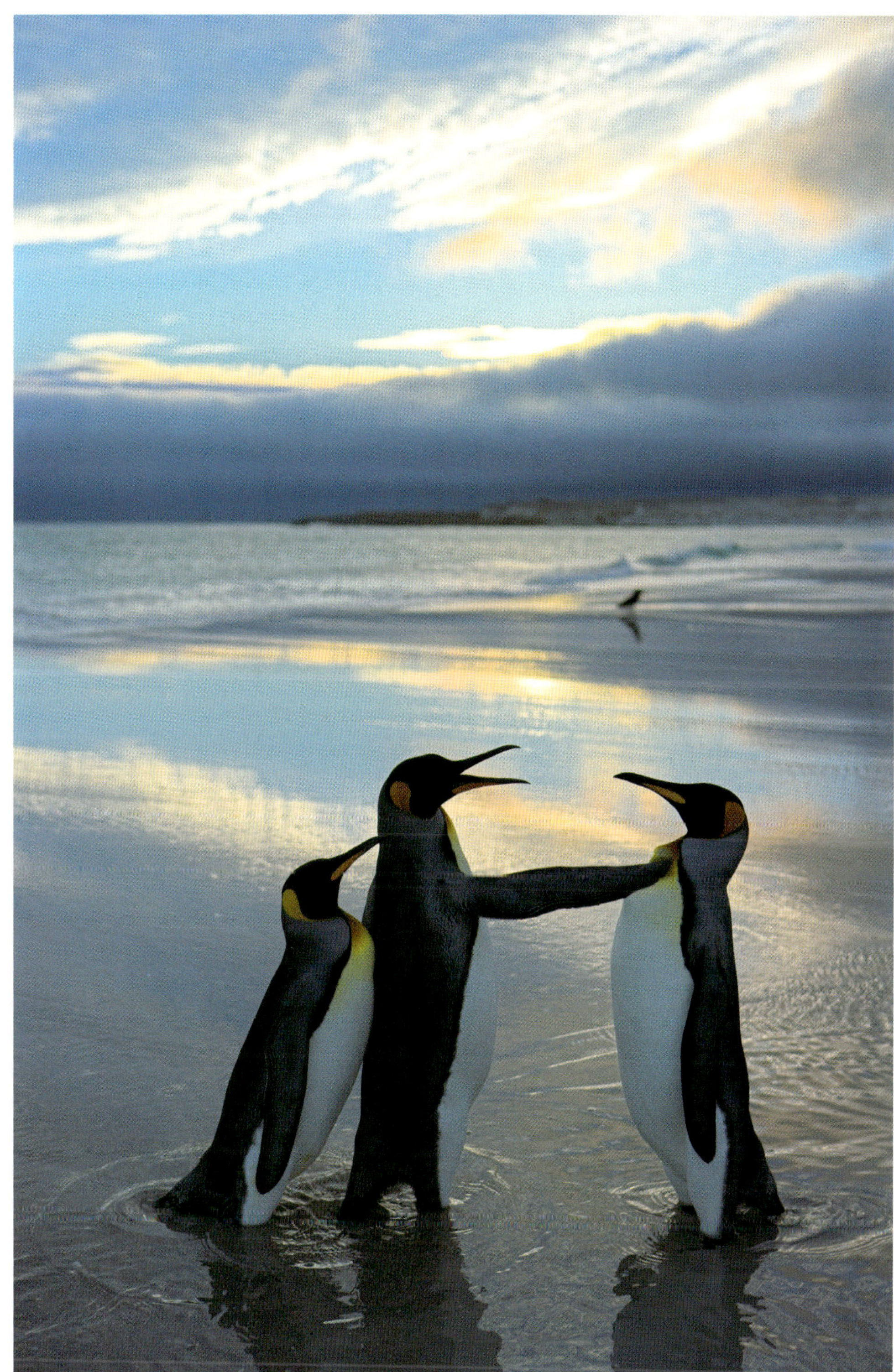

Rival kings

Andy Rouse

UK

Christmas morning on the Falklands was bright and beautiful. 'On the beach I met this squabbling threesome,' says Andy, 'and ended up spending four hours with them, as their antics made me laugh so much.' The penguin on the left is the female, and squabbling over her by slapping each other with their flippers are two males. 'Kings are such cool penguins,' adds Andy, 'but it's the emperors who get all the media attention by hanging out in winter blizzards for months on end. The kings are far more active, though, and therefore much more interesting to photograph.'

Canon EOS-1Ds Mark II with 24-70mm lens; 1/60 sec at f4; 200 ISO.

Eagle poise

Robert O'Toole

USA

Carefully positioned at the top of an Alaskan ice slope, where the wind hit the side and created an updraft, Robert was in the perfect spot to photograph the huge bald eagles soaring overhead, 'but the wind direction kept the birds where the sun was behind them,' he says. 'Now and then, though, one would peel off and turn towards the light for a moment.' When this eagle banked, Robert zoomed in with a short telephoto lens, holding the camera vertically and filling the frame. 'The sun caught the underside of its wings, and the amazing colour and detail were revealed.'

Canon EOS 1D Mark II N with an EF70-200mm L lens; 1/1250 sec at f4; 200 ISO.

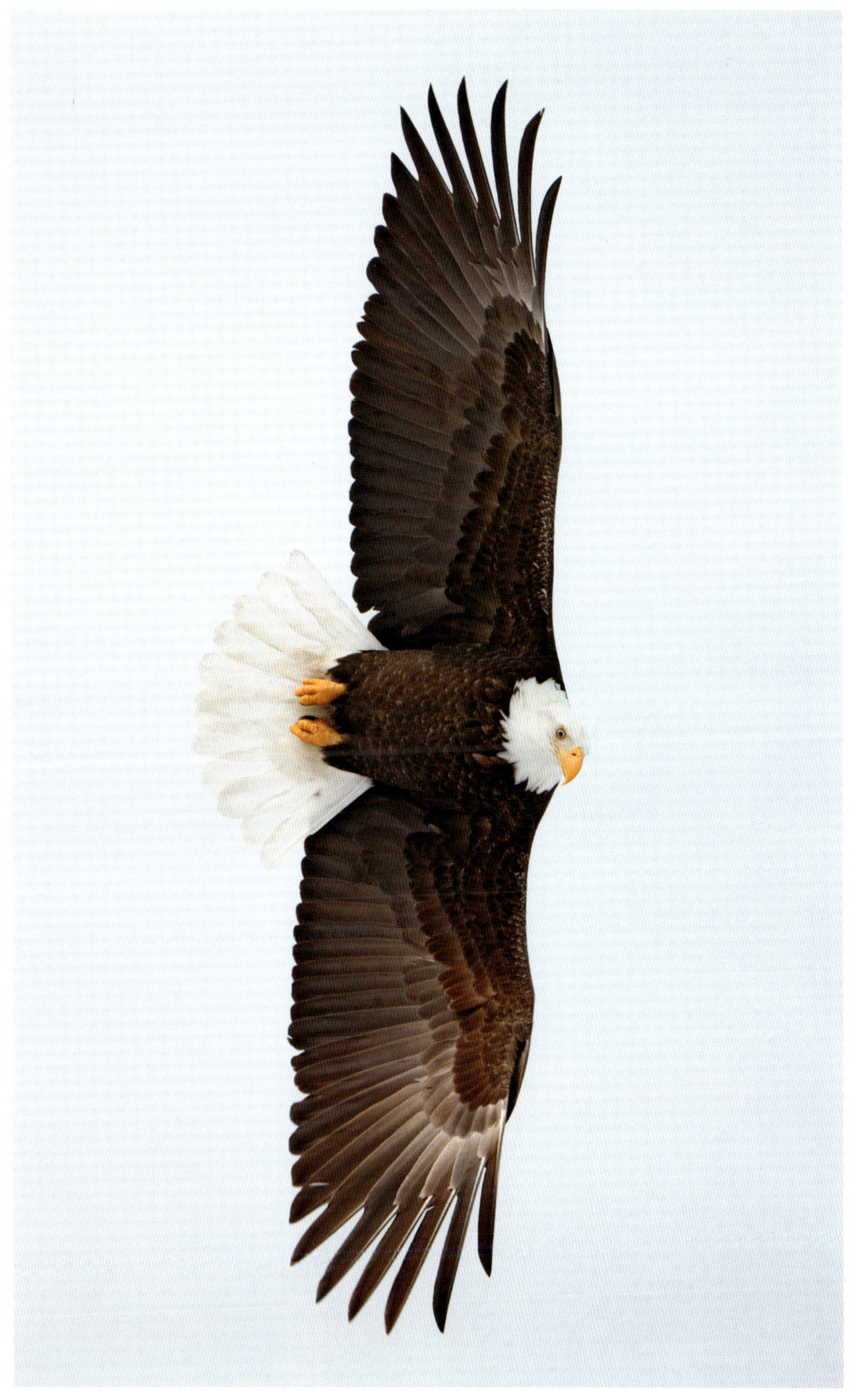

Behaviour All Other Animals

This category offers plenty of scope for interesting pictures, especially when you consider that species other than mammals and birds comprise the majority of animals on Earth and have behaviour that is often little known.

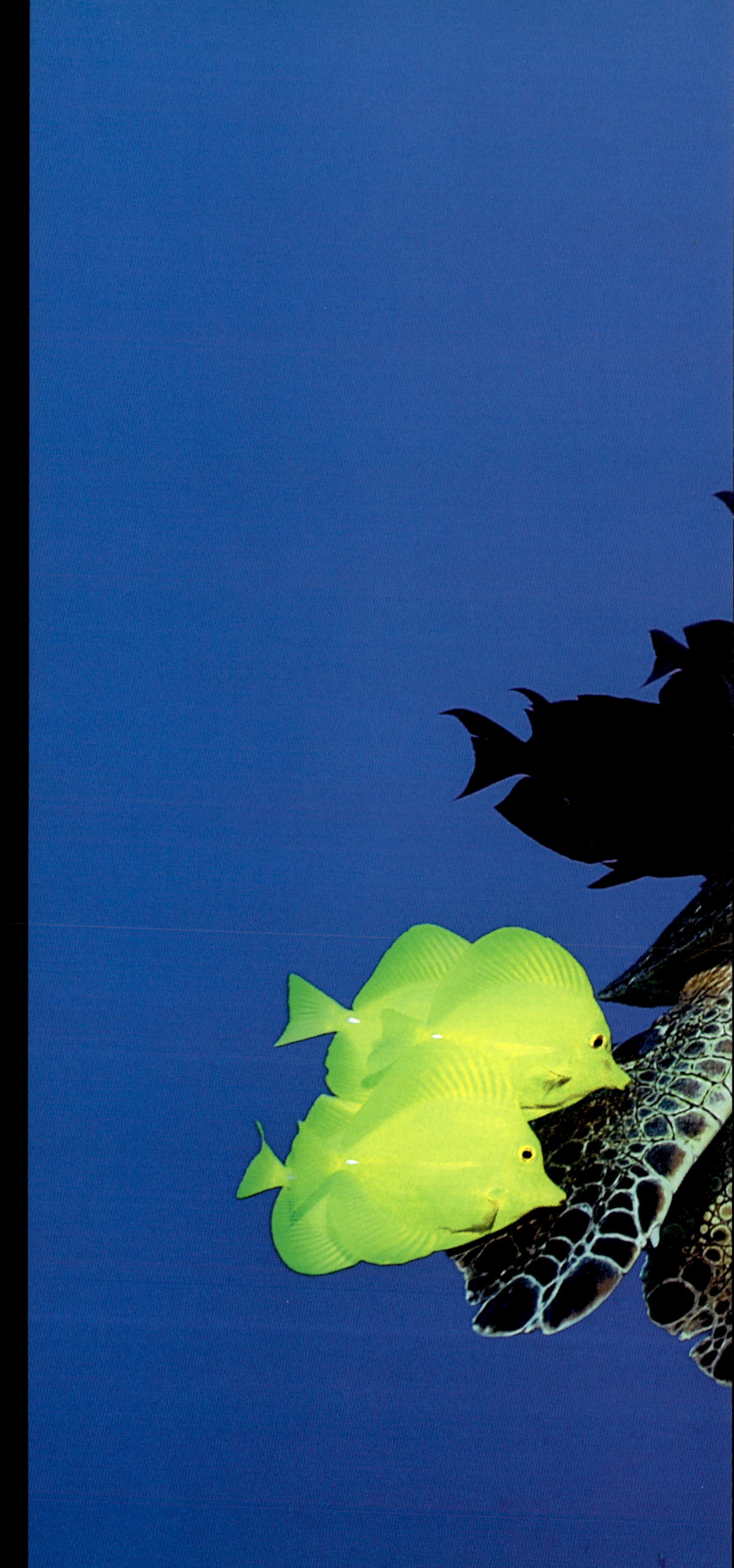

Turtle grooming

WINNER

Andre Seale

BRAZIL / USA

Pure bliss for a green turtle – a full-body cleanse and massage, courtesy of the local fish, whenever it turns up at the designated spot. Turtle Pinnacle, near Honokohau Harbour in Kailua-Kona, Hawaii, boasts such a cleaning-station about 15m (50 feet) down. Sometimes there are several turtles hanging around waiting for service, and typically they don't have to wait long. In this photo, yellow tang, goldring surgeonfish (the blue fish – endemic to the Hawaiian islands) and a saddleback wrasse (underneath – also found only in Hawaii) have nipped up from the reef to nibble off the algae growing on the turtle's shell and skin. 'It seems like a win-win situation for all,' says Andre, 'and certainly for this photographer.'

Nikon D100 with Nikkor 12-24mm lens; 1/80 sec at f8; Nexus Master housing, dual YS90DX strobes.

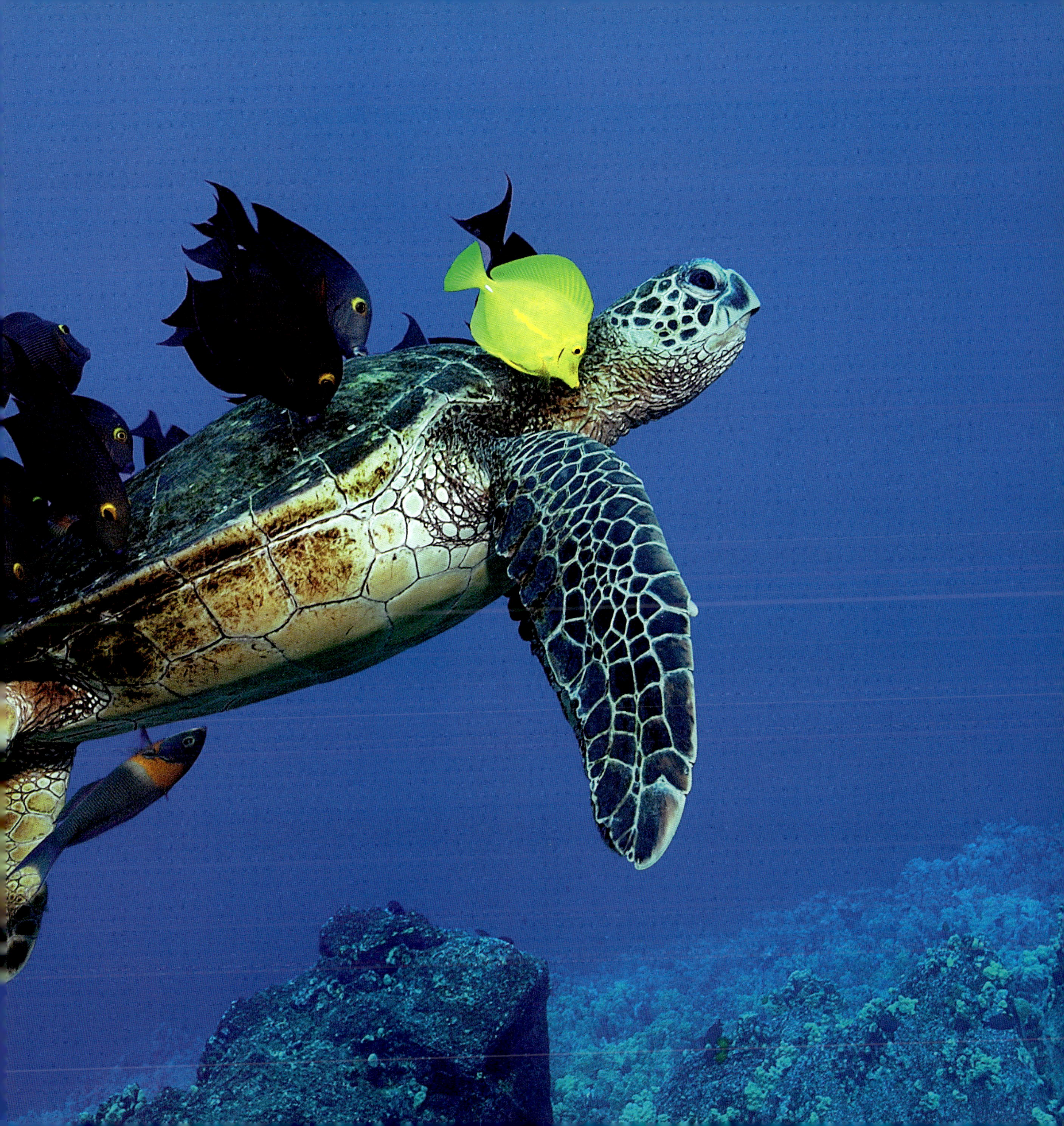

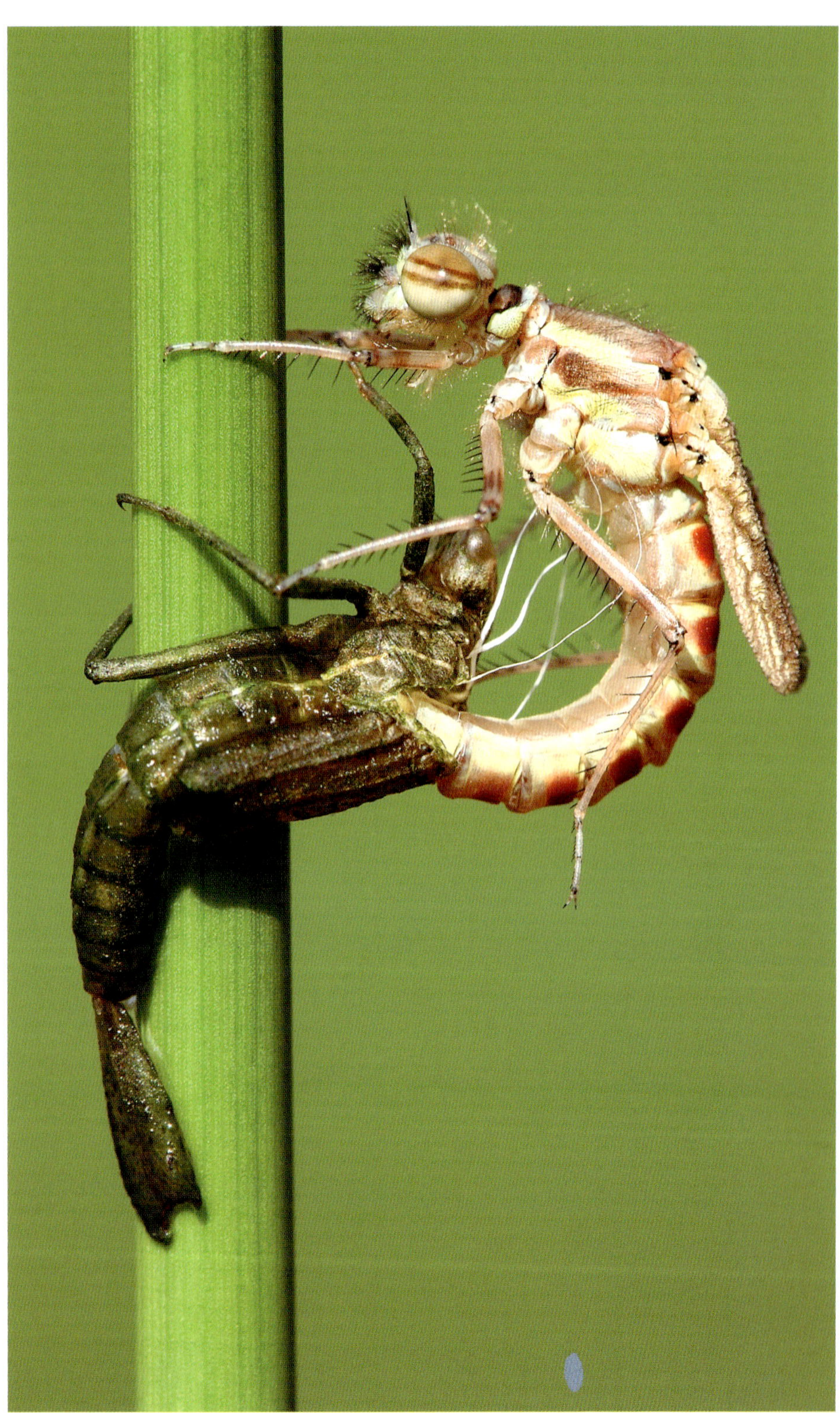

Damsel emerging

RUNNER-UP

Ross Hoddinott

UK

The point when beast turns into a beauty has been one of Ross's favourite wildlife moments ever since he watched the unfolding drama as a child. Every spring, he rises early to try to find dragonflies or damselflies emerging 'before they transform from ugly larvae into striking flying insects'. They are tricky to spot, 'and even when I do find one at an early stage, it is often impractical to take a photograph.' This time, though, he got lucky. Just before its final moult, after two years in the pond, instinct drove a large red damselfly up from the depths 'to climb a reed, close to where I could position my tripod. I allowed enough depth of field to keep the damselfly and reed in sharp focus and the background blurred,' says Ross. An hour later, the insect took its first flight, leaving its monster husk behind.

Nikon D70 with Sigma 150mm macro lens; 1/30 sec at f13; 200 ISO; Manfrotto tripod.

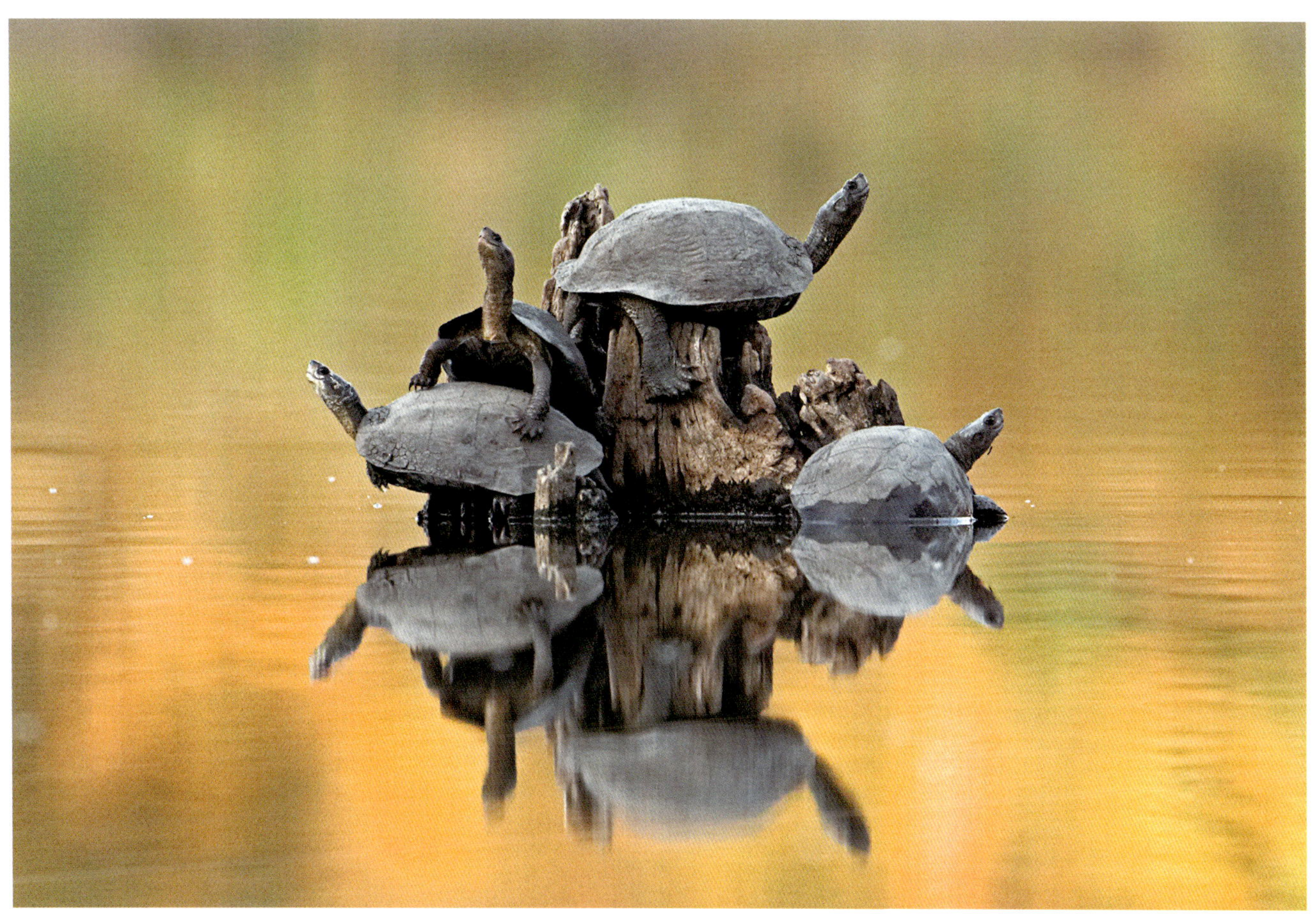

Terrapin hot-spot

Manoj C Sindagi

INDIA

This sculptural arrangement caught Manoj's eye while running a wildlife photography workshop for school students in Nagarahole National Park, south India. 'We were on an evening safari,' says Manoj, 'when we came across these sunbathing Indian pond terrapins, necks outstretched, seemingly offering salutations to the Sun God.' Manoj stalked them until close enough to photograph their reflections against the golden light. 'Just as I pressed the shutter, the turtle pile broke apart and slipped into the water, giving me the opportunity to show my students how important it is for a wildlife photographer to be familiar with an animal's behaviour.'

Canon EOS 20D with EF 500mm f4 lens and 1.4x teleconverter; 1/320 sec at f6.3; 400 ISO; Manfrotto monopod.

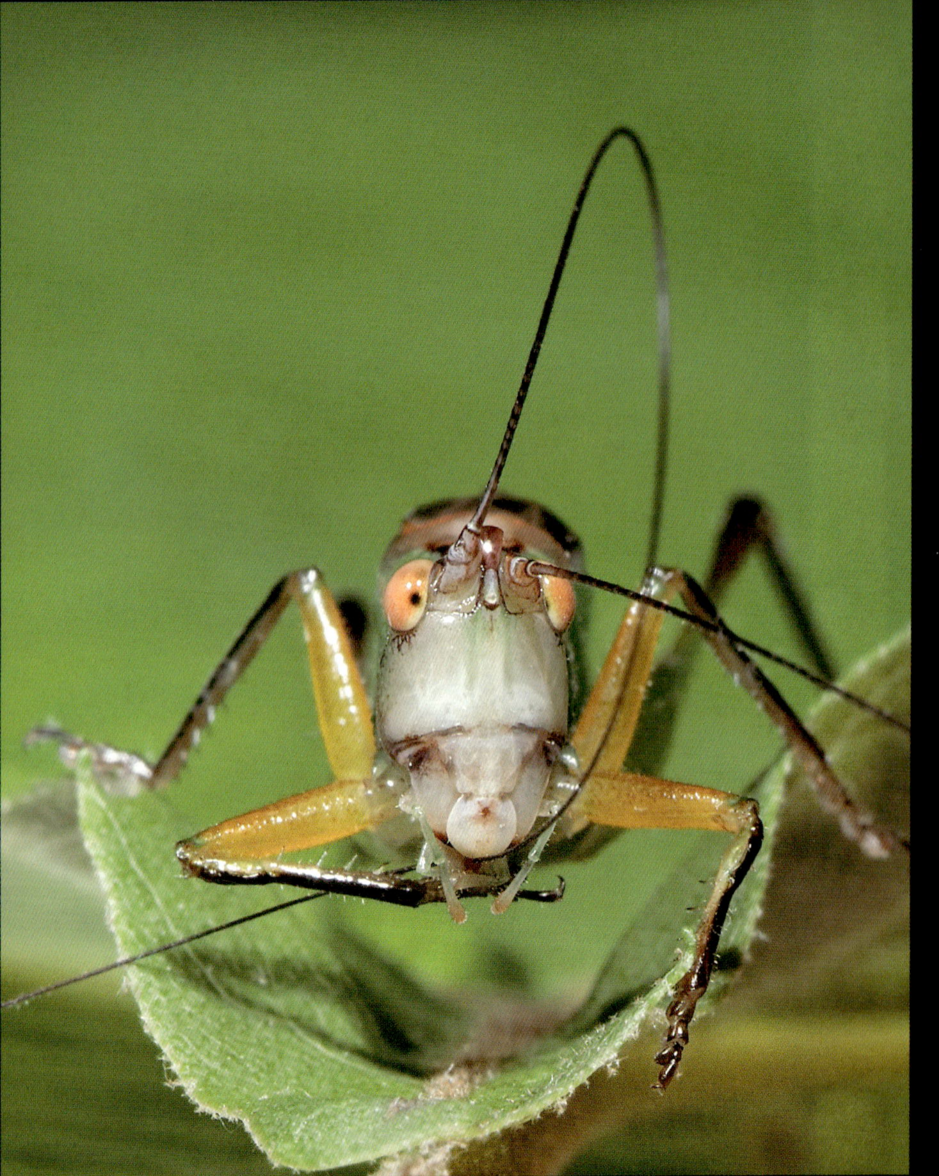

Katydid facial

Wil Hershberger

USA

An insect's-eye view of a creature of the grass is seldom possible, not least because of the difficulty of approaching through a mass of leaves. But Wil managed to get his camera just inches away from this black-legged meadow katydid, which continued to groom, oblivious of the human behind the lens. 'This particular day was spent among river-bottom brambles photographing meadow katydids,' says Wil, 'but none posed as nonchalantly as this one, mouthparts working away to clean its impossibly long antennae.' Katydids' antennae – two or three times the length of their bodies – help them feel their way, find food and be alert to danger. Personal hygiene is therefore essential to keep these life-saving organs in tip-top shape. Katydid is the American name for bush cricket, derived from the 'katy-did, katy-didn't' song of the largest of the North American katydids, the northern true katydid. Their very long antennae help distinguish them from grasshoppers.

Canon EOS-1Ds with 180mm macro f3.5L lens; 1/200 sec at f22 with flash; 200 ISO; Wimberley macro flash brackets and lens plates.

Snappers in synchrony

Alexander Mustard

UK

Swimming off the edge of a coral atoll into the big blue is exciting for a diver but less so for a fish high on the menu of local predators. Guraidhoo Corner off South Malé Atoll, Maldives, is outside the reef and attracts many reef sharks. Paddletail snappers in this exposed environment respond to anything bigger than themselves, including a human diver, by bunching into a tight defensive ball. 'The shape of the formation continually morphed as the fish jostled for position,' says Alex. 'I waited for the fish to create different shapes and took a series of frames. When they formed this perfect sphere, I knew I had an interesting picture.'

Nikon D2X with 17-35mm AFS lens; 1/100 sec at f6.3; 100 ISO; Subal underwater housing.

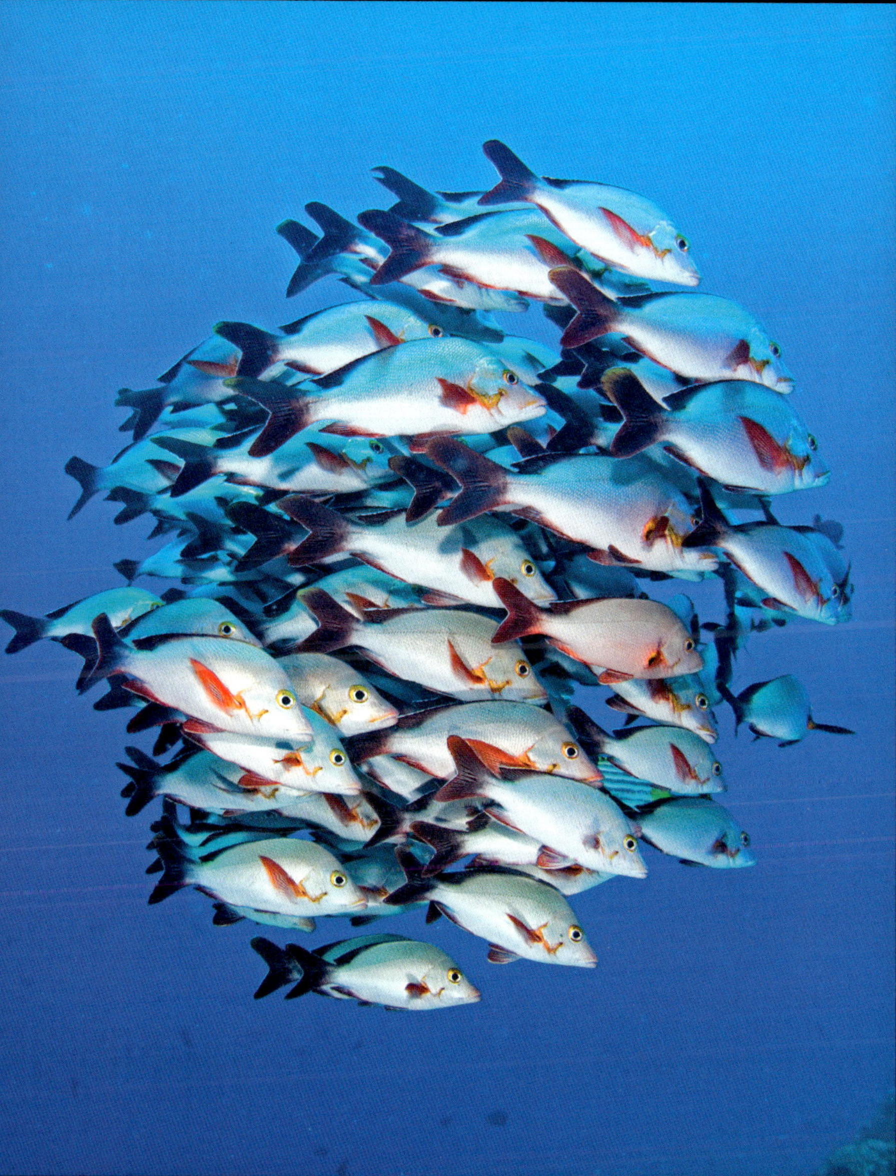

Animals in Their Environment

In this category, a photograph must convey a sense of the relationship between the plant or animal and its habitat, which must be as important a part of the picture as is the subject.

Coconut crab going up

WINNER

Jan Vermeer

THE NETHERLANDS

A beautiful day at one of the remotest places on Earth – Aldabra, in the Indian Ocean – perfect for a walk up a palm tree. The coconut crab is a hermit crab that, as it matures, does away with a need for borrowed shells or, indeed, a normal crab shell. Instead it develops a hard skin, which allows it to grow and grow. And with a leg-tip-to-leg-tip length of up to 1m (40 inches) – making it possibly the biggest arthropod on land – and pincers strong enough to crack a coconut, it is a match for any predator. 'I was struck by the vivid colours of the scene,' says Jan, who was on the island taking photographs for WWF. 'The strong sun and sharp contrast were perfect for revealing just what a magnificent animal this is.'

Nikon D2x with 12-24mm f4 lens; 1/125 sec at f11; 200 ISO.

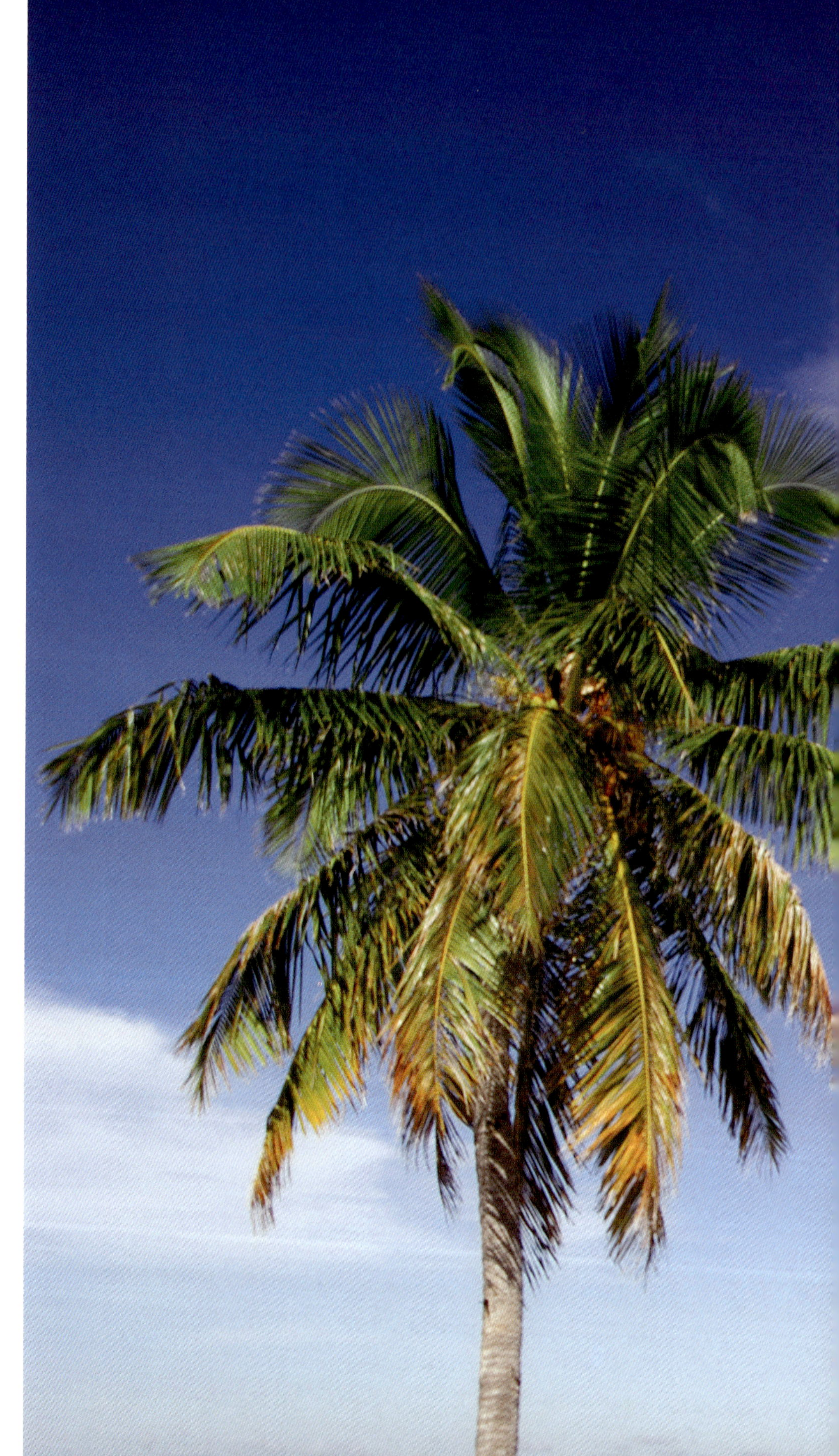

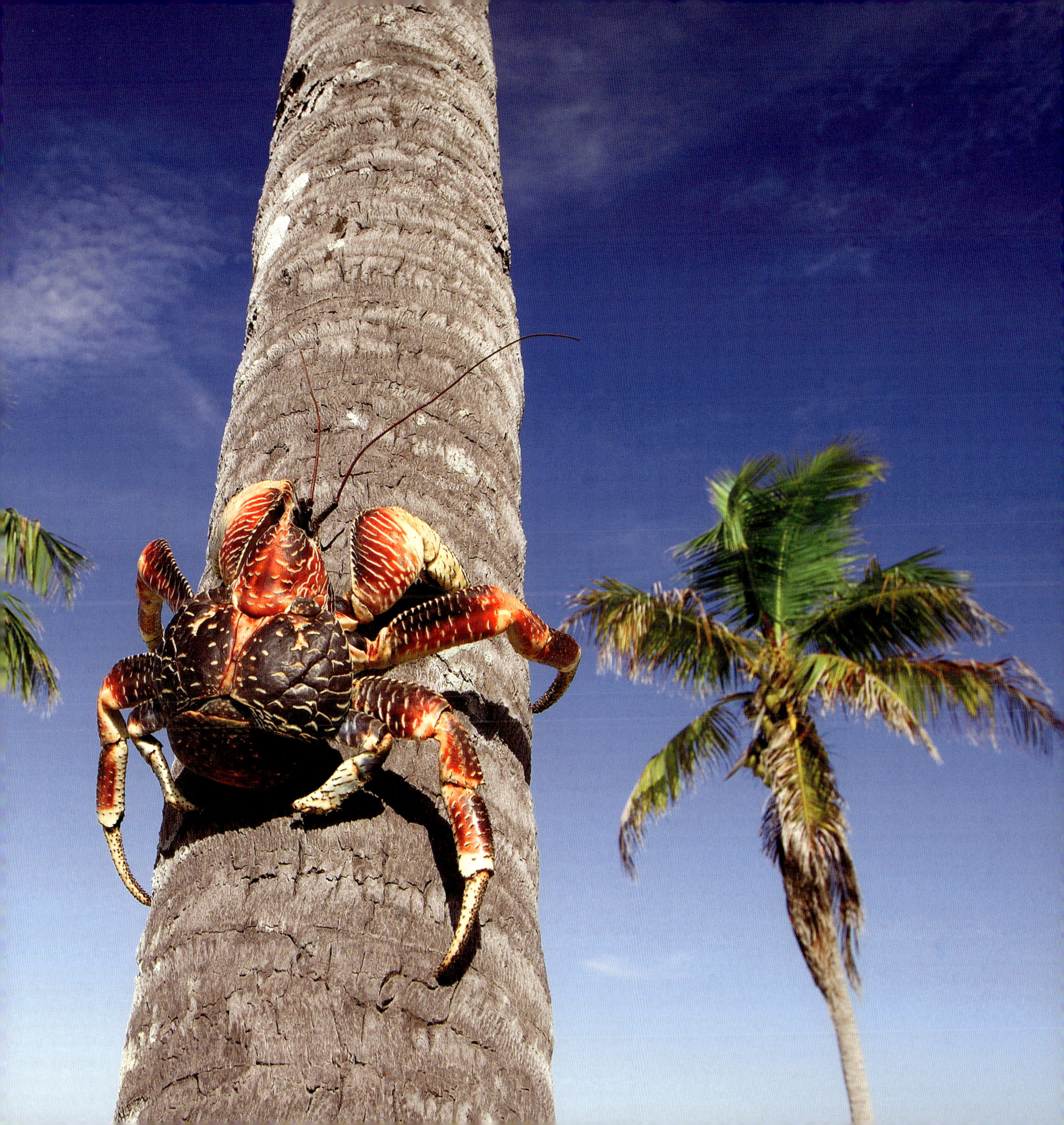

Snow hare

RUNNER-UP

Cheryl A Ertelt

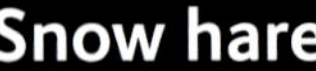

When an Arctic hare is resting, all you are likely to see are its eyes and black ear tips. But in 2005, when less snow than usual fell at Cape Mary in Churchill, Canada, hares sheltering against the lichen-coated rocks became white silhouettes. But this hare was so sure that it was still camouflaged that 'it didn't move a whisker either as I approached or when I retreated,' says Cheryl. 'The overcast light worked well for me, with no shadows to distract from the contrasting colours.'

Canon 1D Mark II with 70-200mm f4 lens; 1/400 sec at f5.6; 400 ISO.

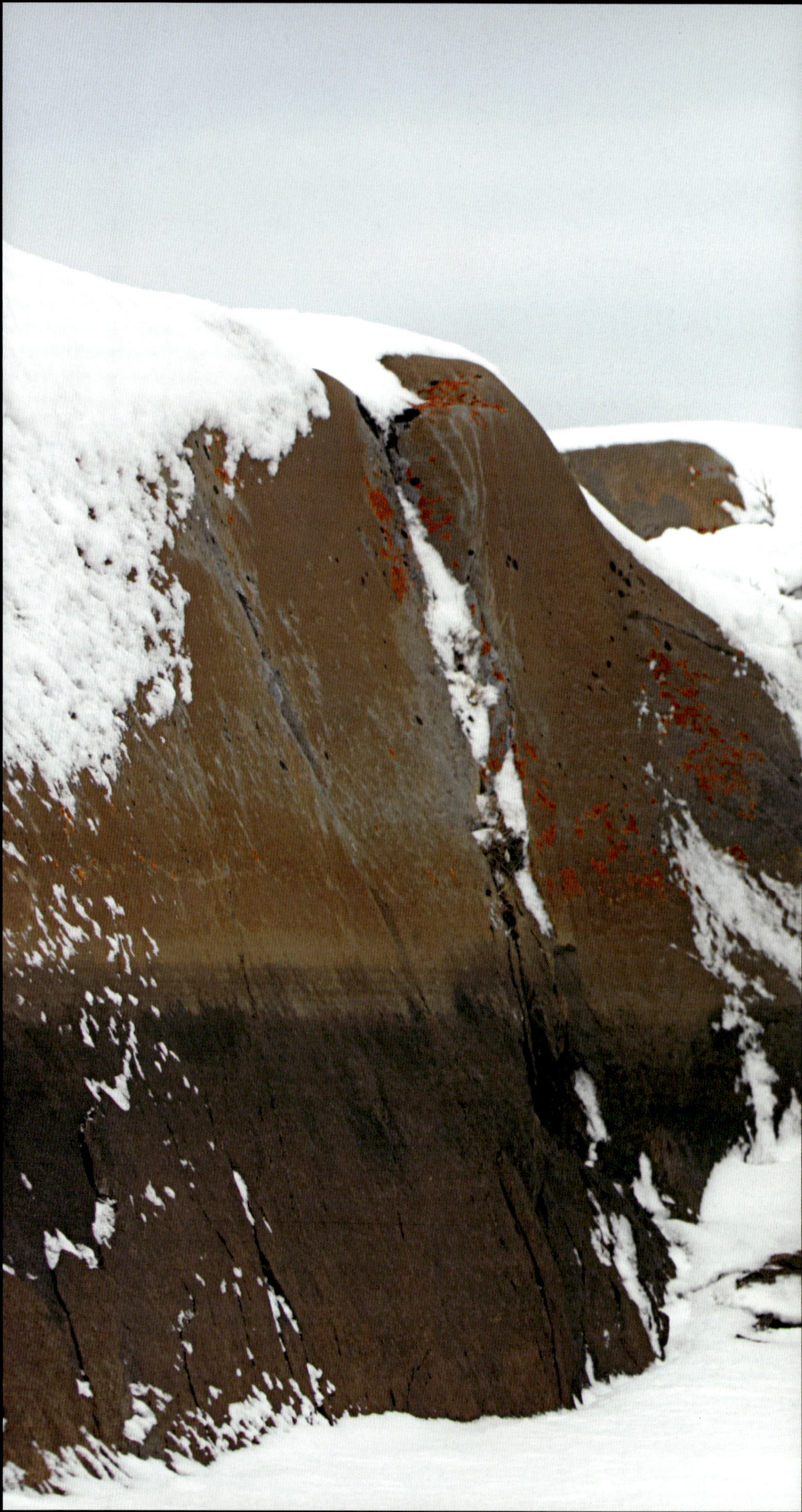

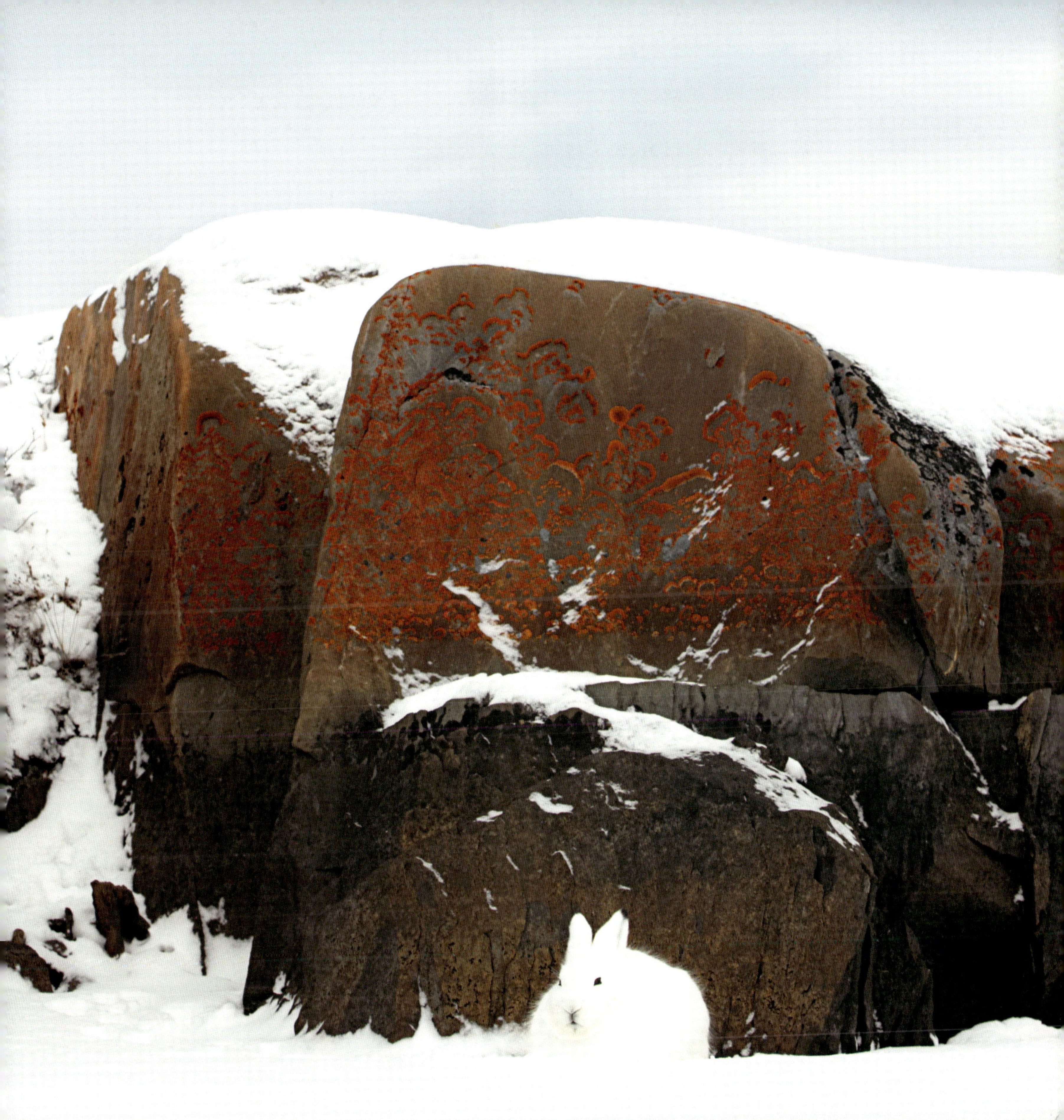

SPECIALLY COMMENDED

Vincent Munier

FRANCE

Vincent waited for hours in freezing conditions for this male snowy owl to appear. When it finally swooped silently across the wind-sculpted snowscape, it was, says Vincent, 'transformed into an angel', wings echoing the gentle curves of the snow. 'It was a magical moment when it turned its head to look at me and our eyes met.' Vincent has taken many photos of animals in their environment but, he adds, 'This is one of my personal favourites. I have rarely managed to capture such poetry in motion'.

Nikon D2x with 70-200mm lens; 1/2000 sec at f6.3; 200 ISO.

Moss mimic

Pete Oxford

UK

Looking like an extra from a sci-fi movie, this katydid has taken natural selection to new heights. In a camouflaged ensemble resembling twigs, mosses and lichens, it blends perfectly with the branch, from its twig-like abdomen right down to its crinkled antennae – ideal for fooling visually orientated predators such as birds and monkeys. 'The katydid was feeding on the moss when I discovered it,' says Pete, who was photographing in the cloudforest of Mindo, on the western slopes of the Andes in Ecuador. 'It made me marvel again at the level of mimicry and camouflage, especially at insect level, that has evolved in this incredibly species-rich habitat.'

Nikon D1x with 105mm f2.8 lens; 1/50 sec at f18; tripod; flash.

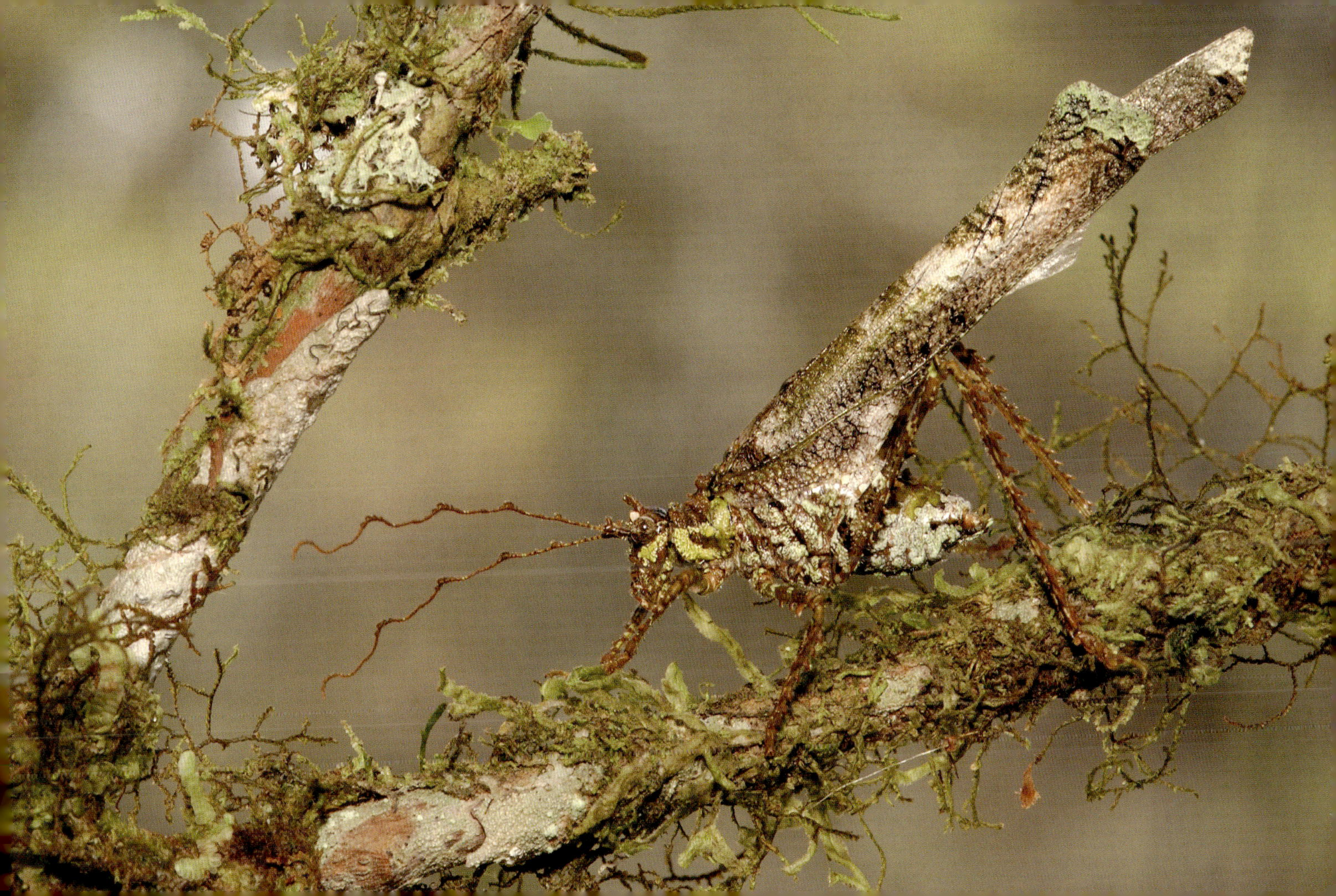

Cranes among the corn

Laszlo Perlaky

USA

Beaks, cobs, legs and stalks – the red caps of sandhill cranes poking above the corn and the white breasts of snow geese emerging from below. The birds winter in their thousands at Bosque del Apache National Wildlife Refuge, New Mexico, in the US. 'At sunrise, the geese take off en masse for the feeding grounds,' says Laszlo. 'The cranes, though, potter around at the roost before leaving in small groups.' Once Laszlo had found where they were feeding, usually in nearby cornfields, he would just watch. 'The cranes would slowly walk along the rows, picking at cobs or corn on the ground, but there would always be some on alert, craning to look for coyotes or other danger.'

Nikon D2x with 600mm lens; 1/250 sec at f5.6; 100 ISO; Gitzo 1548 tripod with Wimberley head.

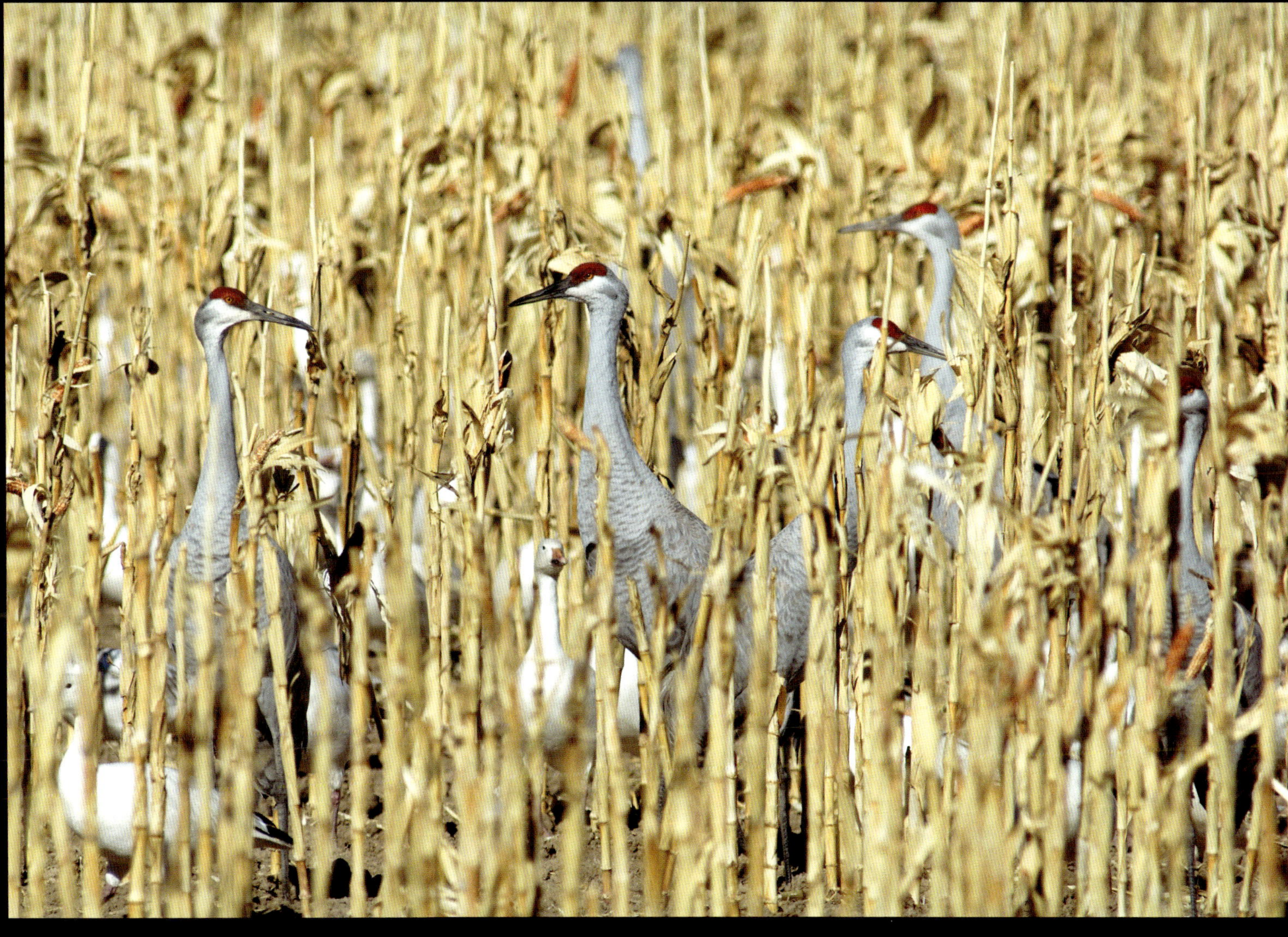

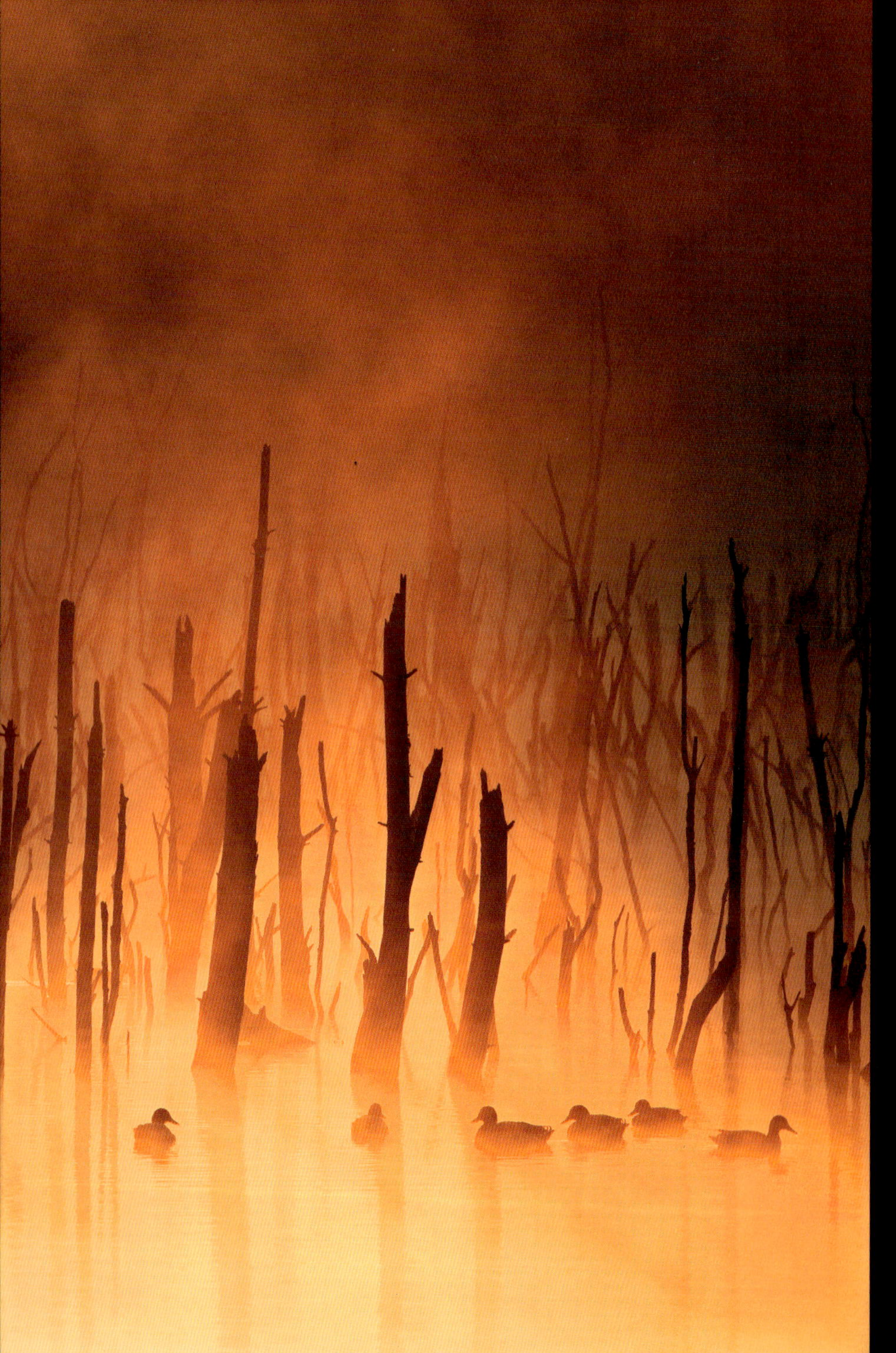

Mallards at dawn

Arnaud Darondeau

FRANCE

'I sat for ages beside this lake before sunrise, convincing myself it would be worth the chilly wait,' says Arnaud, 'but I knew just how magical the light could be at this spot.' After a mellow October day in central France followed by an ice-cold night, the right ingredients merged to create mist, a tangerine glow, the slightest hint of ripples and silhouettes of resting mallard ducks among the reflections. 'A timeless moment well worth the wait,' he concludes.

Nikon D2x with AF-S 500mm f4 lens; 1/250 sec at f11; 200 ISO; tripod.

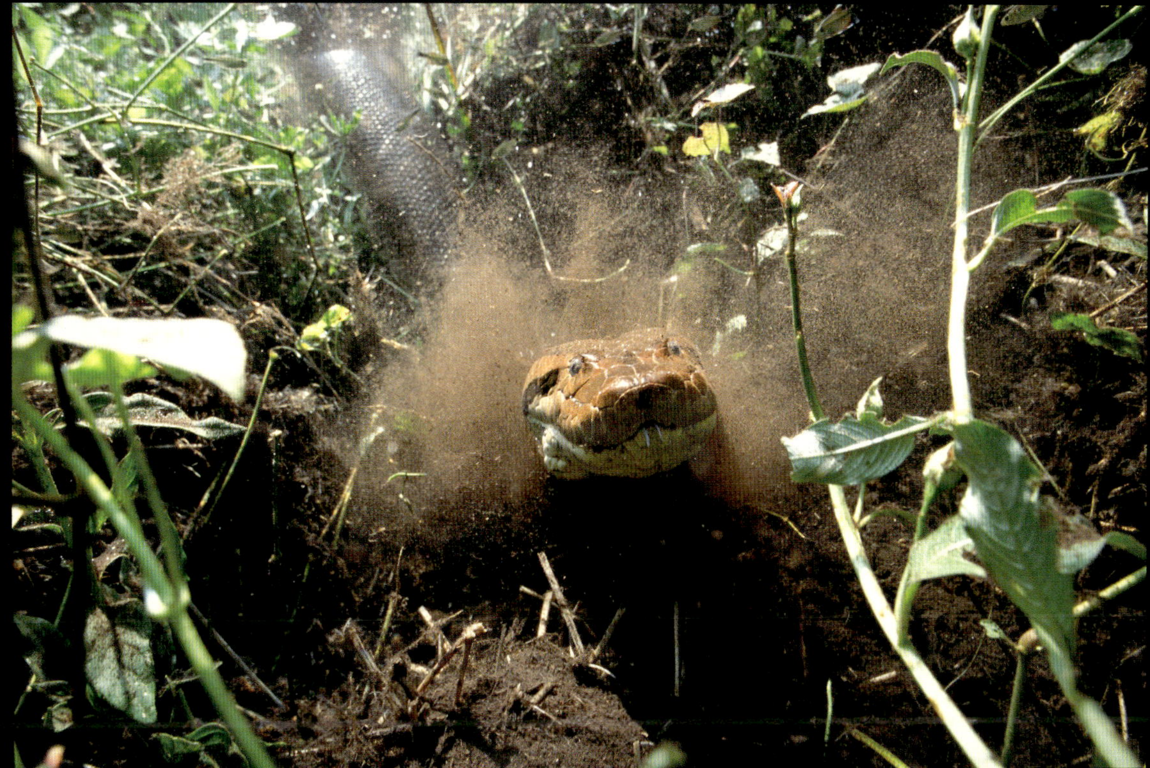

Underwater encounter

Michel Loup

FRANCE

Lying in wait under water or at the river's edge, an anaconda will ambush prey, biting with powerful jaws and pulling it under. The victim may drown or be squeezed to death in the anaconda's coils. So when Michel, positioned in a boat on a river in Brazil, saw this 6m-long (20-foot) female heading down the bank, he slipped into the water to meet it. 'It slid down preparing to hide in the vegetation,' says Michel, 'but then curiosity got the better of it and it came right up to me, looking directly at my lens for what seemed an eternity (10 seconds) from about 20cm (8 inches) away.' Then it turned, and its huge body slid slowly into the gloom. 'I use natural light only for my underwater photography,' adds Michel, 'and so I was very lucky that the water in this area is so clear.'

Nikonos V with 15mm f2.8 lens; 1/125 sec at f11; Fujichrome Provia 400F.

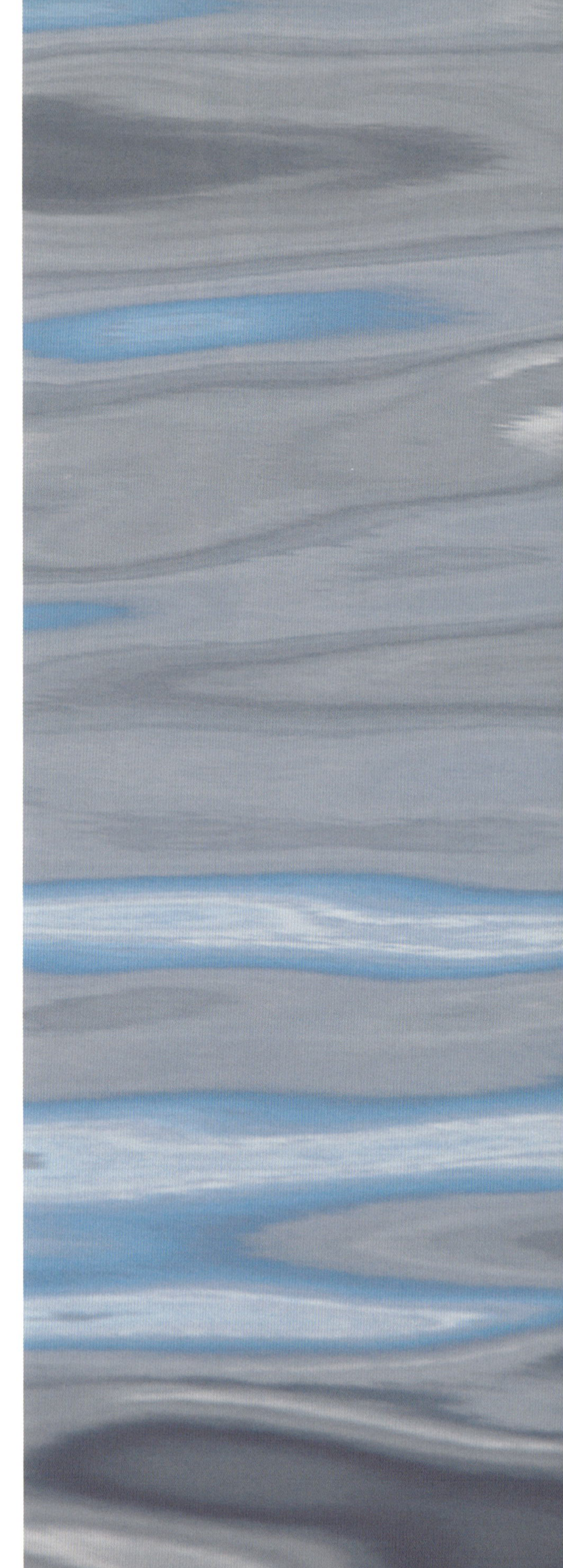

Flight of the albatross

Pat Douglass
UK

Friend to the sailor and icon of the long-distance traveller, an albatross is capable of soaring for thousands of miles without touching land. South of the Falkland Islands, on a ship heading for South Georgia, Pat was enjoying a calm, sunny afternoon on deck, 'trying to photograph birds as they skimmed along the water, rising and falling on the air currents at the stern'. As this black-browed albatross dipped close to the water, its wave-rippled reflection provided the extra dimension she was after. 'It was only the second day at sea with many more to come,' explains Pat, 'but I knew that I had caught an image that would be symbolic of my journey in the Southern Ocean.' It is also an image that few may be able to photograph in the future, as so many albatrosses have died on the hooks of longline fisheries that the species is now highly endangered.

Canon 5D with 300mm f4 lens and 1.4x converter; 1/640 sec at f8; 200 ISO.

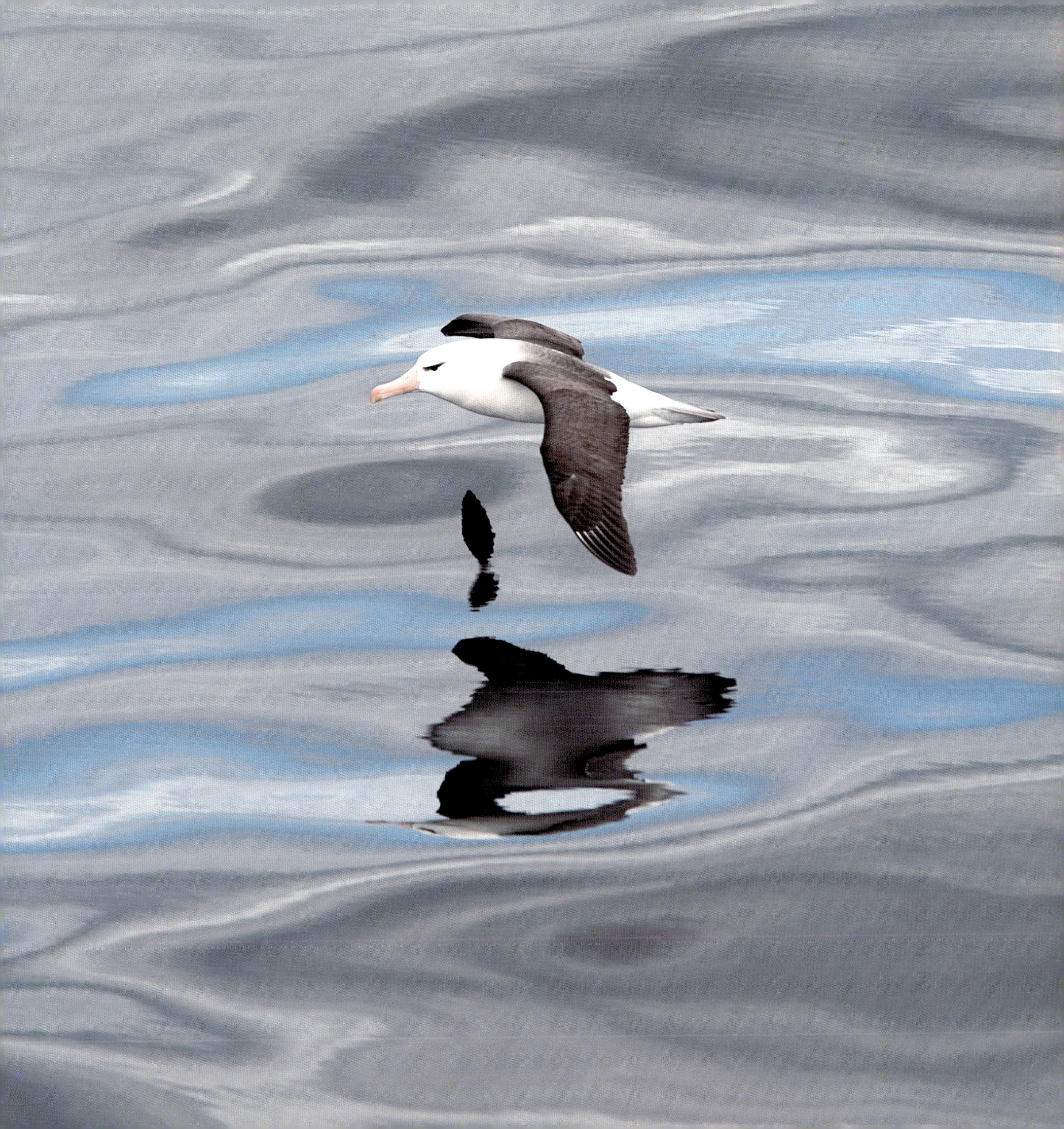

The Underwater World

Here the subjects can be marine or freshwater, but as with land subjects, images must be memorable, either because of the behaviour displayed or because of their aesthetic appeal.

The great mimic

WINNER

Michael AW

SINGAPORE

Diving off Banka Island, Manado, in north Sulawesi, Michael spotted a strange eel moving along a sandy slope. For the next hour he swam with it as it hunted over the sand, watching it assume the movement and shape of various marine creatures, including a sole, a ray and even a sea snake. What he'd met was the master of disguises, the Indo-Malayan mimic octopus – here sporting its 'normal' brown-and-white striped coat. This species takes intelligence to a new level – it can even discern which dangerous sea creature to imitate to present the greatest threat to any predator it's confronted with. Only discovered in 1998, the mimic's repertoire of hunting or hiding disguises includes hermit crabs, sand anemones, crinoids, jellyfish, sea cucumbers, blennies, jawfish and lionfish. Already a fan of octopuses, Michael has 'long since given up eating them'.

Nikon D2X with 12-24mm lens; 1/100 sec at f14; 160 ISO; Seacam housing, single S200 Ikelite strobe.

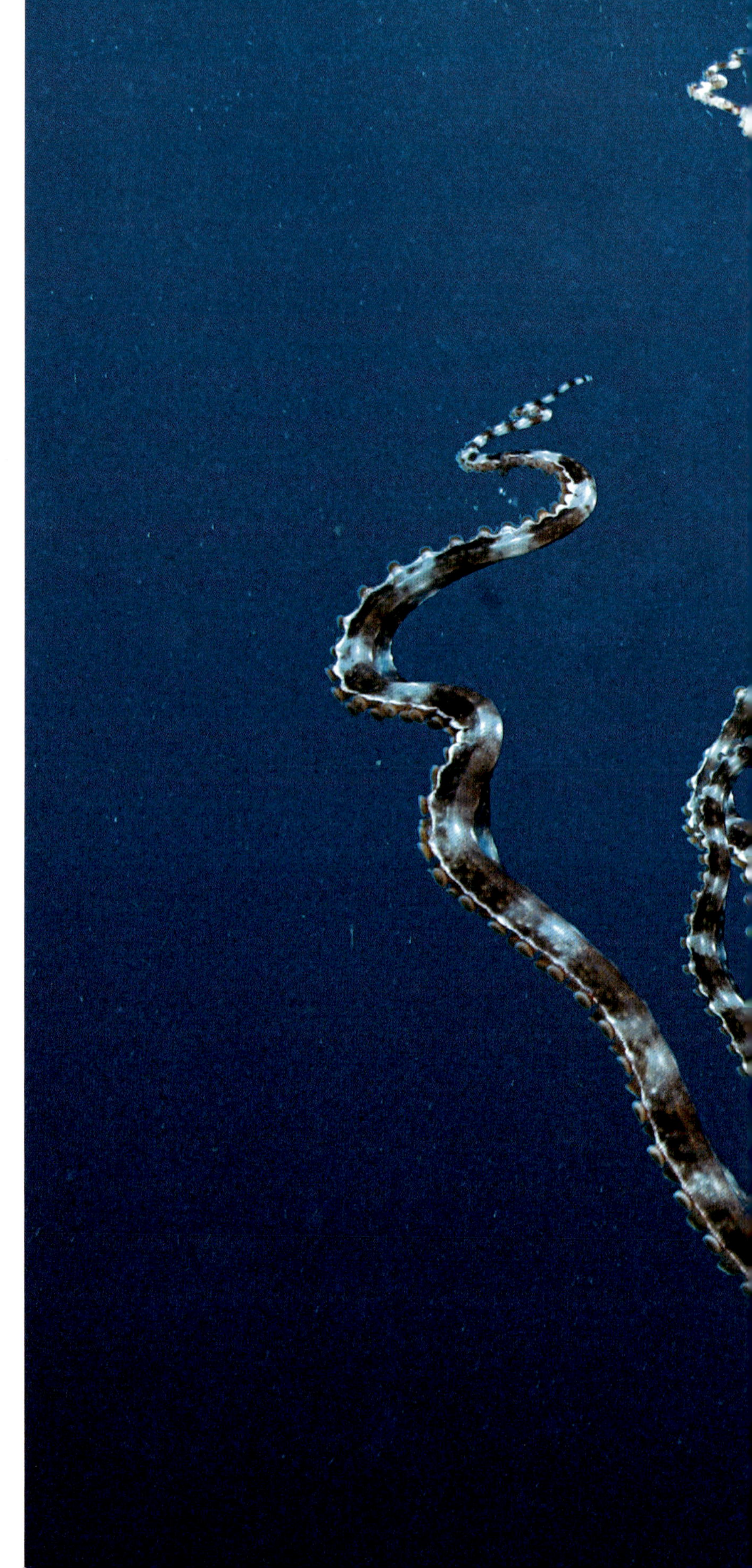

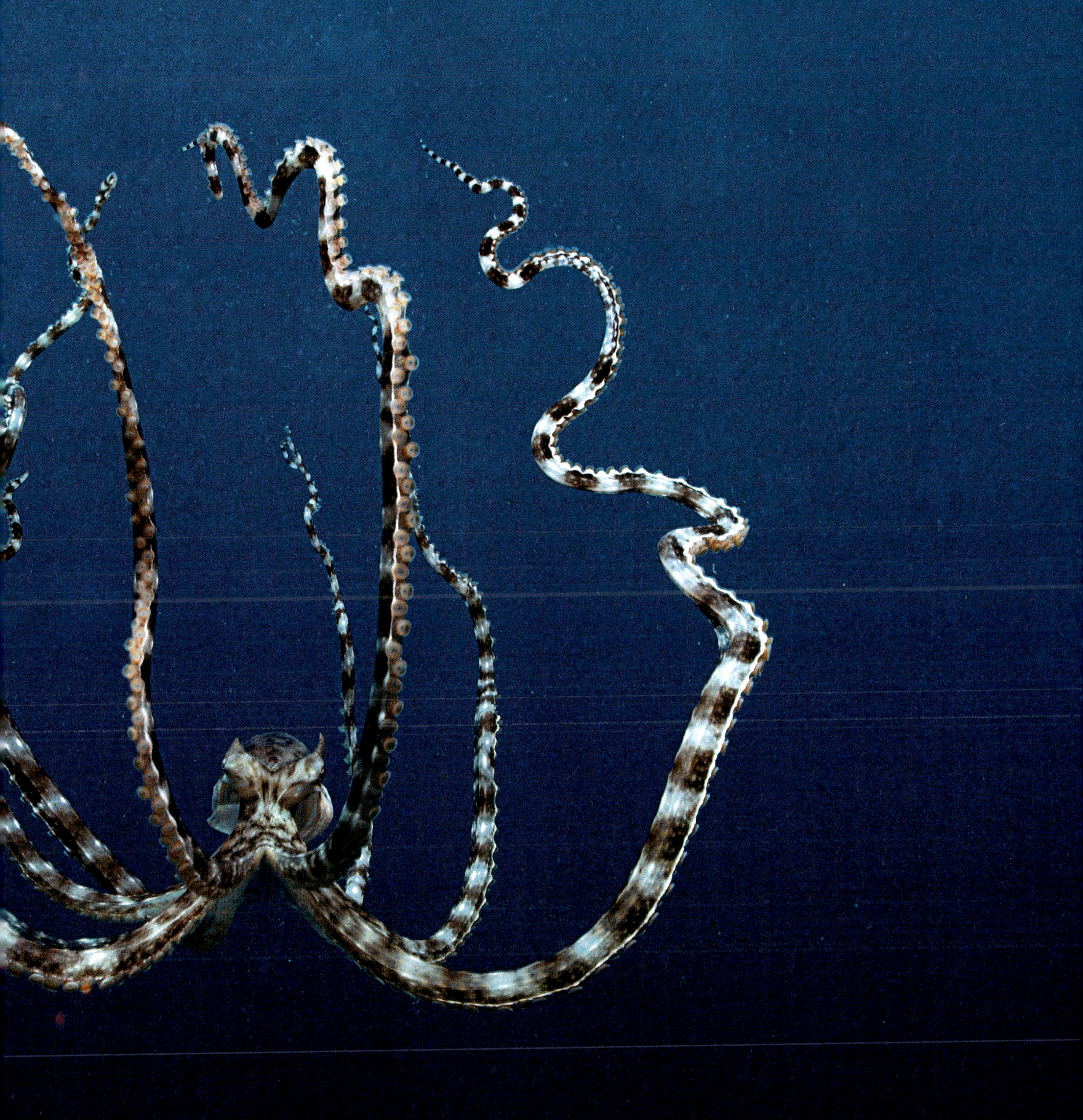

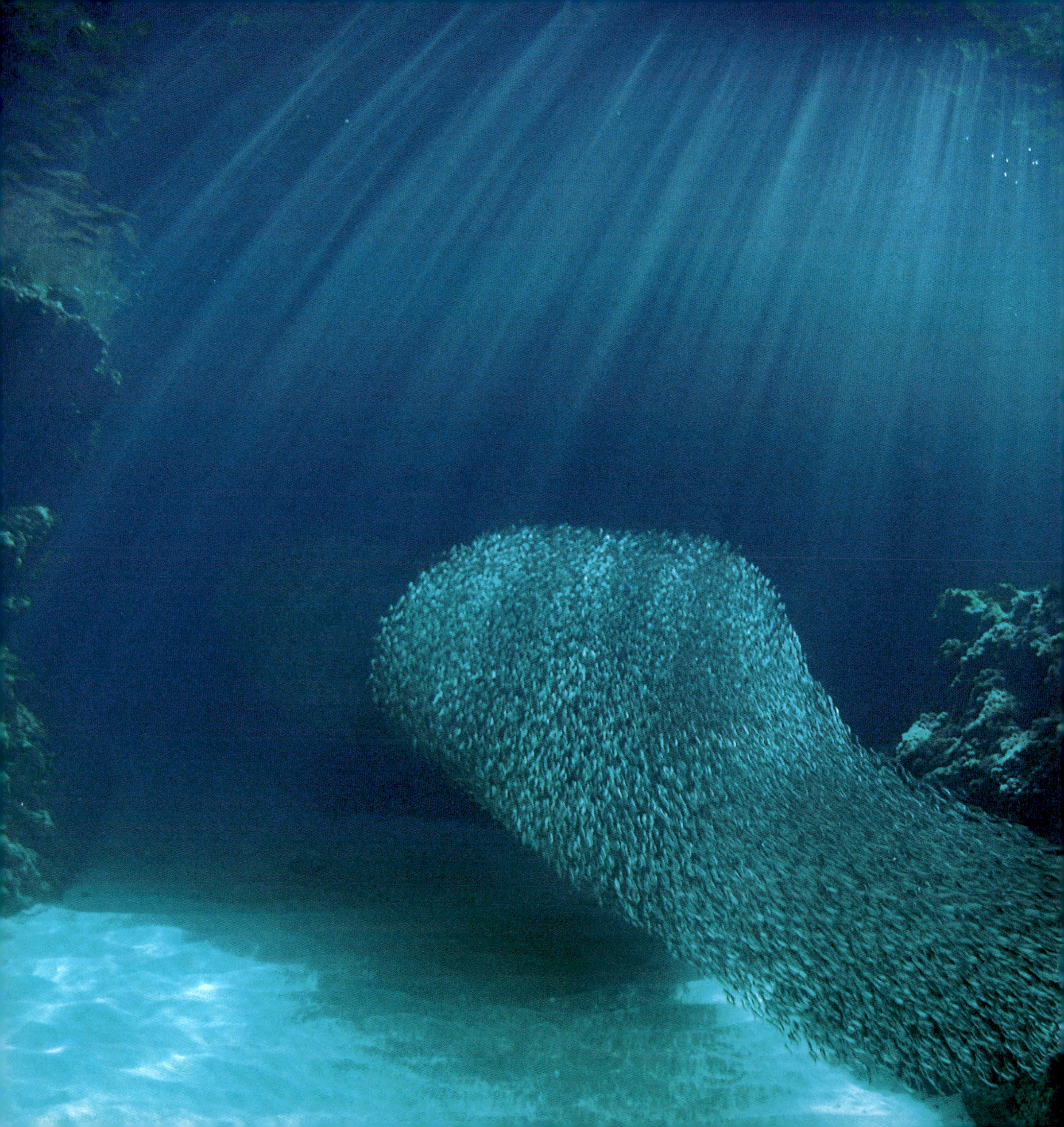

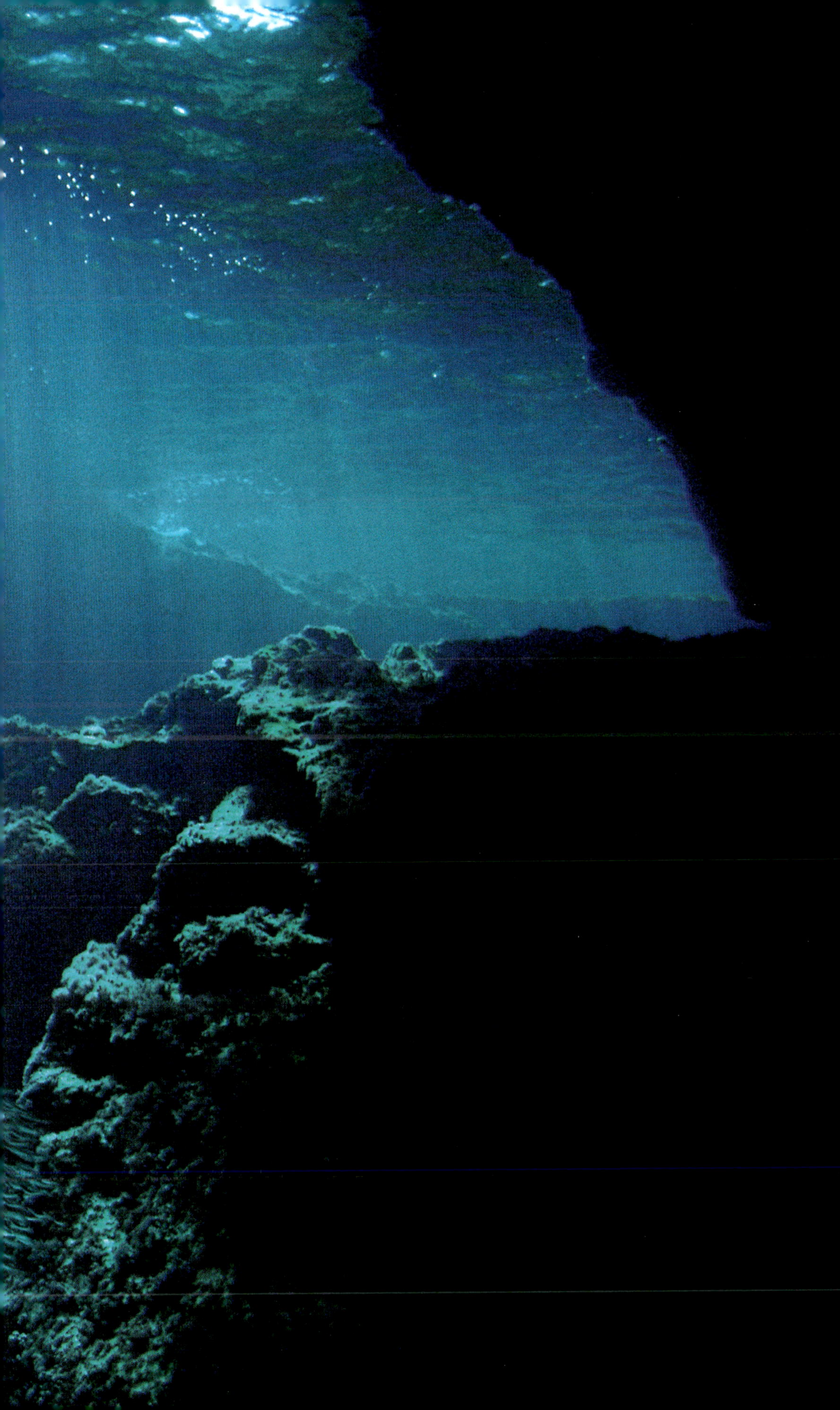

The swirling shoal

RUNNER-UP

Manu San Félix

SPAIN

Snorkelling off Formentera, one of the Balearic islands in the Mediterranean, camera at the ready, Manu became absorbed by the light filtering down from above. As he passed over a cave, a massive creature suddenly emerged and swirled away into the ocean. It was a shoal of thousands and thousands of fishes – one of many shoals of juvenile pelagic (open ocean) species, from pilchards and anchovies to mackerel, that come in close to shore in autumn to shelter from bigger predatory fish, including their own species. 'It was magic,' says Manu. 'They moved as if they were one individual, swirling in perfect synchrony.'

Nikon F5 with 16mm lens; 1/160 sec at f8; Ektachrome 100; Aquatica housing.

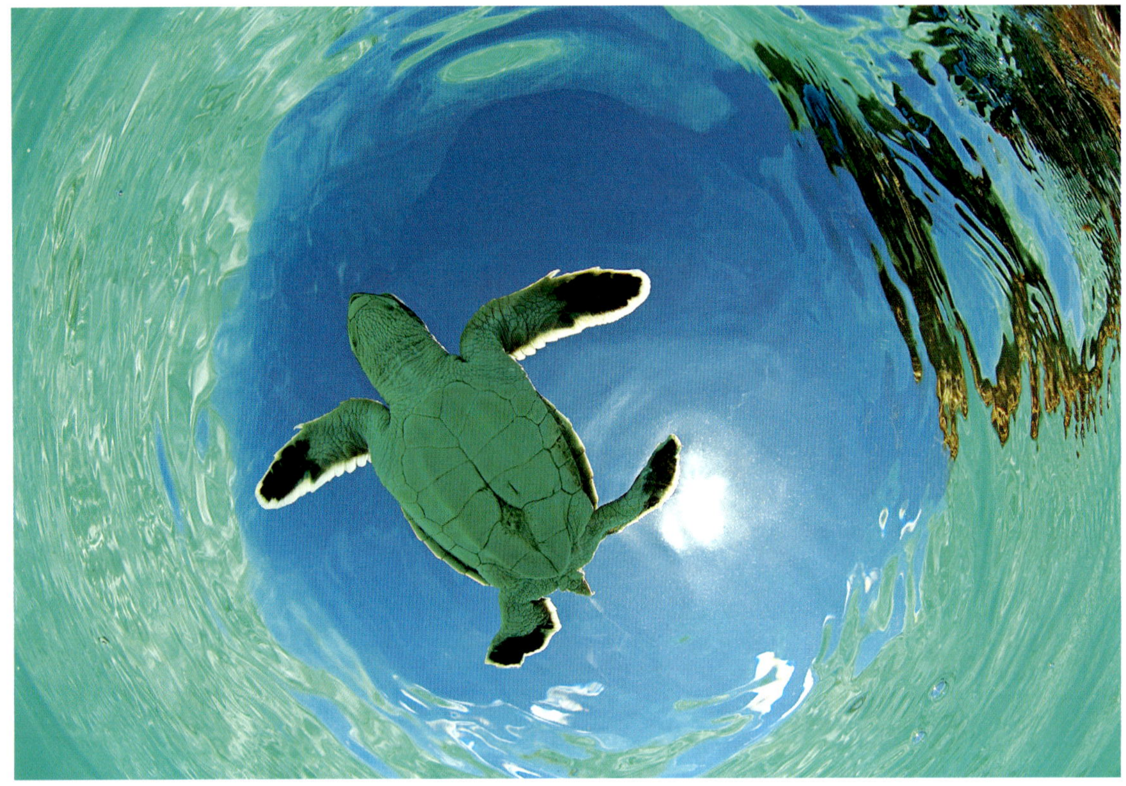

Swimming for life

Willem Kolvoort
THE NETHERLANDS

This newly hatched green turtle had a bleak outlook. Even if it had succeeded in climbing out of the deep pit that it was stuck in, it would have had to scramble over a sand ridge and cross a wide beach on Aldabra before facing sharks in the shallows. But when the weary turtle was rescued from its hole and released into the sea, it seemed to perk up. 'I swam out with it, beyond the blacktip reef sharks I was photographing,' says Willem. Following the baby turtle into deeper water, he took lots of pictures of it using a fisheye lens, and then 'watched it disappear into the blue beyond.'

Nikon D70 with 10.5mm fisheye lens; 1/800 sec at f14; 200 ISO; Seacam housing.

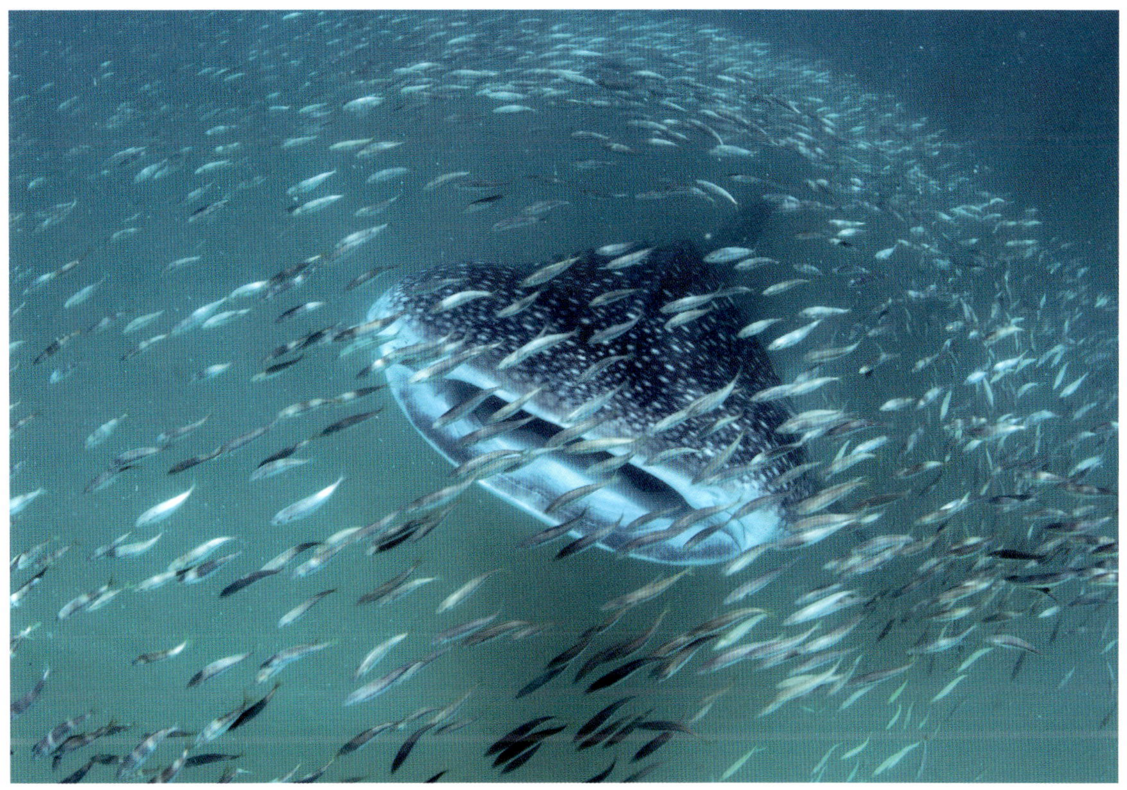

Big fish, little fishes

Gavin Parsons

UK

The world's largest fishes – whale sharks, which can be up to 20m (65 feet) long – gather off Mafia Island, Tanzania, between November and January to filter-feed on the masses of plankton there. Local fishermen use them to locate shoals of small fishes, which shelter around them, and Gavin used fishing boats to locate the giants. 'We found a shark being shadowed by a couple of boats,' says Gavin. 'It moved under our boat and just hung there, possibly sheltering from the glare. As I slipped into the sea and it lifted its huge head, the little fishes fled for fear of being chased to the surface.'

Nikon D70 with 16mm fisheye lens; 1/125 sec at f8; 200 ISO; Sea & Sea housing with fisheye dome port.

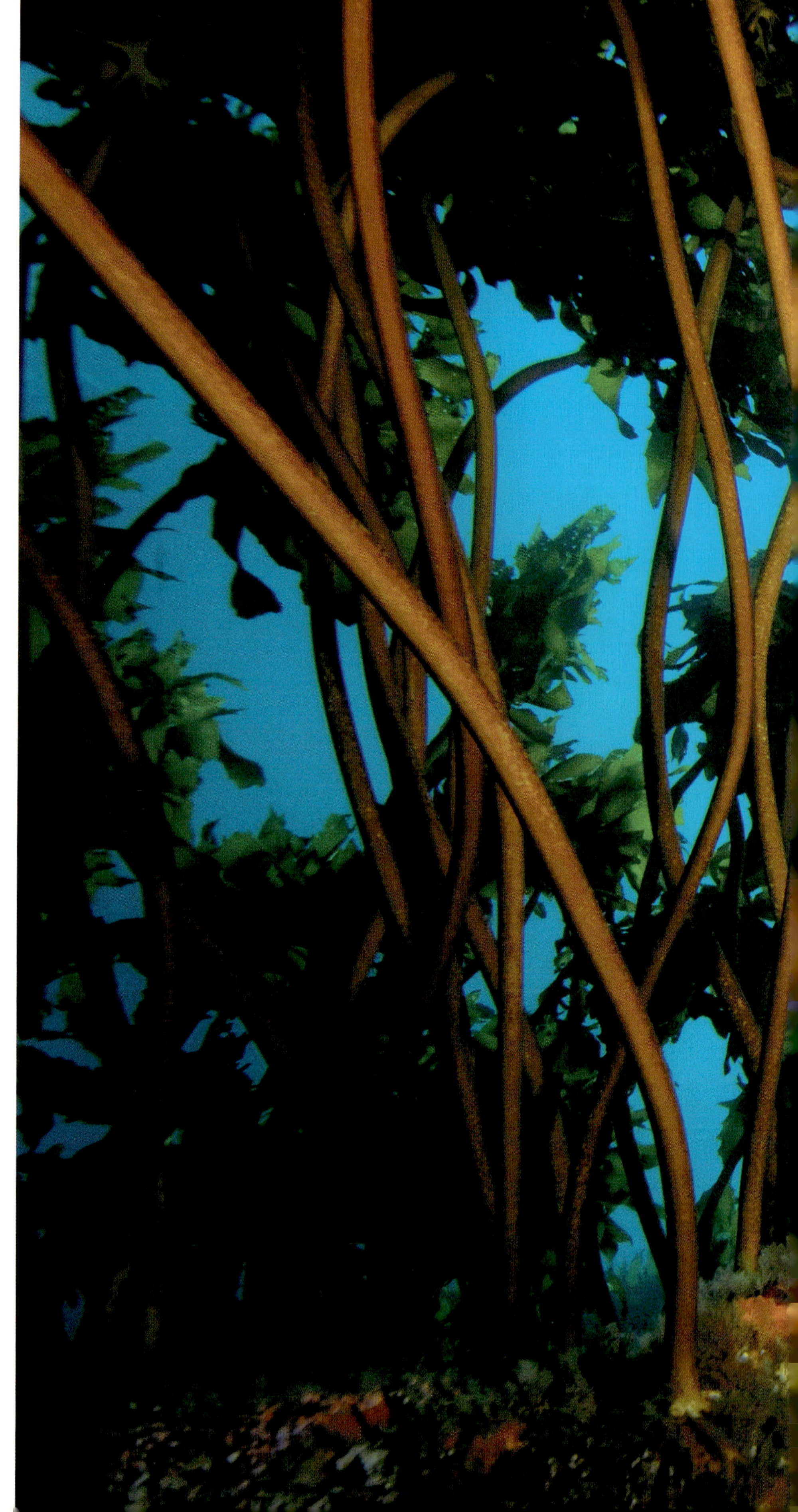

Pigfish in kelp

Ross Armstrong

NEW ZEALAND

Viewed from above water, dense kelp beds appear full of menace, hiding any number of fearsome creatures. Ross, though, loves to explore these mysterious habitats. *Ecklonia*-kelp-coated reefs occur around the Poor Knights Islands off northeast New Zealand. 'I tried to find an exposed reef edge so that I could get below the kelp,' says Ross. 'Looking upwards gives the feel of being in an underwater forest.' A curious female redpig fish swam back and forth, keeping an eye on the underwater intruder: 'The perfect contrast for my composition.'

Nikon D70 with Nikkor 12-24mm DX zoom lens; 1/250 sec at f8; 200 ISO; Nexus housing and two strobes.

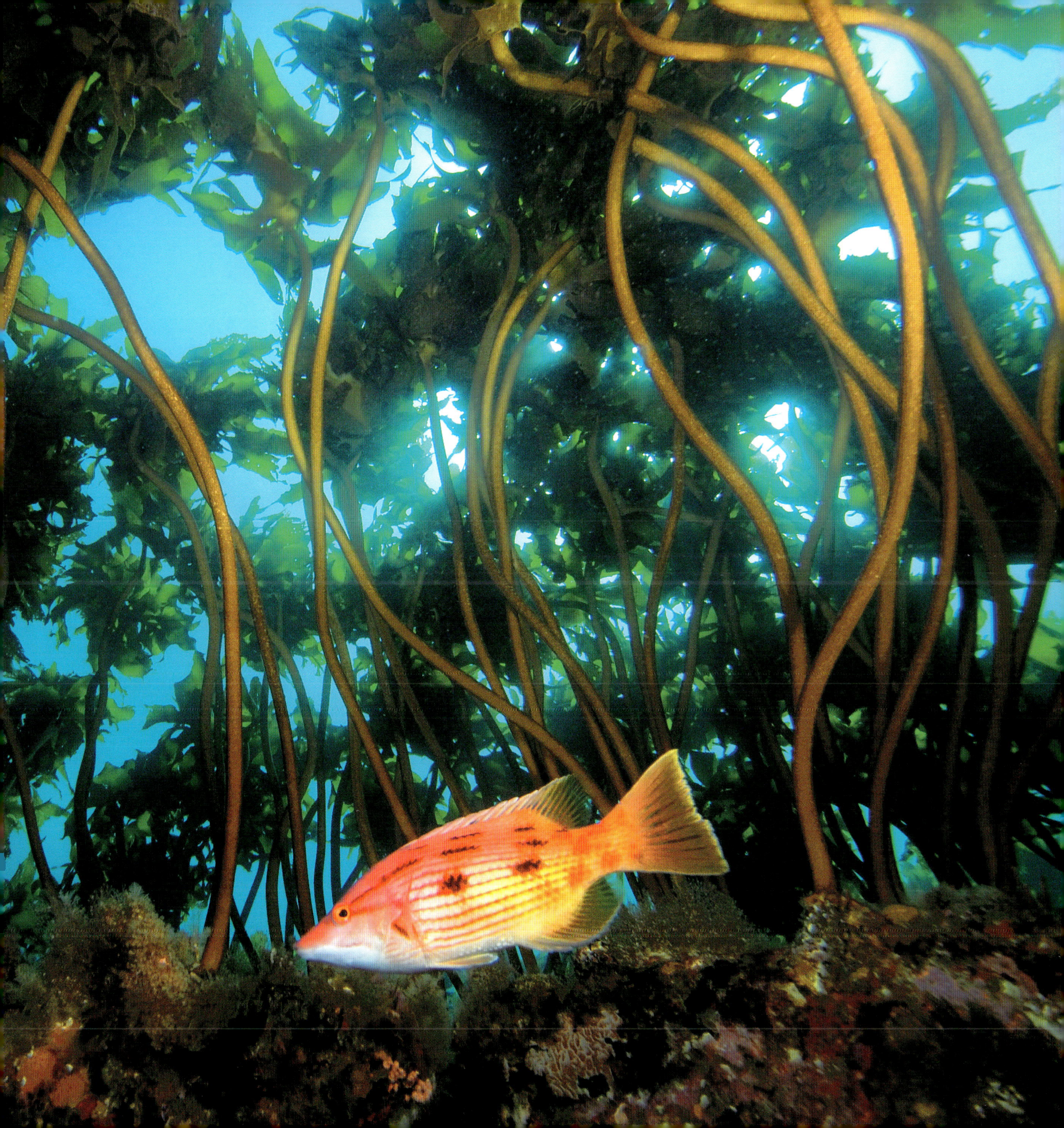

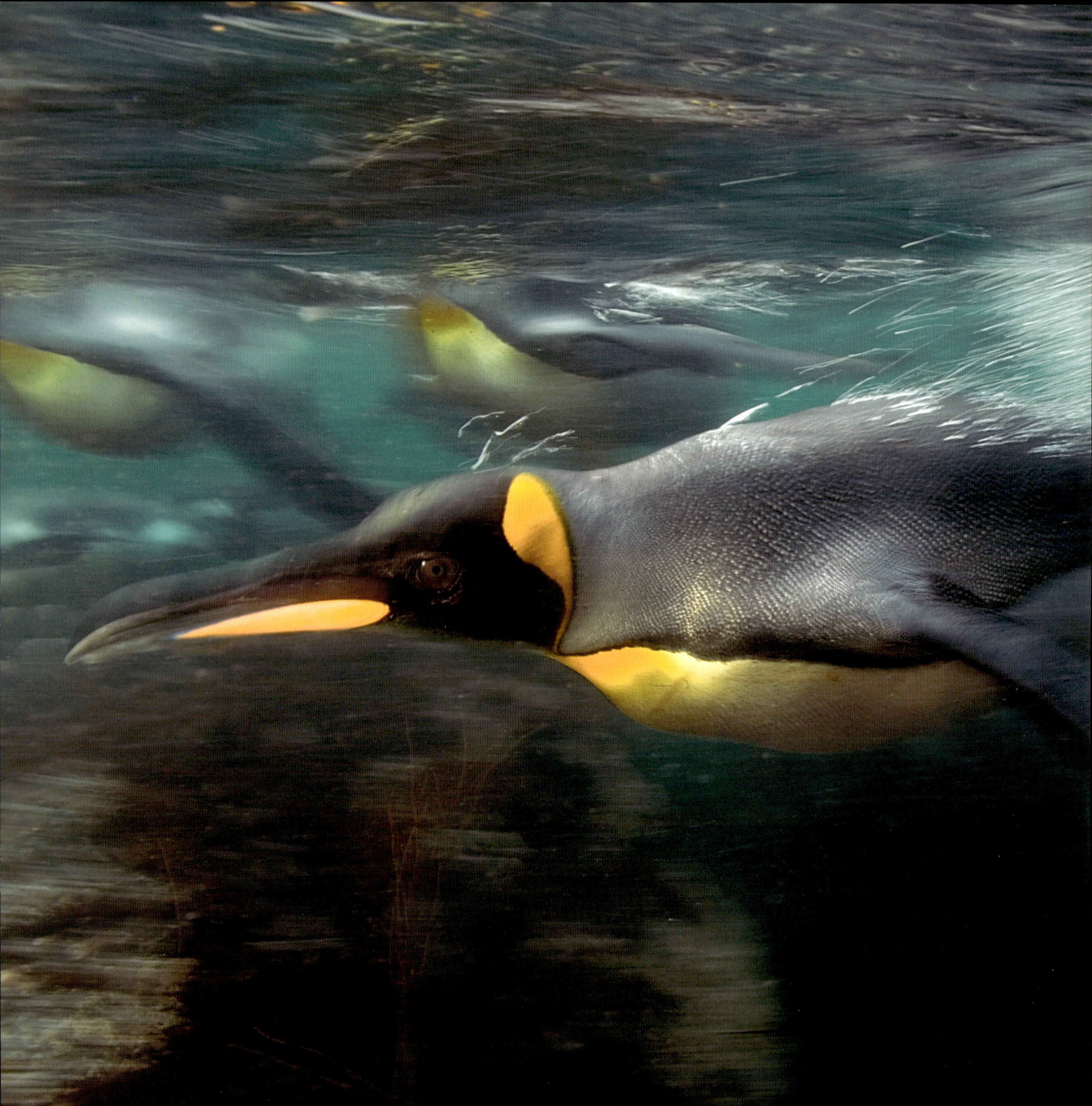

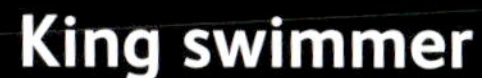

King swimmer

Tobias Bernhard

GERMANY

The king penguin colony at Sandy Bay on Maquarie Island in the sub-Antarctic is camped around a tidal pool for easy access to the tempestuous Southern Ocean. Tobias positioned himself in the water near one of the penguins' favourite launch sites to watch the busy thoroughfare of penguins rushing back and forth. 'The birds didn't hang around,' says Tobias. 'They were on a mission to fill their bellies.' Here one flies past the photographer on its way out to sea, its eye on the camera. 'They were so unfazed by me', adds Tobias, 'that some of them cheekily used my back as a diving board while I was bent over half in the water with my eye glued to the viewfinder.'

Nikon D2x with 14mm f2.8 lens; f15 at 20 sec; 100 ISO; Subal housing.

Animal Portraits

This category – one of the most popular in the competition – invites portraits that capture the character or spirit of the subject they focus on.

Great barracuda

WINNER

Tibor Dombovári

HUNGARY

Unlike a dolphin whose 'smiling' snout endears it to people, the barracuda with its protruding lower jaw, formidable teeth and thuggish expression has a few problems with its PR. Tibor, however, saw only beauty when he came across this great barracuda lurking beneath his dive boat in Papua New Guinea. 'I grabbed a tank of air and a wide-angle lens,' he says, 'and jumped straight in.' He then set about getting to know the barracuda and gaining its trust. 'We were mutually curious and followed each other around for nearly two hours.' Great barracudas are top-of-the-range, opportunistic predators, with huge, powerful jaws that enable them to eat a variety of prey. Unprovoked attacks on humans are extremely rare, though.

Nikon D70s with Nikkor 12-24mm f4G AFS DX lens; 1/200 sec at f7.1; 200 ISO; Subal housing, two Ikelite DS125 strobes.

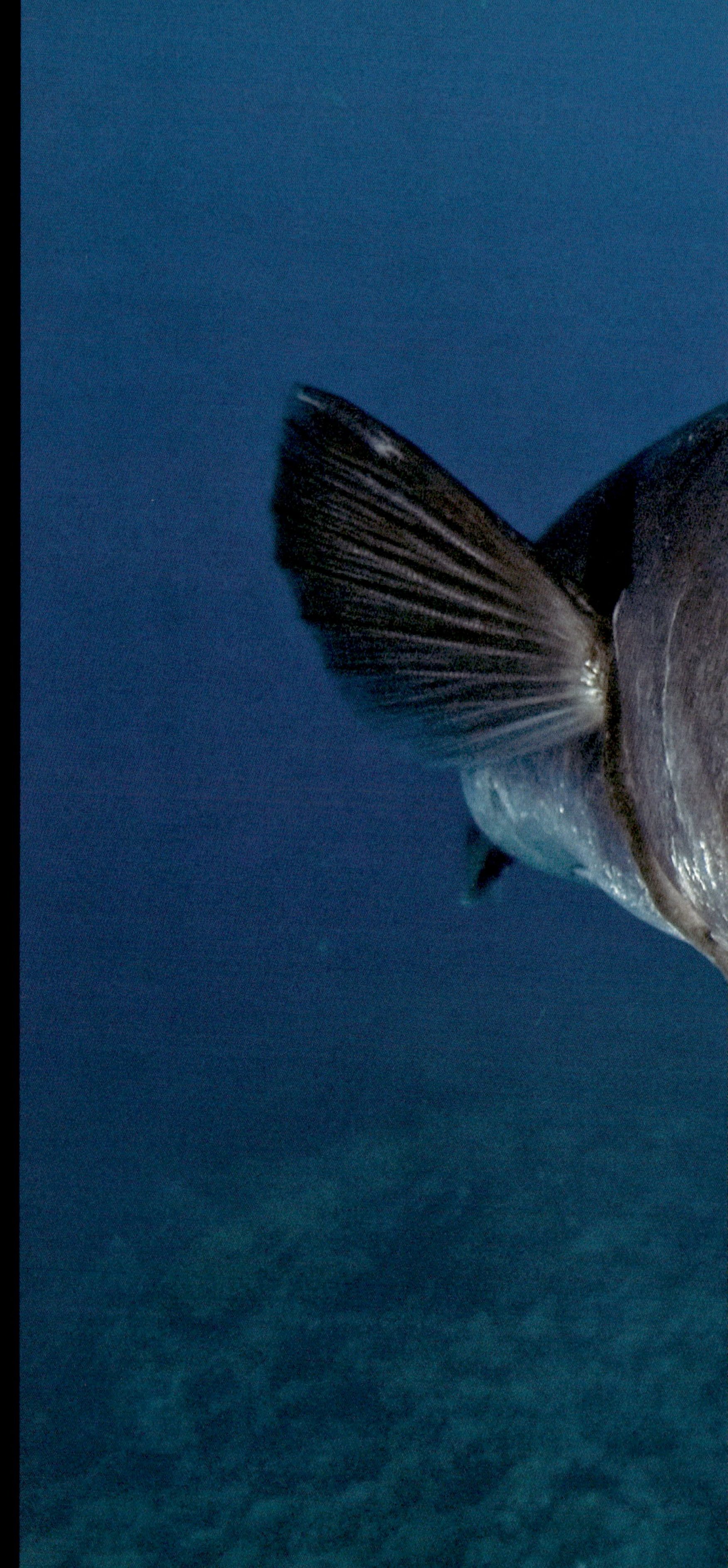

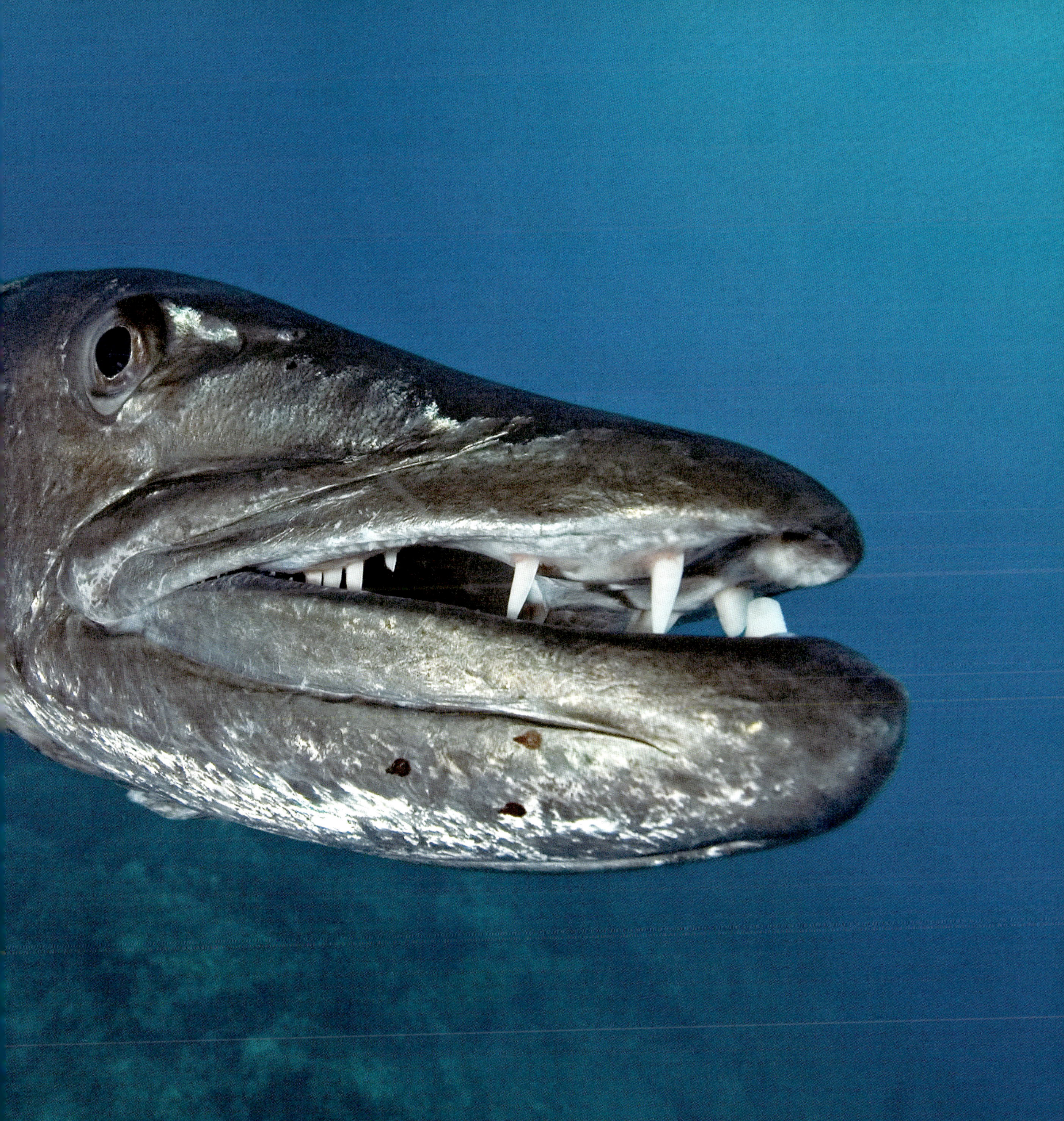

Ice hole

RUNNER-UP

Baard Næss

NORWAY

Baard wasn't having a good day in his search for polar bears. Bitter winds, snowstorms and heavy clouds on Svalbard made the going tough. 'When we got off the snow-scooters for a rest,' says Baard, 'I spotted a seal breathing hole and saw stirrings. I waited motionlessly right next to it – a bit like a polar bear might do – until a head popped up.' In the event, the grey light was perfect – any harsher and the subtle colours would have been lost and the contrast between the ringed seal and its icy environment would have been too great.

Canon 1D Mark II with 70-200mm f2.8L lens; 1/200 sec at f5.6; 400 ISO.

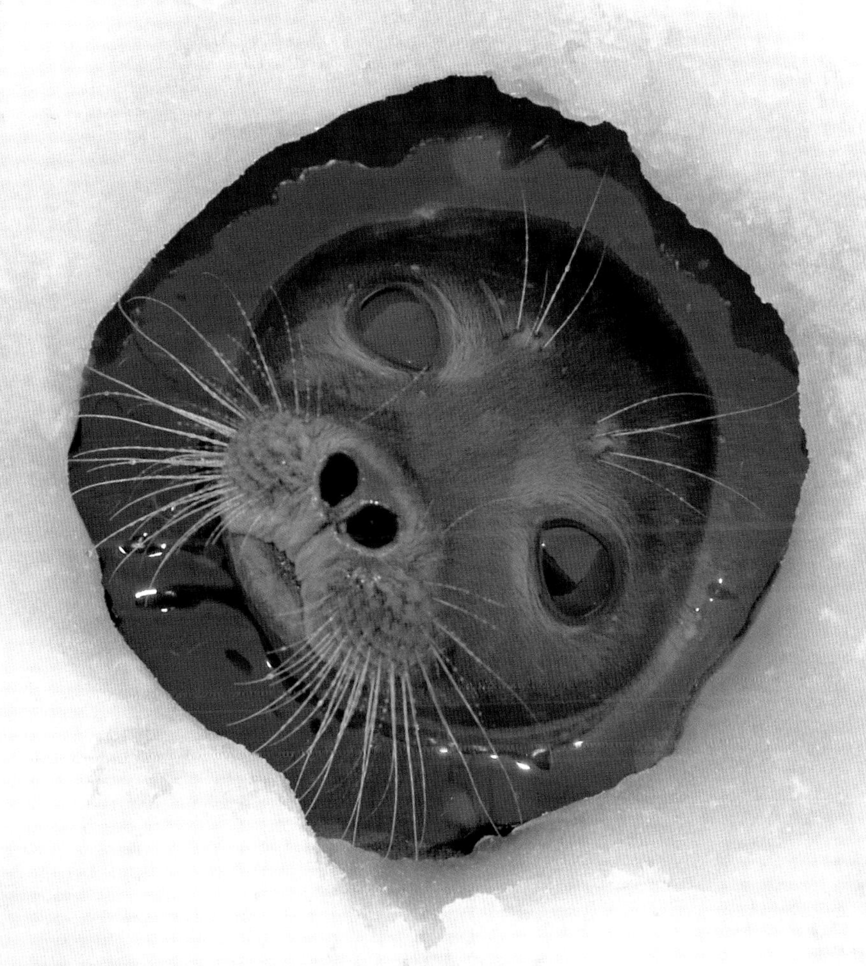

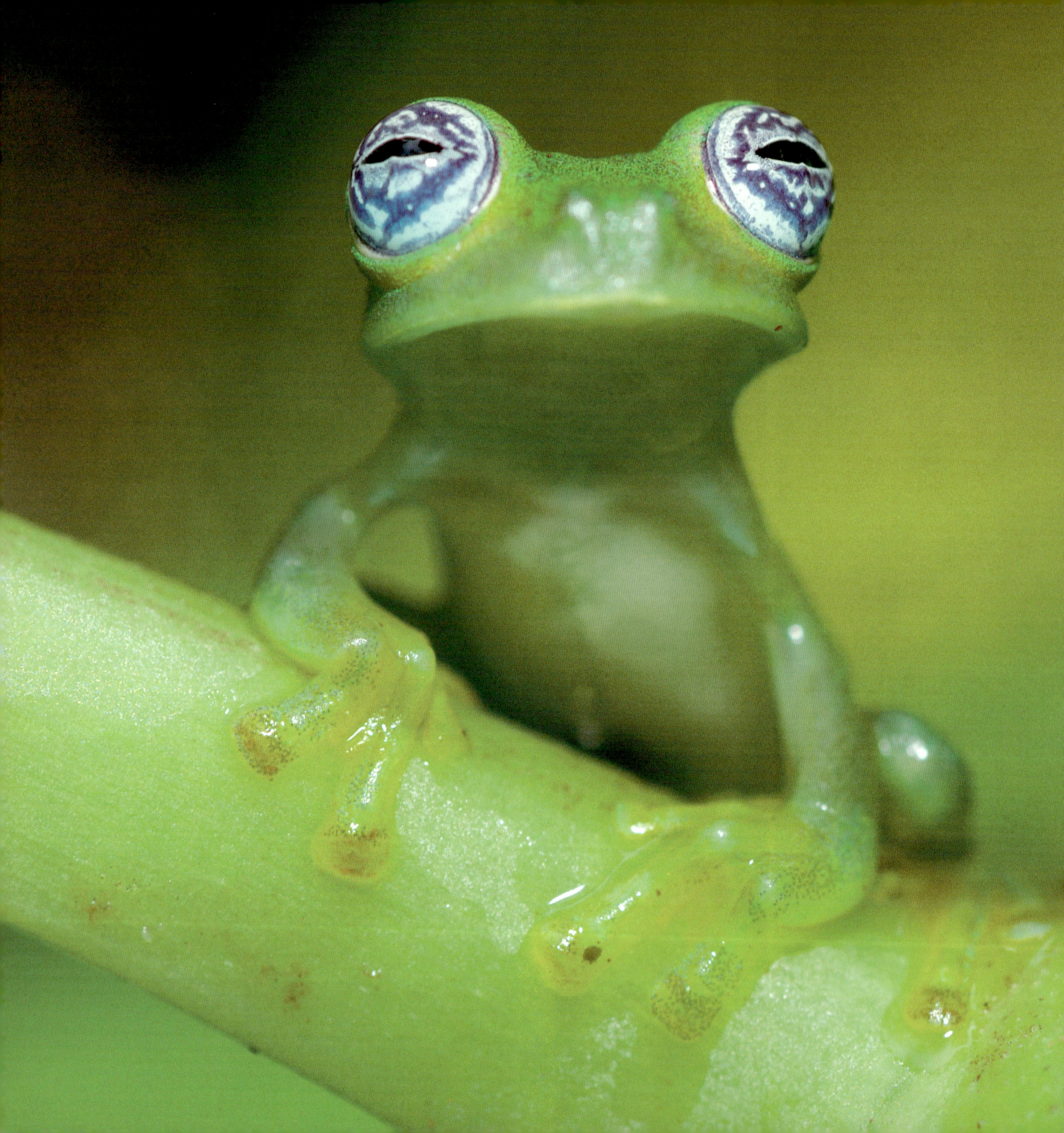

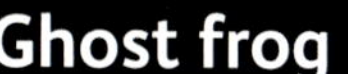

Ghost frog

SPECIALLY COMMENDED

Edwin Giesbers

THE NETHERLANDS

Many species of frog in Costa Rica have disappeared over the past couple of decades, believed to be victims of a combination of a deadly fungus and the stresses of climate change. Ghost glass frogs are still relatively widespread but difficult to find – Edwin's guide hadn't seen one for a year – and so the discovery was even more exciting than that of the mountain lion footprints in the mud nearby. 'I stood in a stream to get as close as I could,' says Edwin. 'The frog remained motionless as I took its portrait, completely confident in its ability to morph into the plant it was attached to.' Glass frogs get their name from the transparent skin on their bellies through which you can see their organs and even their circulating blood.

Nikon D70 with Tamron 90mm macro lens; f4; 400 ISO.

Dusk flight

Vincent Munier

FRANCE

'The worse the weather conditions,' says Vincent, 'the closer I feel to snowy owls.' To get this portrait, he sat for hours through wind and freezing snowstorms, snow crystals lashing across the Canadian landscape. Feeling nothing but awe for these birds of prey, he adds, 'Their resistance is simply unbelievable.' This male (juveniles and females have dark bars on their plumage) was one Vincent got to know well. At dusk, it would choose the same spot to hunt, close to a farm where it could find plenty of rodent prey. 'You would never believe from the mellow lighting just how cold it was,' says Vincent. 'The fine snow is blown in such a way you could be forgiven for thinking it was the Sahara.'

Nikon D2x with 300mm f2.8 AFS lens; 1/6400 sec at f4; 250 ISO; tripod.

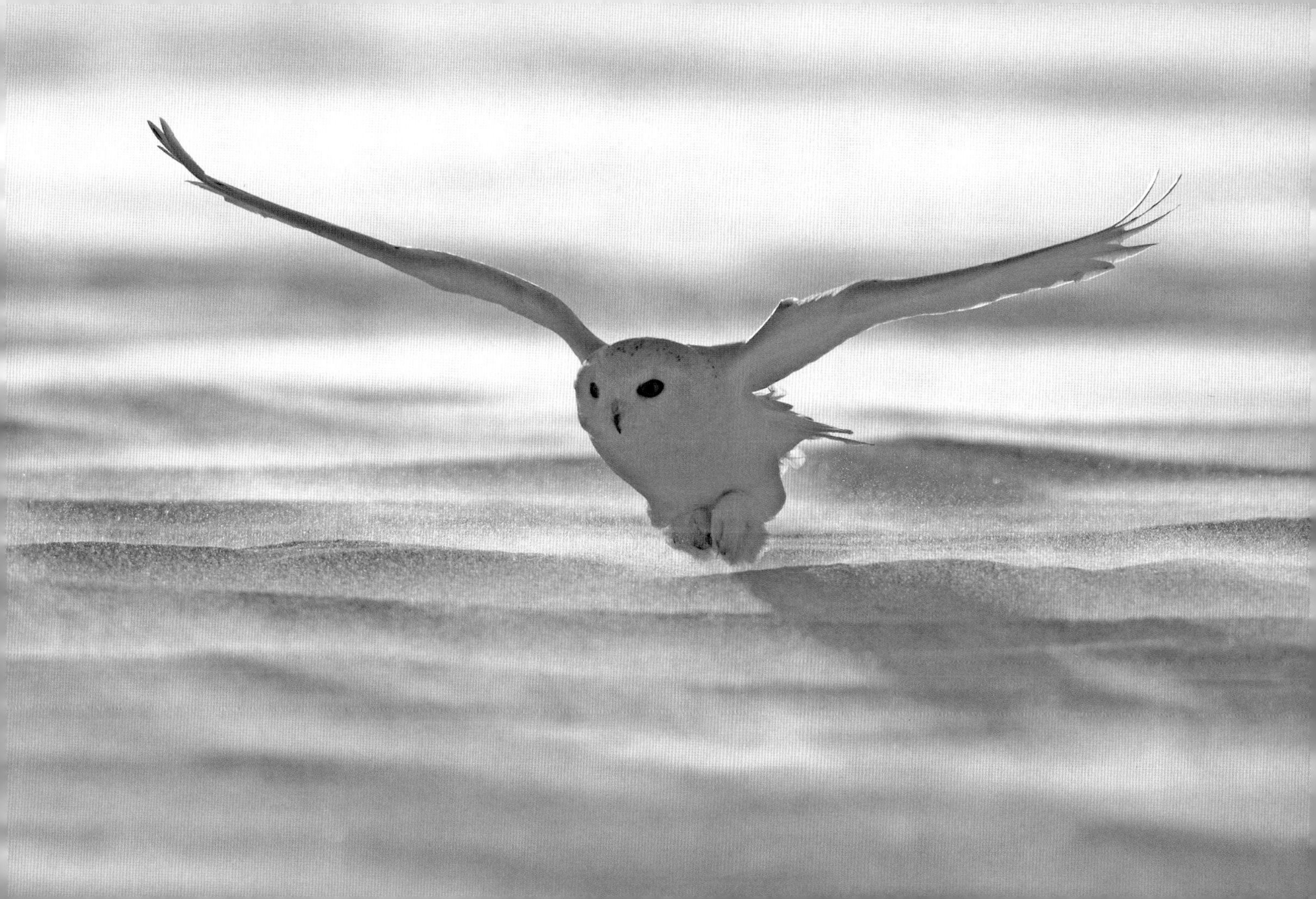

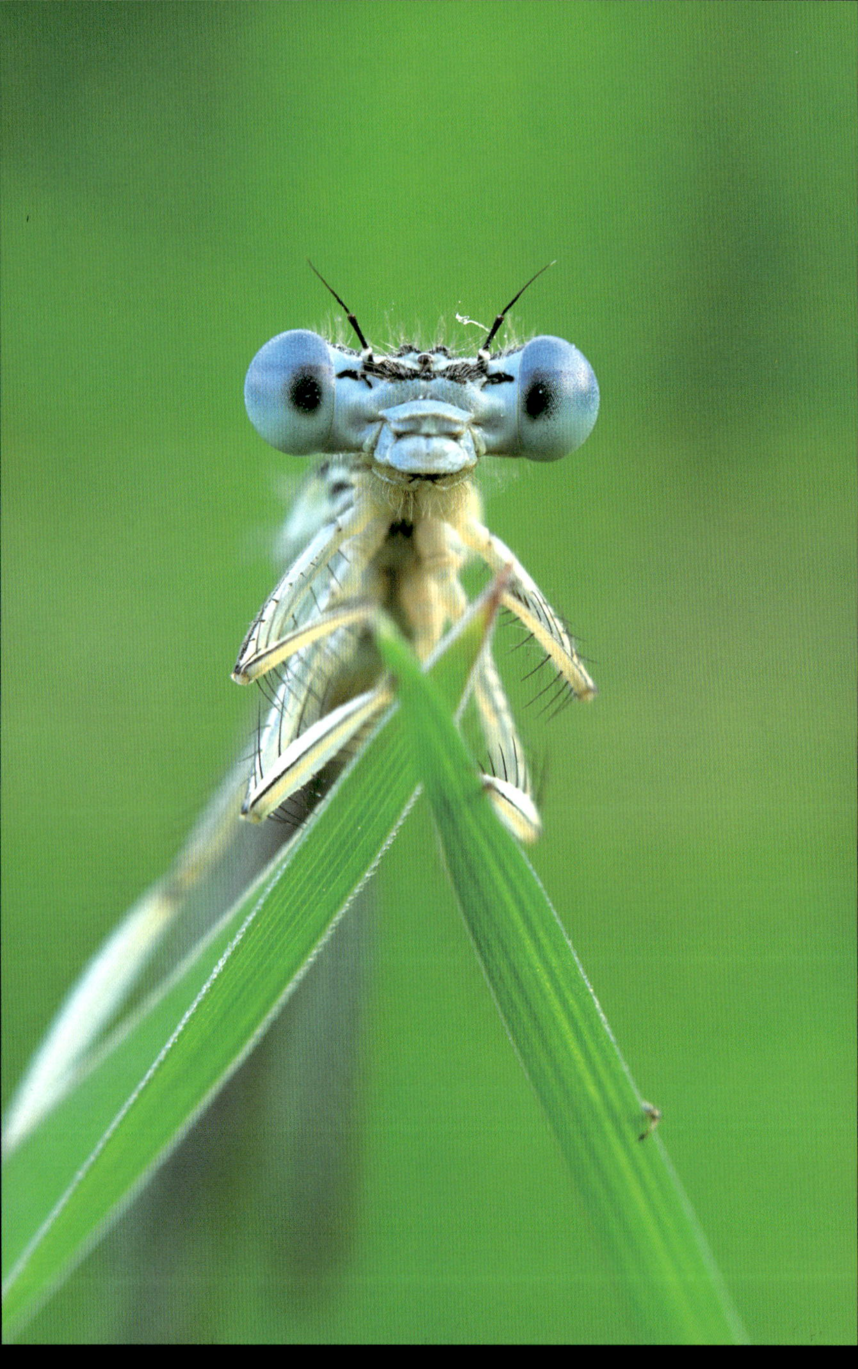

Eye-to-eye

Theo Bosboom

THE NETHERLANDS

This white-legged damselfly posed one May evening for more than an hour on symmetrically crossed grasses, seemingly as transfixed by the photographer as he was by it. 'After a couple of photos from a distance,' says Theo, 'I crept closer and closer, trying not to make any unexpected movements. An hour or so and a lot of shots later, I had got really close. But it still maintained eye contact while I fired off shot after shot.' The resulting detail reveals not only its beautiful colours but also its spiked hair and 'goatee' beard, together with its armoury of sensory leg bristles.

Canon EOS 30 with 100mm f2.8 macro lens, 25mm extension tube and 1.4 extender; Fujichrome Velvia 50 rated at 40; tripod, cable release and mirror lock-up.

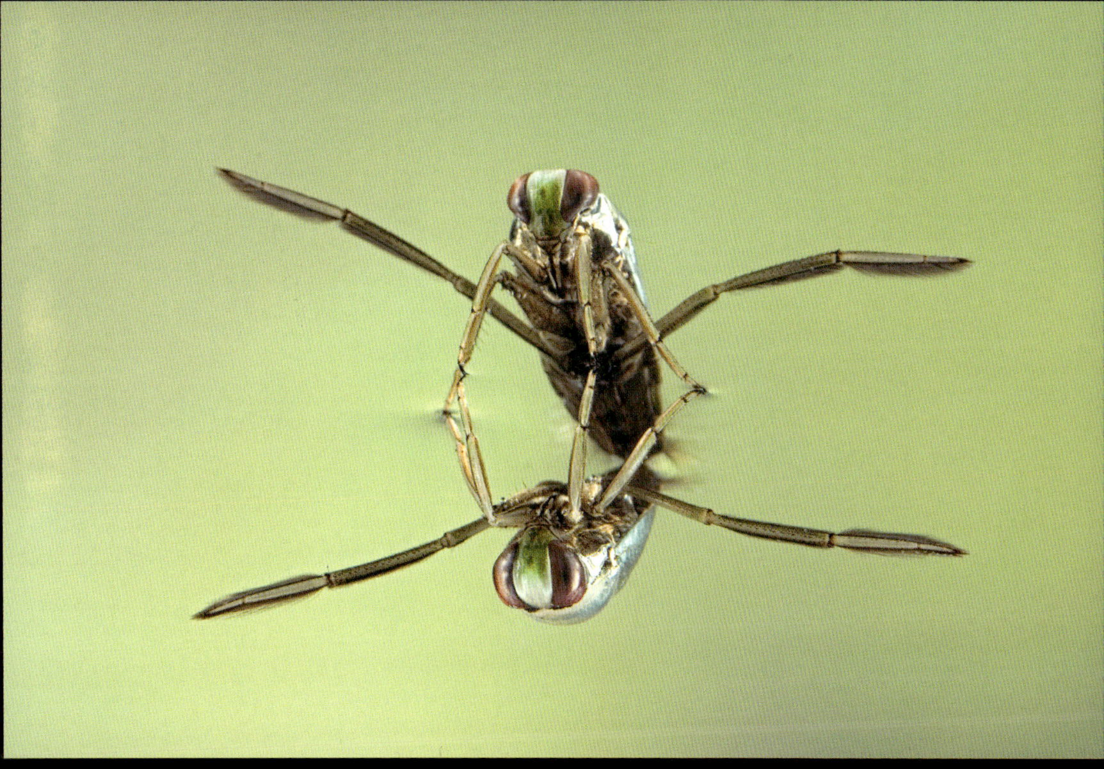

Reflection

Ingo Arndt

GERMANY

A beautifully crafted optical illusion captures the essence of a water boatman. Hanging from the water film, its reflection becomes the portrait. 'I made it a home in an aquarium so I could position my camera for the right shot,' says Ingo. 'The dimples – its footprints – are what you will see on a still summer day when the bug waits patiently to grab passing prey on the surface.' Perfect lighting and focus reveal the

Ice leopard

Carlos Villoch

SPAIN

After an uneventful ice dive, photographing penguin chicks making their first leap into Antarctic waters – a dangerous feat, as leopard seals are usually lurking close by – Carlos was returning to his boat in an inflatable when he spotted a leopard seal swimming around a chunk of ice. His oxygen tank was empty, and so he decided just to snorkel. 'As I slipped into the water, thoughts of how these huge seals can turn aggressive, with fatal consequences, escalated in my mind.' Melting ice made the visibility terrible, maybe only a couple of metres, but the silhouette of the 3m- (10-foot) long seal against the ice loomed large. 'As it grew more confident,' he says, 'I grew less. When it suddenly zoomed from the gloom to look at itself in my camera lens, my heart nearly stopped.' He adds: 'Goodness knows how a penguin must feel.'

Nikon D70 with 10.5mm lens; 1/400 sec at f7.1; 200 ISO; Ikelite housing; double Ikelite strobes.

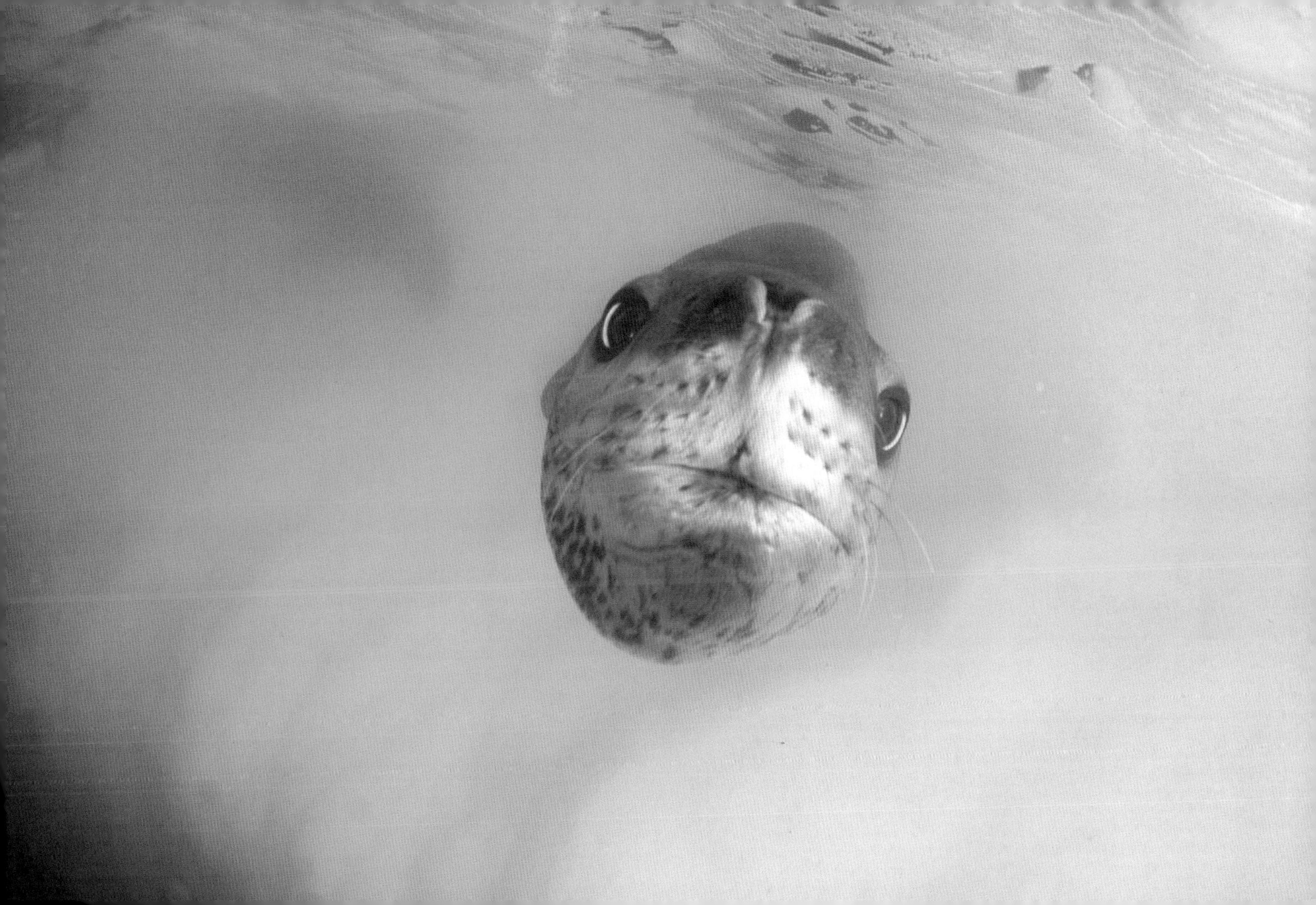

In Praise of Plants

The aim of this category is to showcase the beauty and importance of flowering and non-flowering plants, whether by featuring them in close-up or as part of the habitat.

Lily leaf

WINNER

Dirk Heckmann

GERMANY

Fascinated by leaves – the multitude of different shades of green and variety of textures and shapes – Dirk chose to spend a day in Berlin's Botanic Garden. What attracted him to this water-lily leaf was its relationship with the water – how it controlled the amount of water on its surface, the way the water changed the colours and, sliding into its centre, magnified the details of the leaf, and the shape the water itself took. 'The difficulty was angling the tripod so that I could shoot down on the leaf,' adds Dirk. 'I took very many images before I was satisfied.'

Canon EOS 10D with 100mm f2.8 macro lens; 1/40 sec at f7.1; tripod.

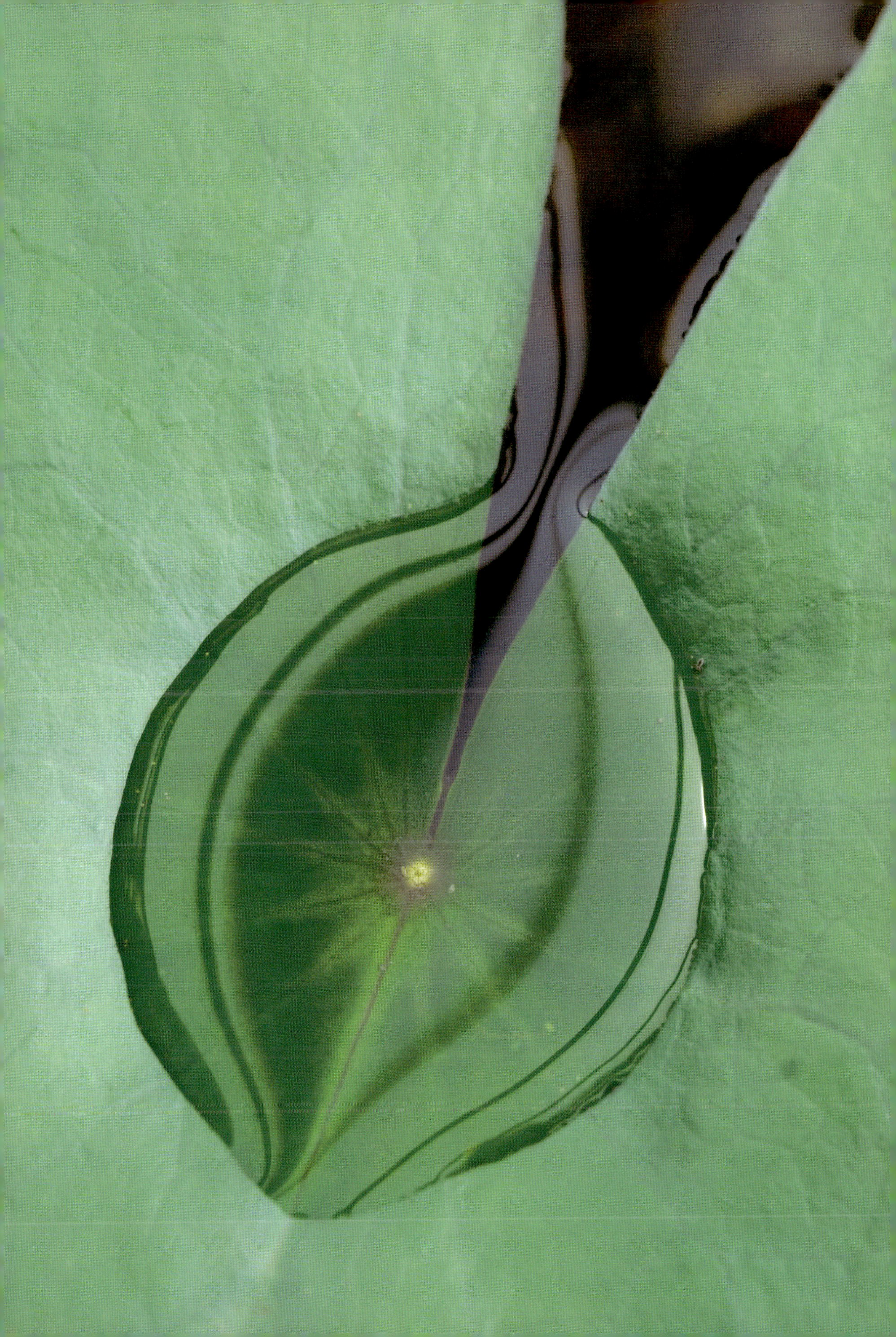

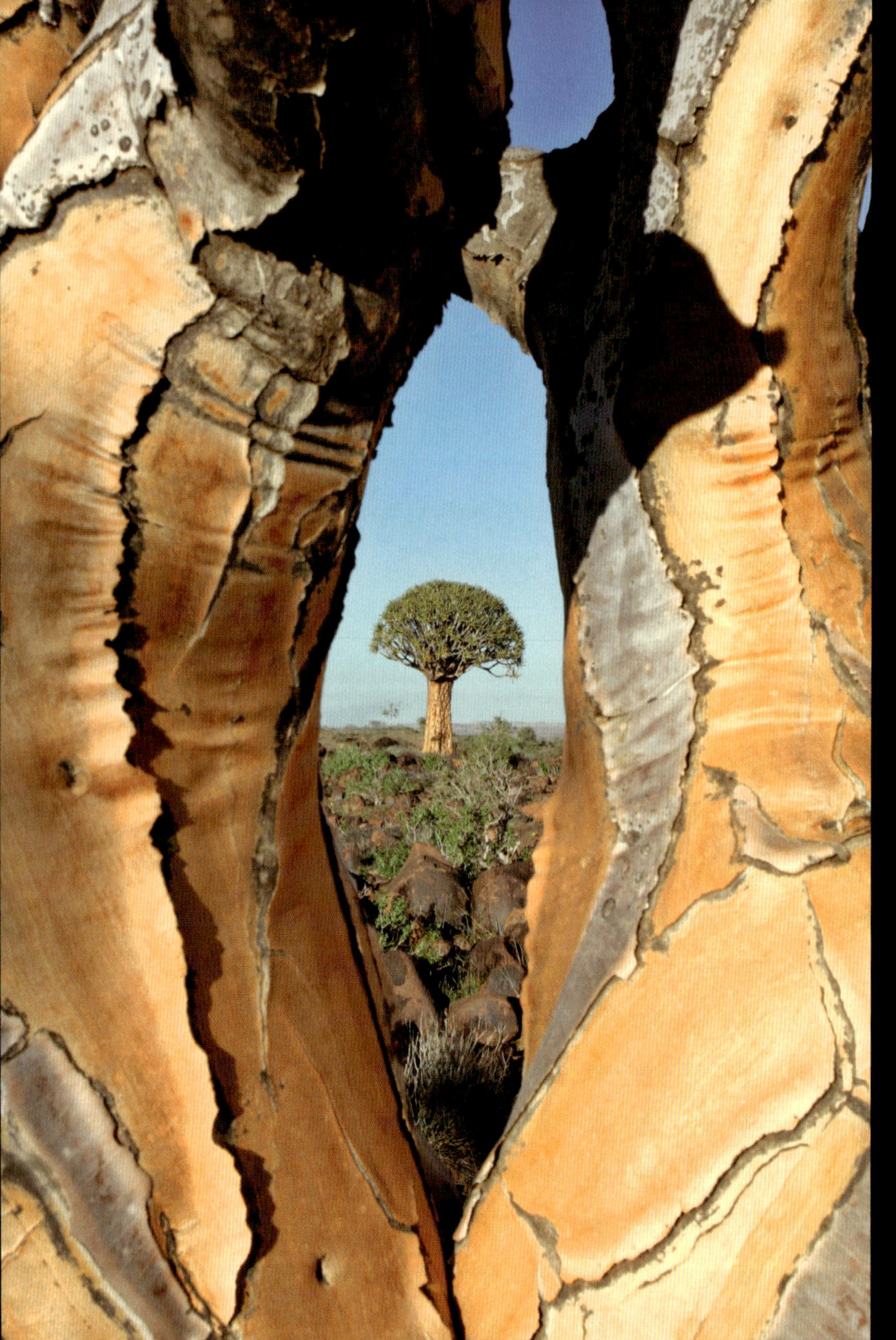

Quiver tree frame

Steffen Sailer

GERMANY

'When I came across this wonderful old plant,' says Steffen, 'I knew I had found the image I'd been looking for. The golden-brown gnarled branches make the perfect frame, and your eye is drawn directly to the perfectly shaped quiver tree in the distance.' The location is the Quiver Tree Forest in the semi-desert environment of Namibia, and the thick, cracked bark is part of the aloe's adaptation to the extreme conditions, protecting the tissues underneath.

Canon EOS 1D Mark II with 17-40mm lens; 1/60 sec at f22; 400 ISO; tripod.

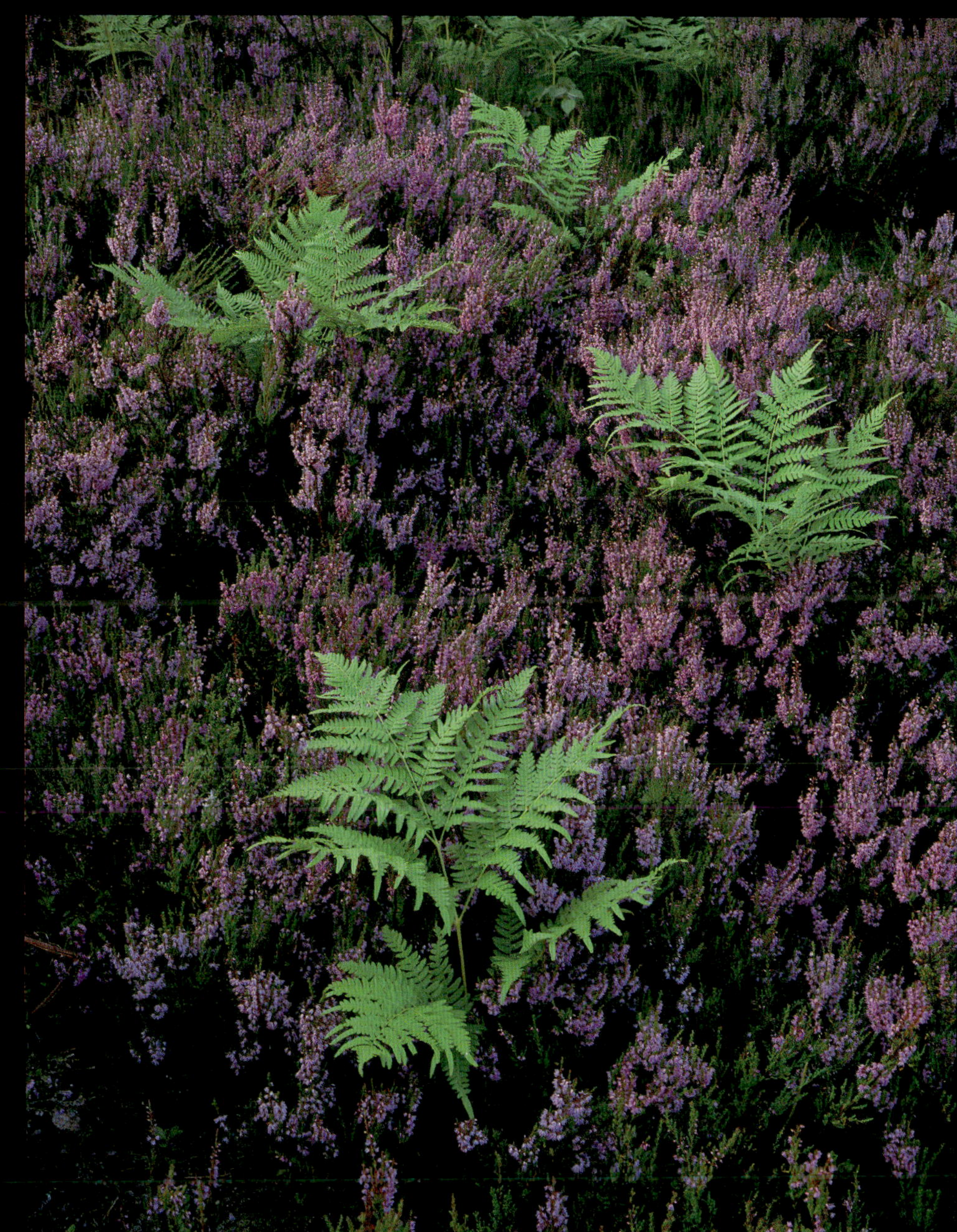

Bracken among heather

Per-Olov Eriksson

SWEDEN

Walking through woodland early one August morning in the western part of county Nàrke, Per-Olov came across a glorious carpet of heather. 'The impact of the colour and the fragrance took my breath away,' he says, 'and it was hard to represent the beauty of the scene.' Early morning in this part of Sweden can be 'truly magic,' he adds, 'poetry for both mind and soul'.

Pentax 67 with 135mm macro lens; 4 sec at f32; Fujichrome Velvia 50.

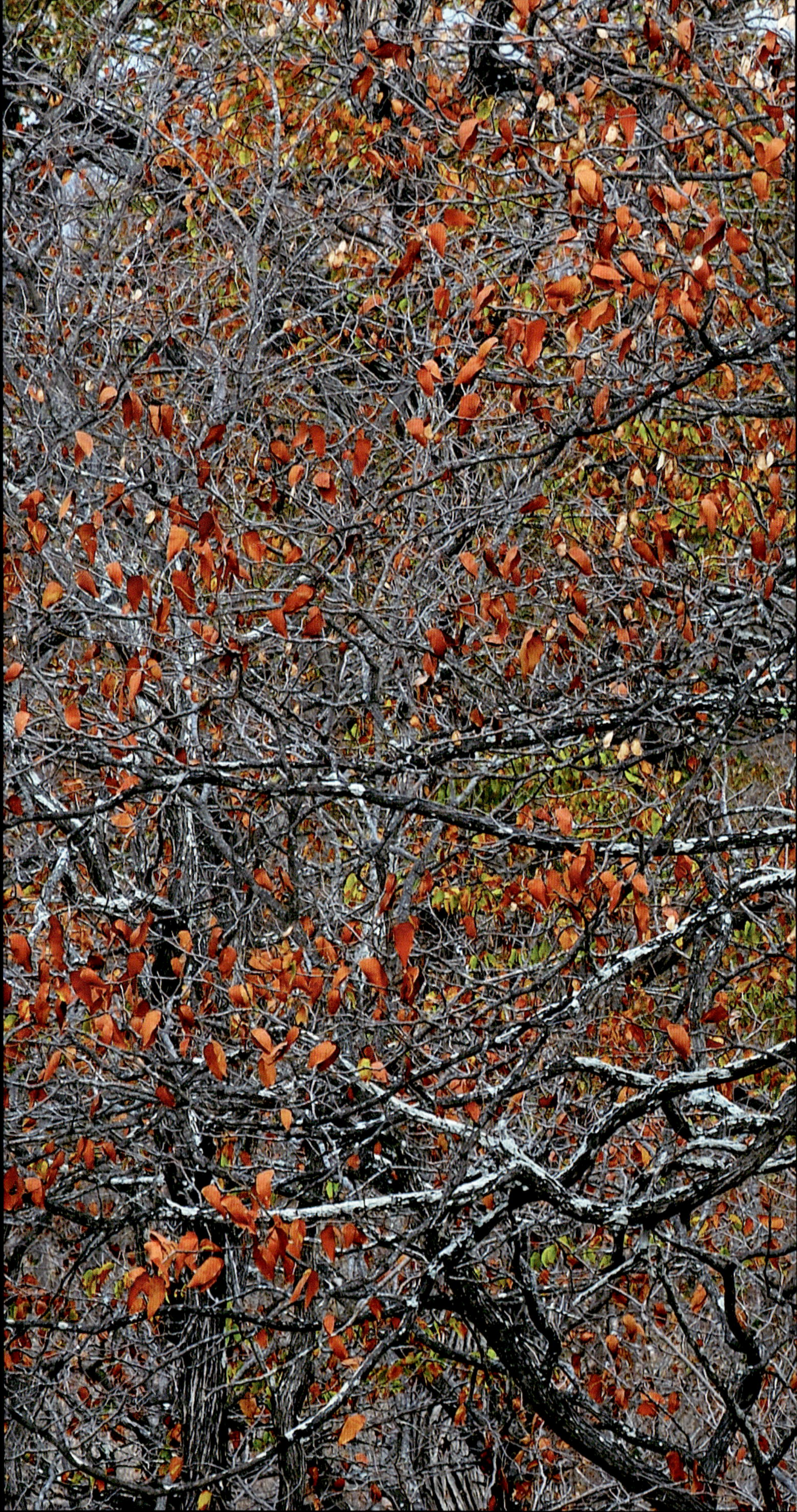

Mopane mosaic

Johann C Mader

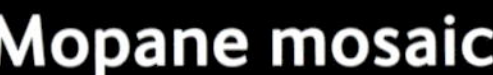

'In autumn, the mopane woodland explodes with colour,' says Johann. 'The angular, lichen-draped branches of this particular tree provided the ideal contrast in a composition of pattern and colour.' The mopane is the most common tree in the northern parts of South Africa's Kruger National Park – easily recognized by its butterfly-shaped leaves – and is also a favourite with elephants, who feast on its high-protein leaves and seeds.

Nikon D70 with VR 70-200mm f2.8 lens; 1/30 sec at f19; 200 ISO; beanbag.

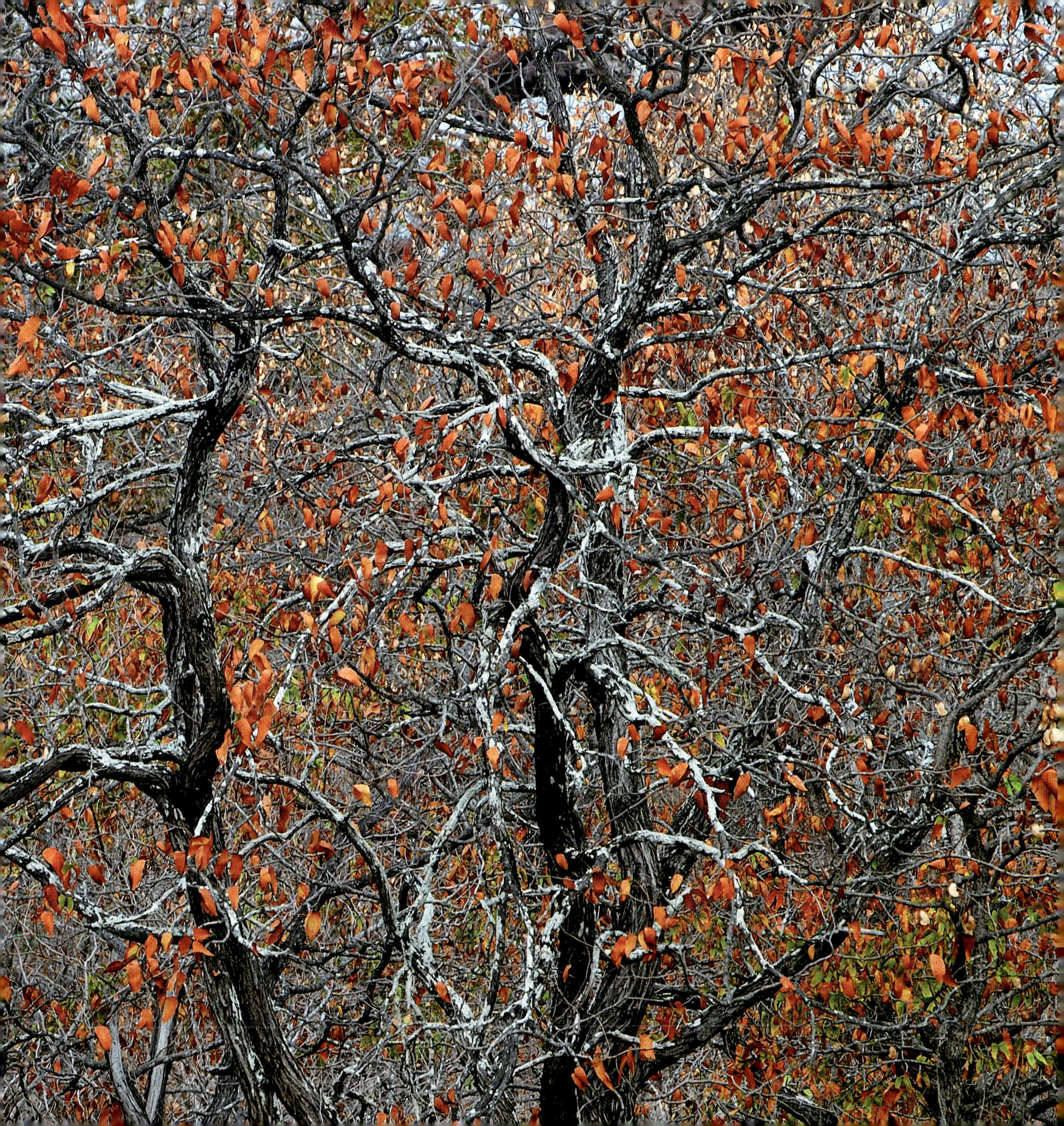

While working early one morning in his cabin on the Kamchatka Peninsula in the Russian Far East, Igor heard a noise in his porch. 'Thinking it was my colleague who lived next door,' says Igor, 'I invited her in, saying the door was open.' Receiving no response, he got up and pushed the door open with his foot. When the door bumped against something, he stuck his head through to apologise. It wasn't the scientist at all but a bear, which had prised open the outside door and was having a good nose around. 'He looked up at me in a rather friendly manner,' says Igor, 'but nevertheless, I quickly closed the door.' The bear turned around to leave, knocking things over as it left. As Igor went back inside to get his camera, there was the bear, peeping at him through the window by standing on the snowdrift. 'This was the only photo I had time to take before the bear left. I had put out the lemons on the window sill to ripen, never imagining that they would add the final touch to such a surreal still life.'

Nikon D2x with AFS Nikkor 12-24mm f1.4G lens; 1/60 sec at f4; 100 ISO.

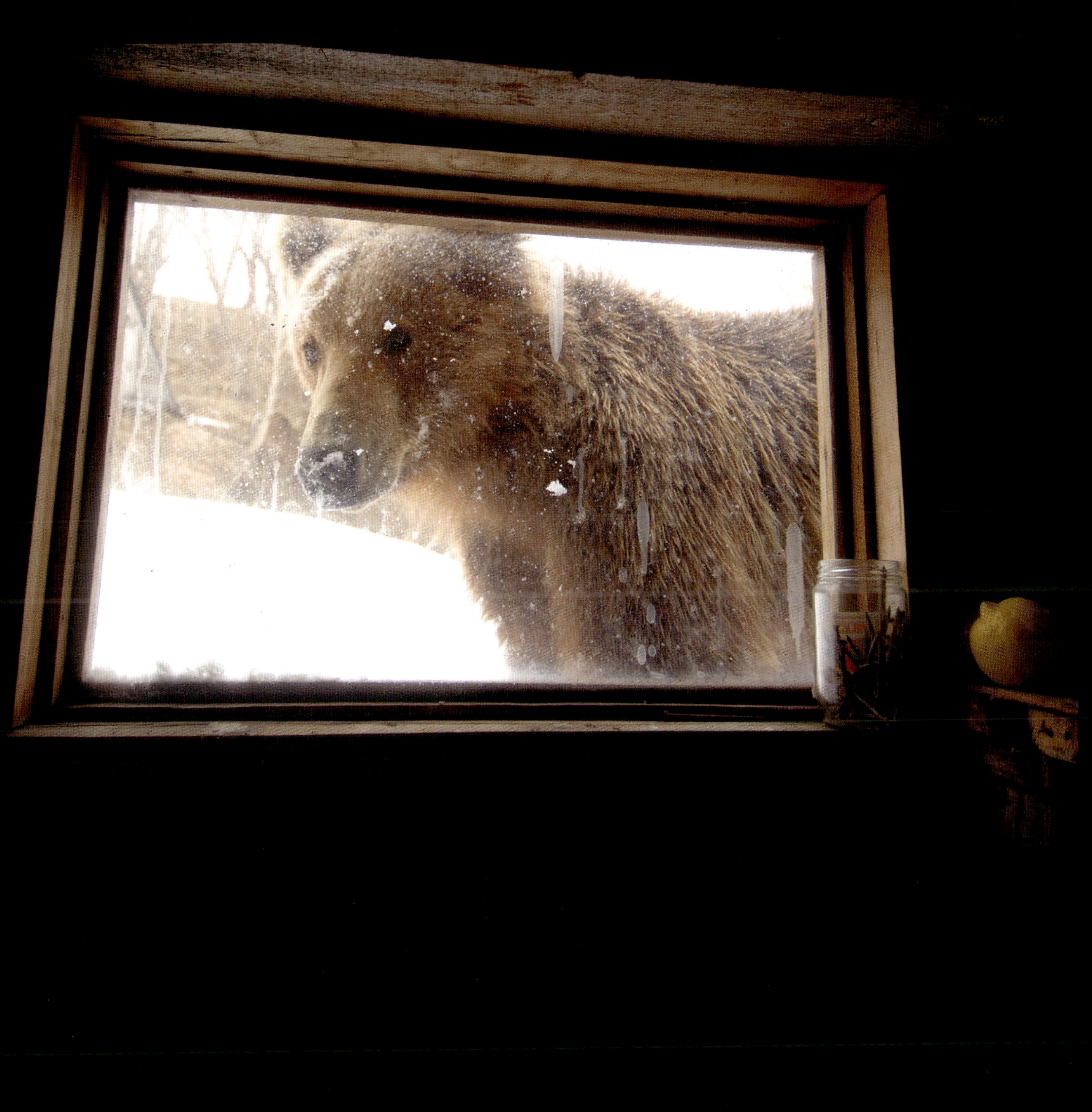

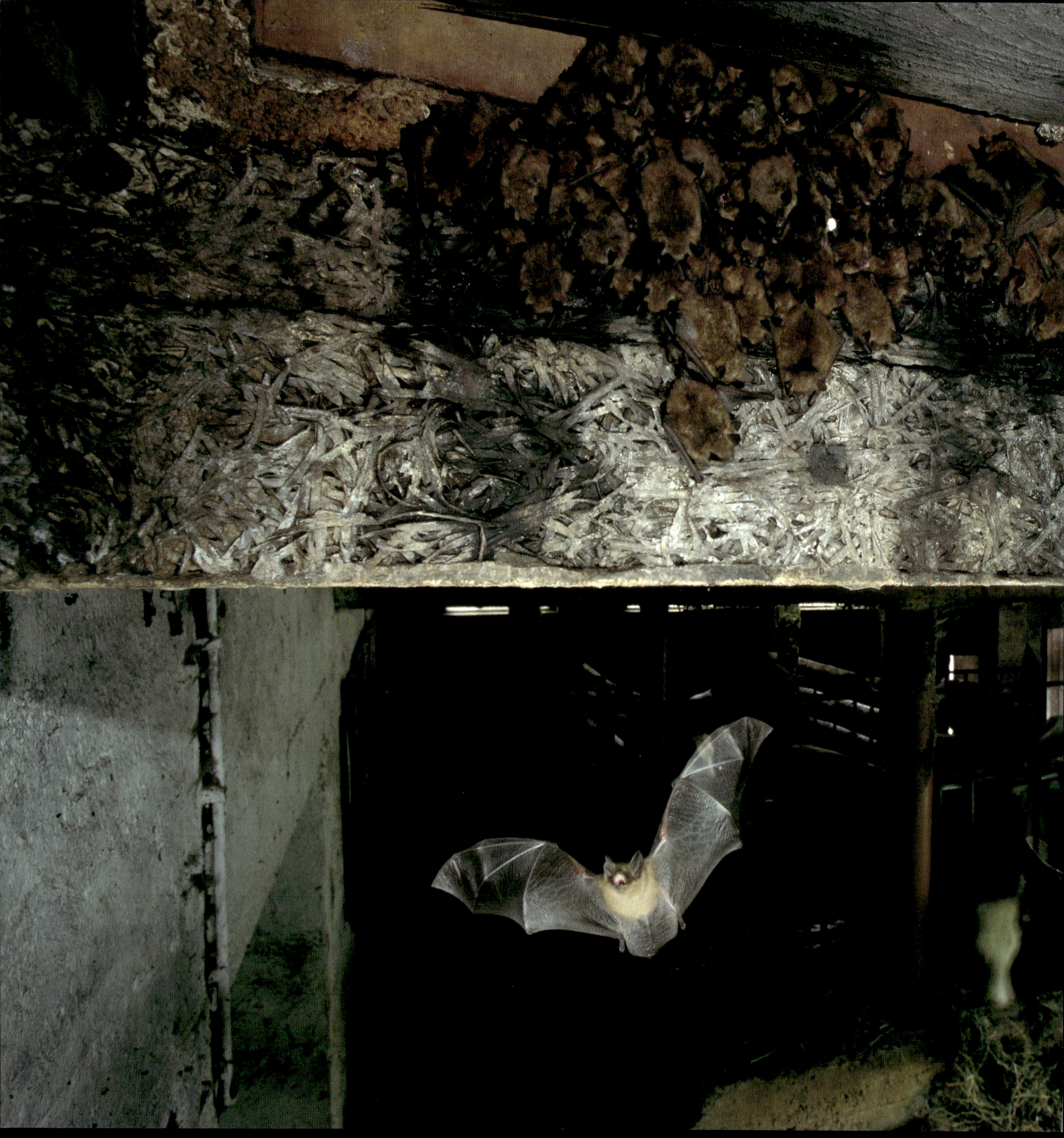

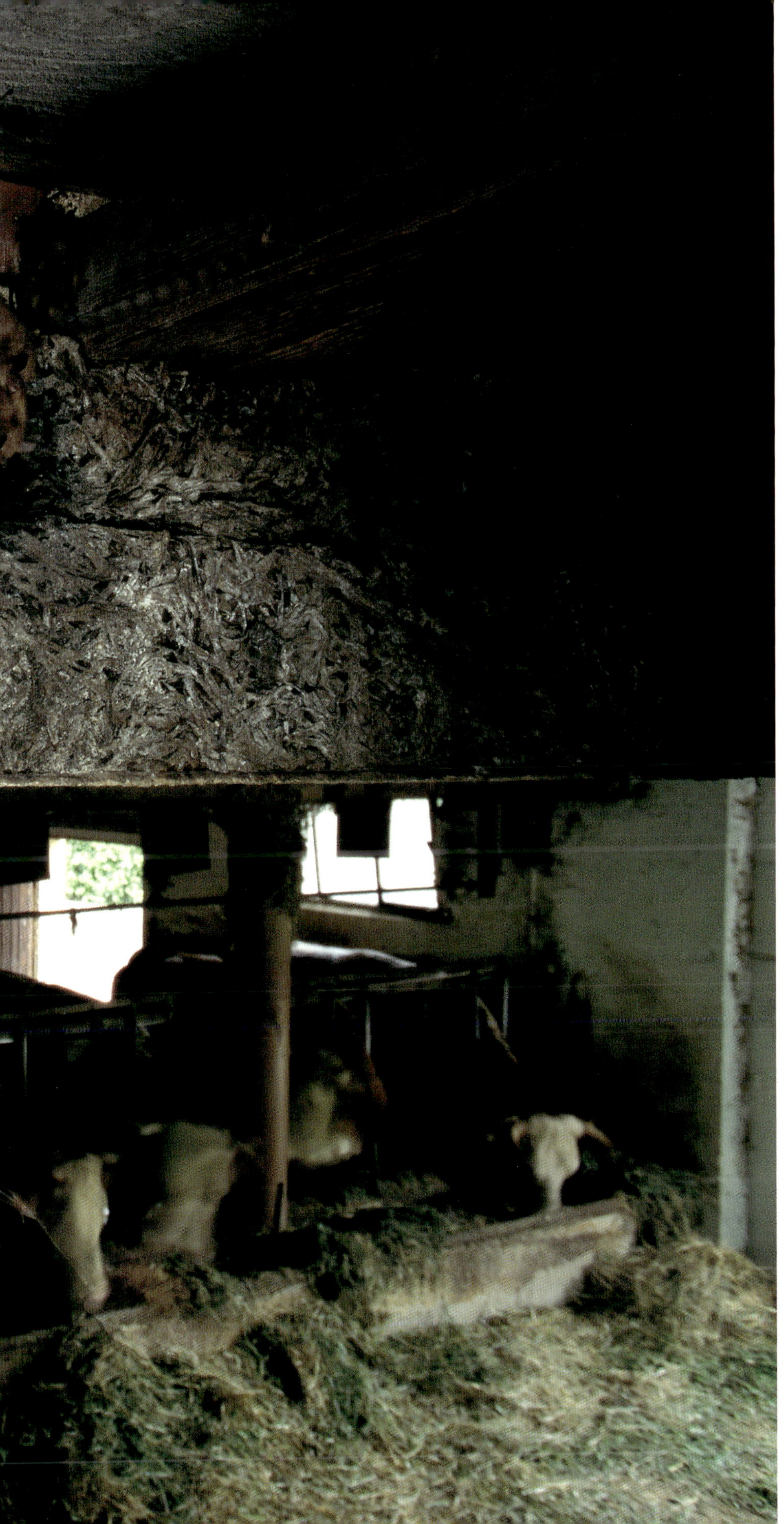

The cowshed bats

RUNNER-UP

Klaus Echle

GERMANY

Klaus has for many years worked to help conserve bats in Germany. One of his favourites is the rare and endangered Geoffroy's bat – a medium-sized quite furry bat, not found in the UK. In Baden-Württemberg, it spends the winter roosting mainly in caves and old mines, but in May and June, one population of females chooses farmer Friedhelm's cowshed to rear their babies. 'Friedhelm is very proud that the bats choose his shed and looks after them,' says Klaus. 'Watching the bats over time, I noticed that a few bats would have a quick fly around the shed during the day, perhaps stretching their wings. The return flight was the moment I wanted for my picture. All I needed was just a little luck and a lot of patience.'

Canon 1N Rs with 8-20mm 1:2 lens; f14; Fujichrome Sensia 100; 3 flashes, remote control.

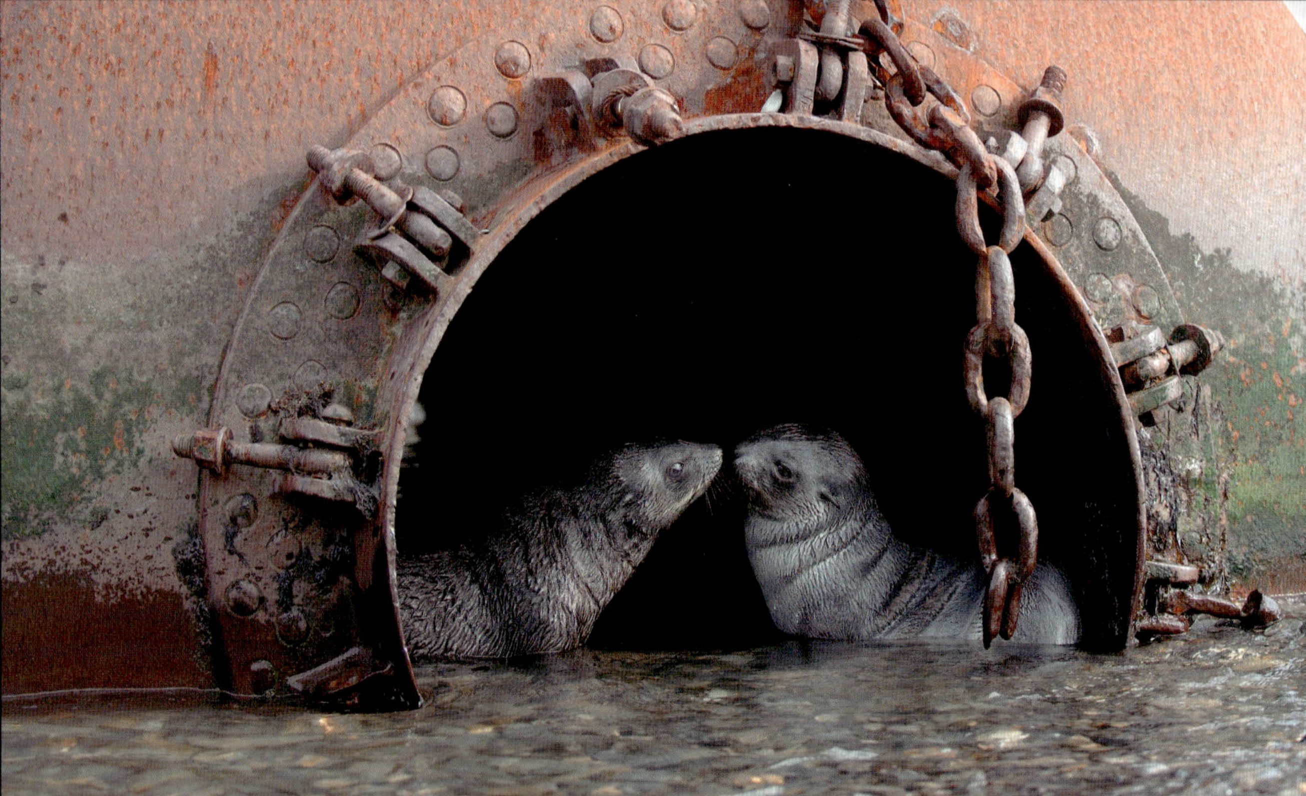

Fur seal playground

SPECIALLY COMMENDED

Fanus Weldhagen

SOUTH AFRICA

The rusting hulks of whale-oil pipes in the abandoned whaling station at Husvik, South Georgia, today provide an adventure playground for young Antarctic fur seals. Fanus watched this pair while waiting for his boat to unload supplies for the Antarctic island. 'They played endless games of hide-and-seek,' he says, 'their contagious enthusiasm reminding me of my own children playing.' Antarctic fur seals were hunted almost to extinction by commercial sealing, but today there are thought to be around 4 million, 95 per cent of which breed on South Georgia. 'In this photograph', adds Fanus, 'the pair have just found each other again and are greeting like long-lost friends.'

Nikon D2x with Nikkor AFS 70-200mm lens; 1/640 sec at f2.8; 200 ISO; Gitzo tripod.

Ermine at home

Peter Lilja

SWEDEN

Driving through the countryside in February, when snow was on the ground, Peter passed an old house in a small village where the owner was feeding the birds. He stopped to photograph a woodpecker and was concentrating so hard that he 'nearly missed a flicker of movement under the house'. A stoat in full ermine was peeping through a hole. Returning a couple of days later, Peter set up watch. 'What luck', he adds, 'that the stoat should have popped up just in the spot where the granite stone and wall contrast so well. It stared at me for a few seconds before disappearing.'

Nikon D2x with 200-400mm f4 lens; 1/60 sec at f5.6; 280 ISO; beanbag.

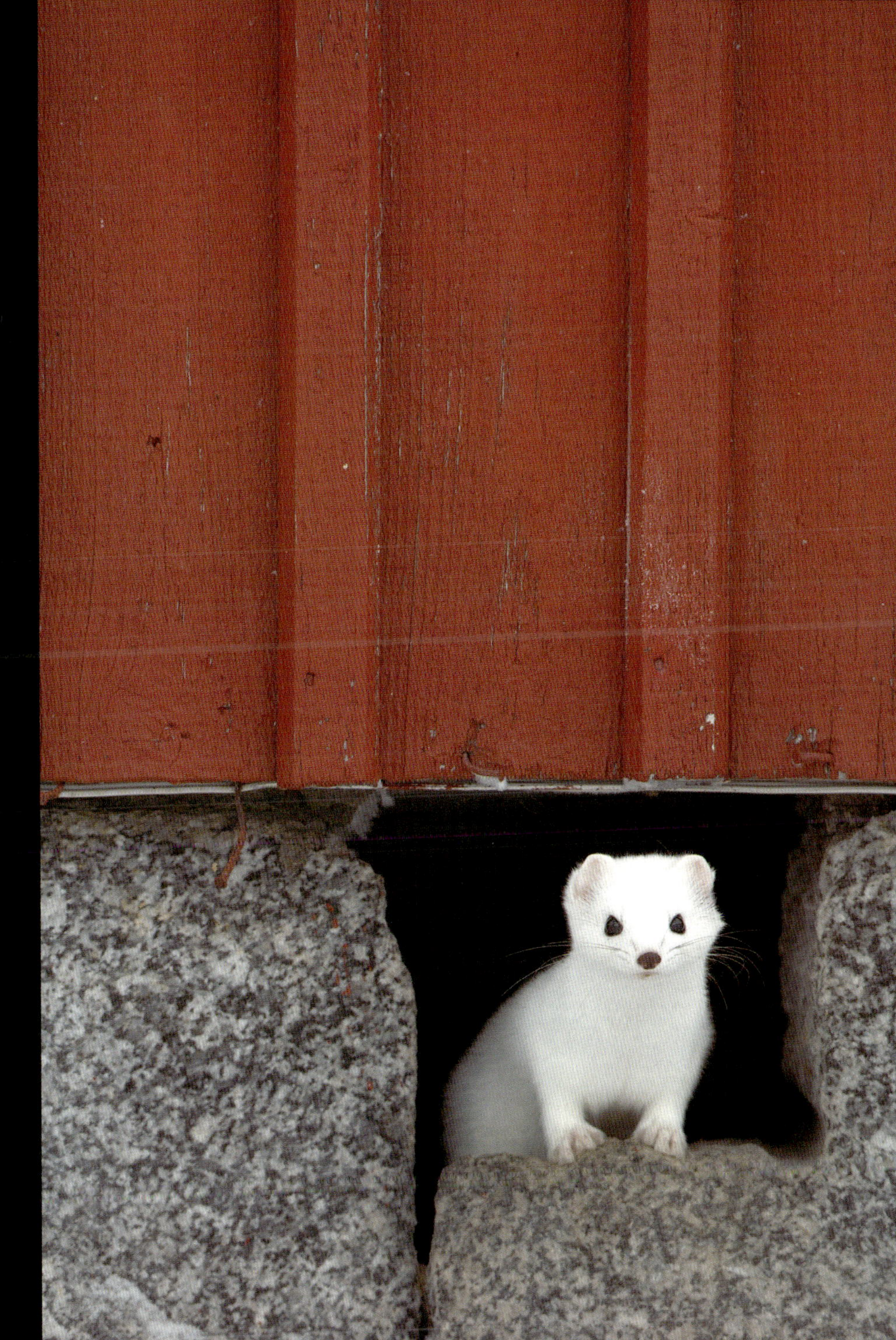

Creative Visions of Nature

Pictures in this category should take inspiration from nature but reveal new ways of seeing natural subjects or scenes. They can be figurative, abstract or conceptual but must provoke thought or emotional reactions, whether through their beauty or imaginative interpretation.

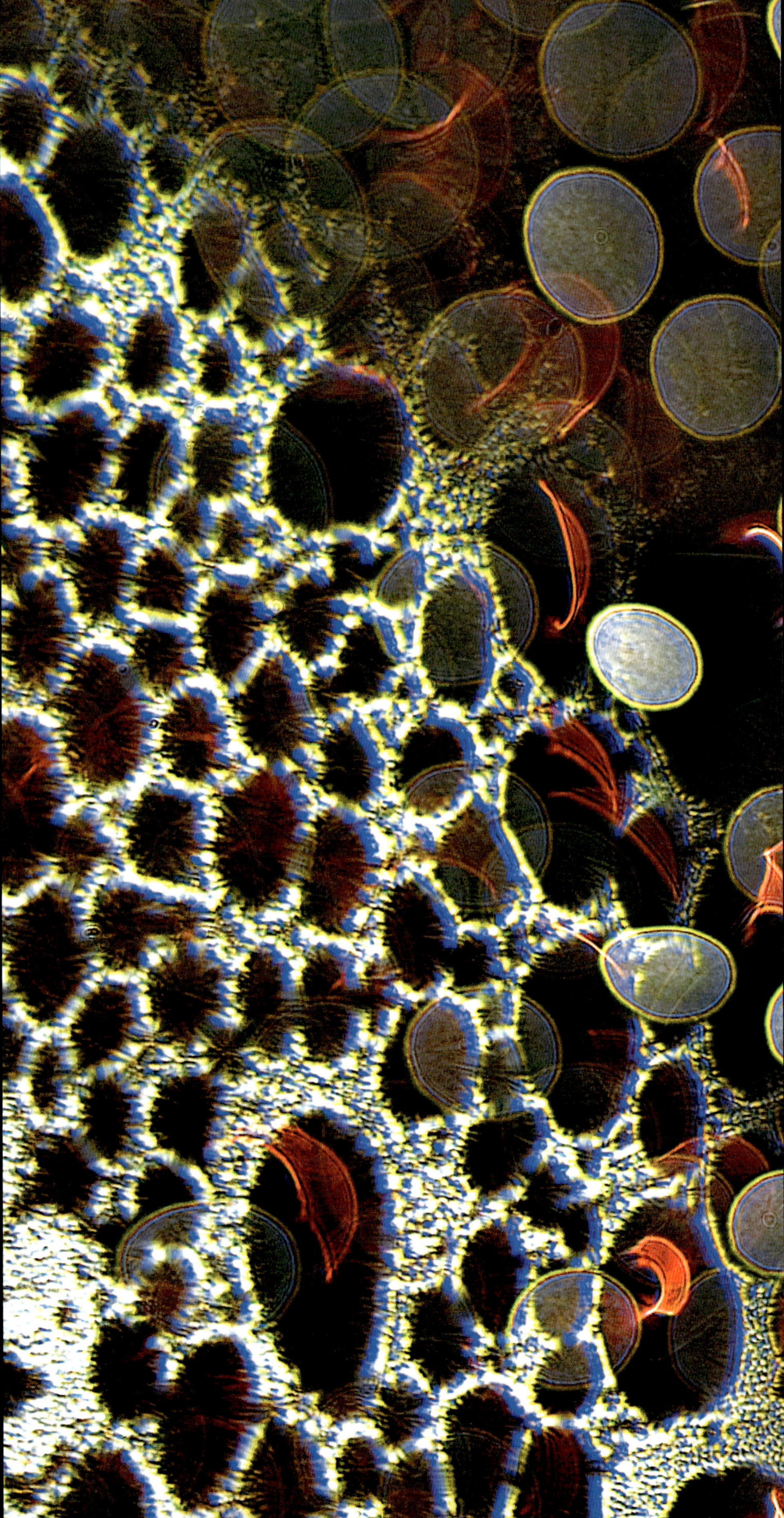

Dewdrops

WINNER

Juhani Kosonen

FINLAND

'When I look at this picture,' says Juhani, 'I think of the universe – of planets and stars.' He has photographed dew many times on the same window pane and is always astonished at how it can change. 'A tiny shift in the light affects the reflected array of colours and can make a dramatic difference.' In this case, the picture was created at night, with the only light reflected in the droplets coming from outside. A slight change in camera angle or focus point generated a totally different scene, but this was the composition he finally chose.

Canon EOS 10D with Sigma 105mm f2.8 macro lens; 13 sec at f2.8; 100 ISO; tripod.

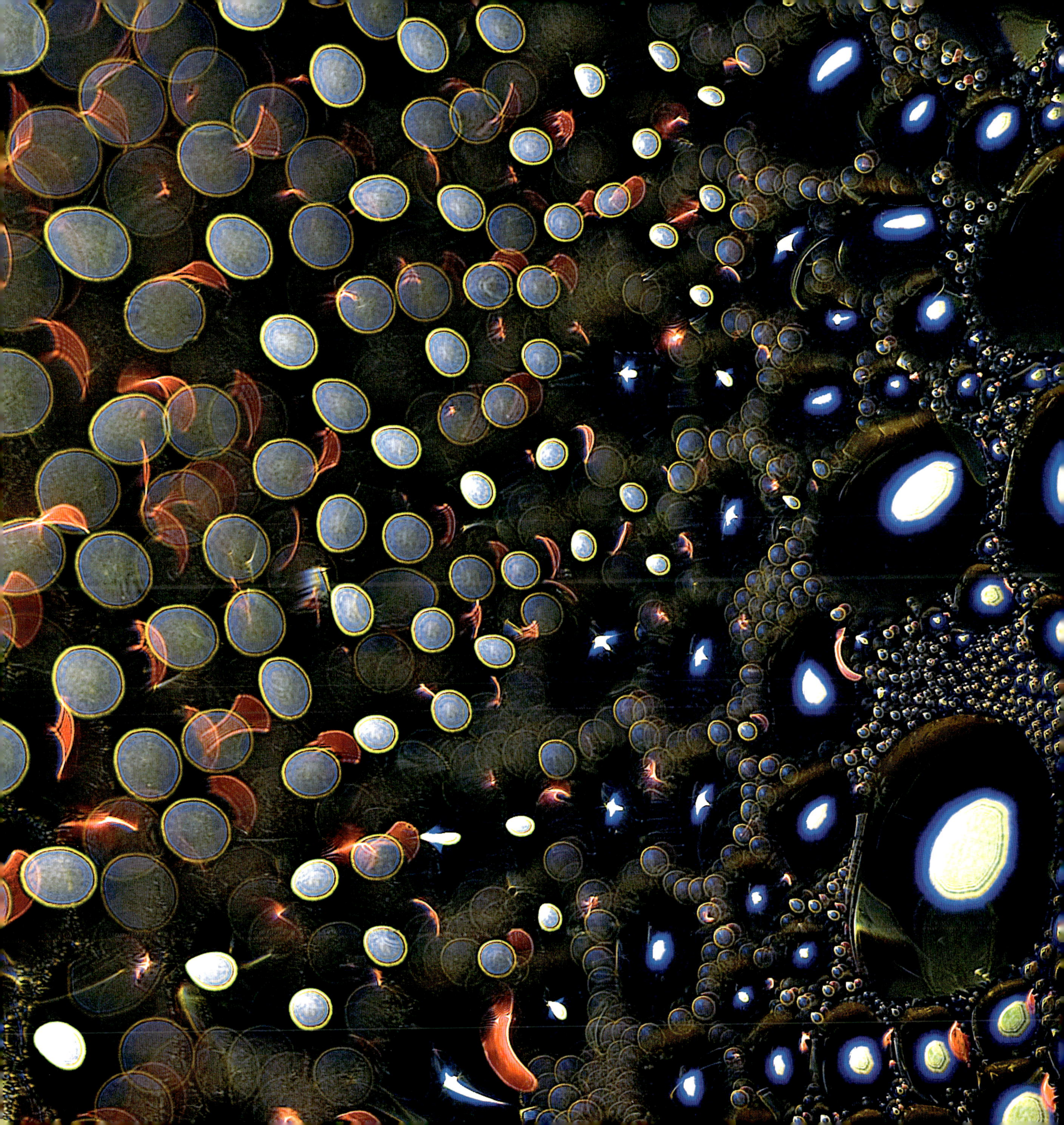

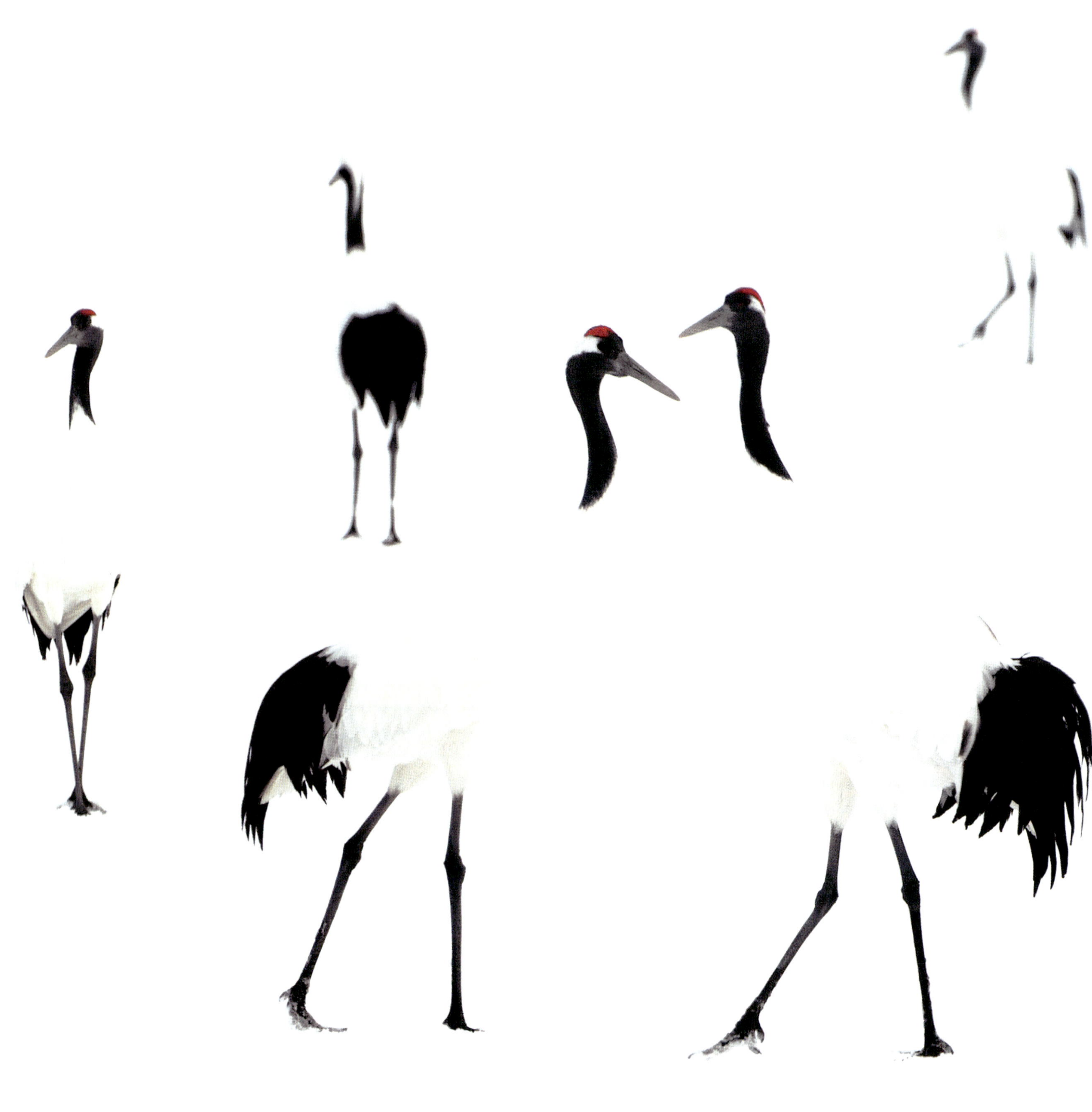

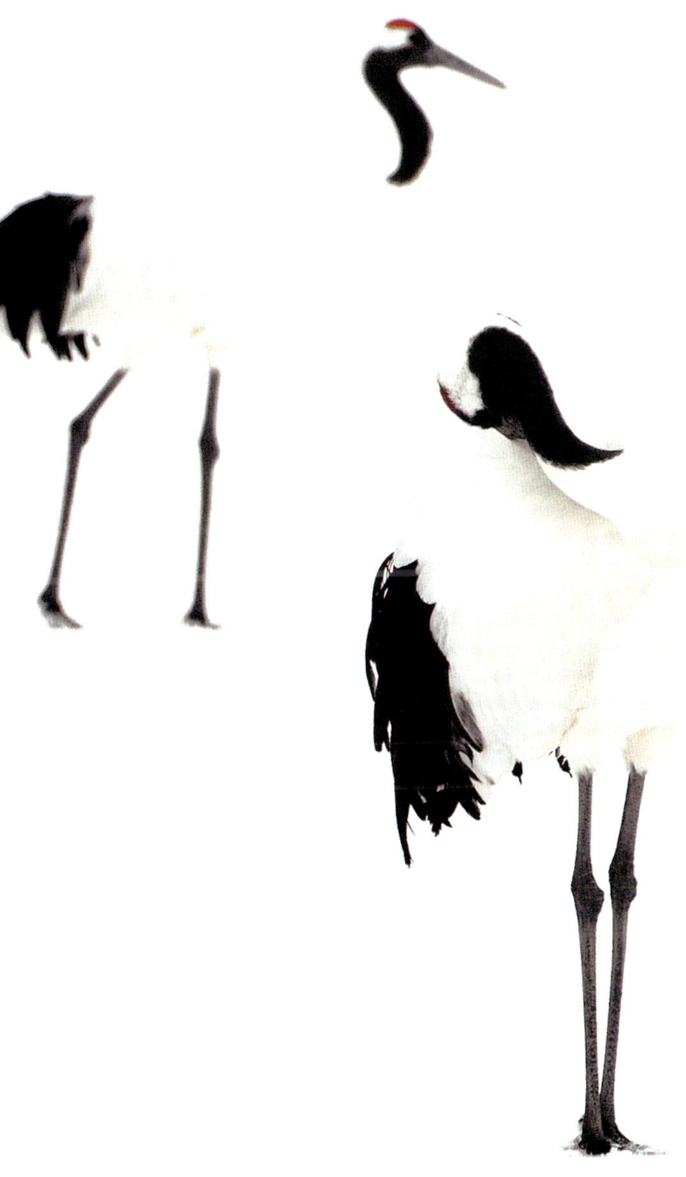

Japanese crane dance

RUNNER-UP

Jan Vermeer

THE NETHERLANDS

Japanese red-crowned cranes are possibly the most artistic of all the birds, much loved by photographers – elegant in a truly Japanese way. Locally, they are symbols of peace, longevity and fortune – and fidelity, too, as they pair for life. Captivated by their spectacular courtship dance, Jan recalls how 'their choreography on the snow field was perfect.'
The beauty of the scene is accentuated by the positioning of the birds on the edges of the dance floor around the leading couple, on a background exposed to almost total whiteness. The Japanese crane is the largest of all the cranes at around 1.3m (4 feet) tall and with a wingspan of more than 2m (6.5 feet). Highly endangered, it occurs only in northeastern Asia and is resident only in Japan, mainly on the northern island of Hokkaido – which is where Jan watched the performance.

Nikon D2x with 500mm f4 lens; 1/1250 sec at f8; 200 ISO.

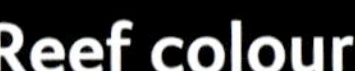

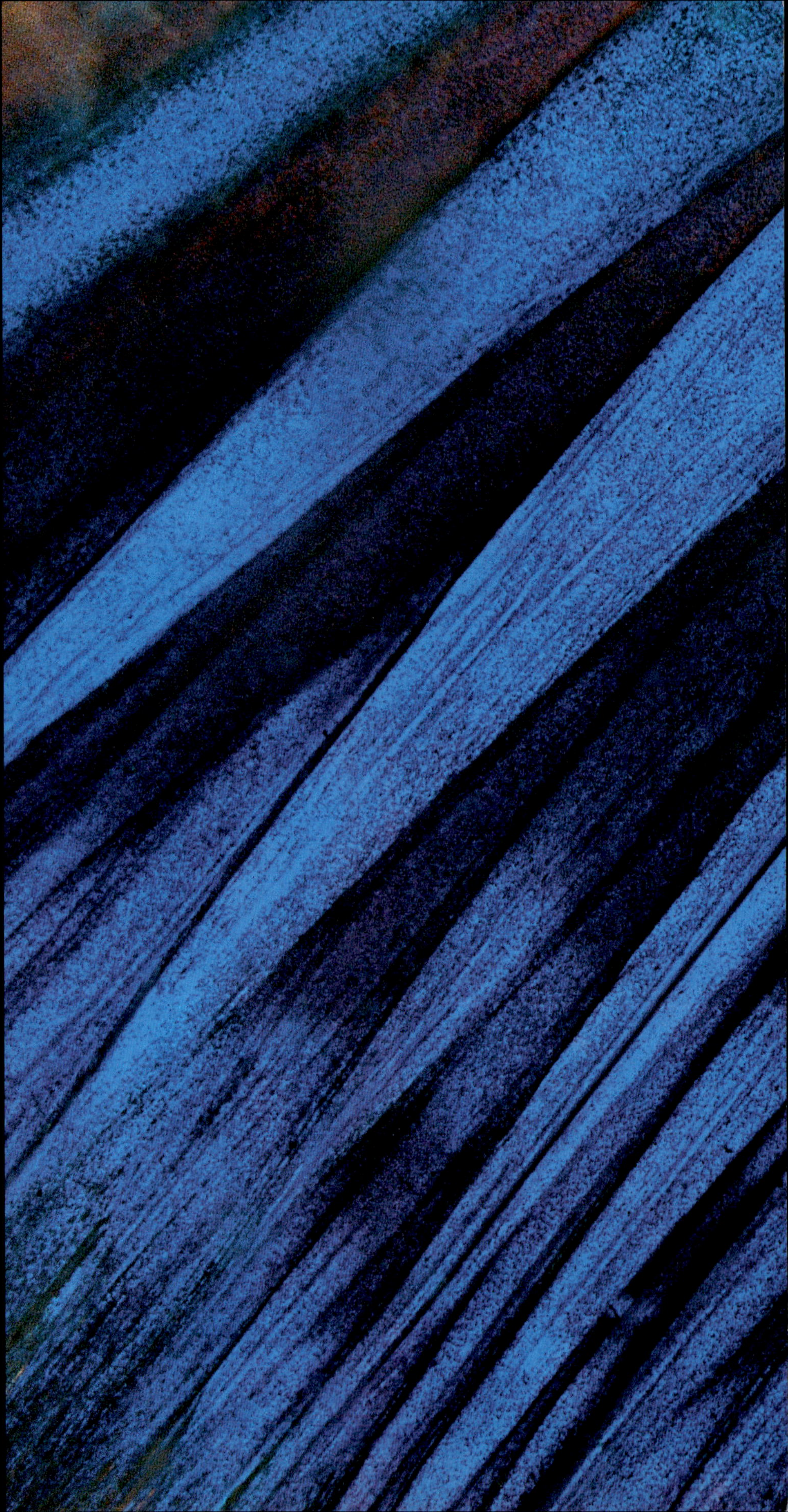

Reef colour

Magnus Lundgren

SWEDEN

On a night dive in the Red Sea, Magnus found a parrotfish sleeping under a coral overhang. Using his macro lens, he concentrated on looking for new angles and patterns, becoming mesmerized by the iridescent colours. 'I took more than 100 images,' he says, 'and this one, from the base of the tail, is my favourite.' The colour of a parrotfish alters depending on what phase it is in and what sex (secondary males are born female but can become male, depending on the sex ratio in the area), providing a never-ending palette for the nature photographer.

Nikon D70 with 105mm macro lens; 1/250 sec at f32; 200 ISO; underwater housing; double strobes.

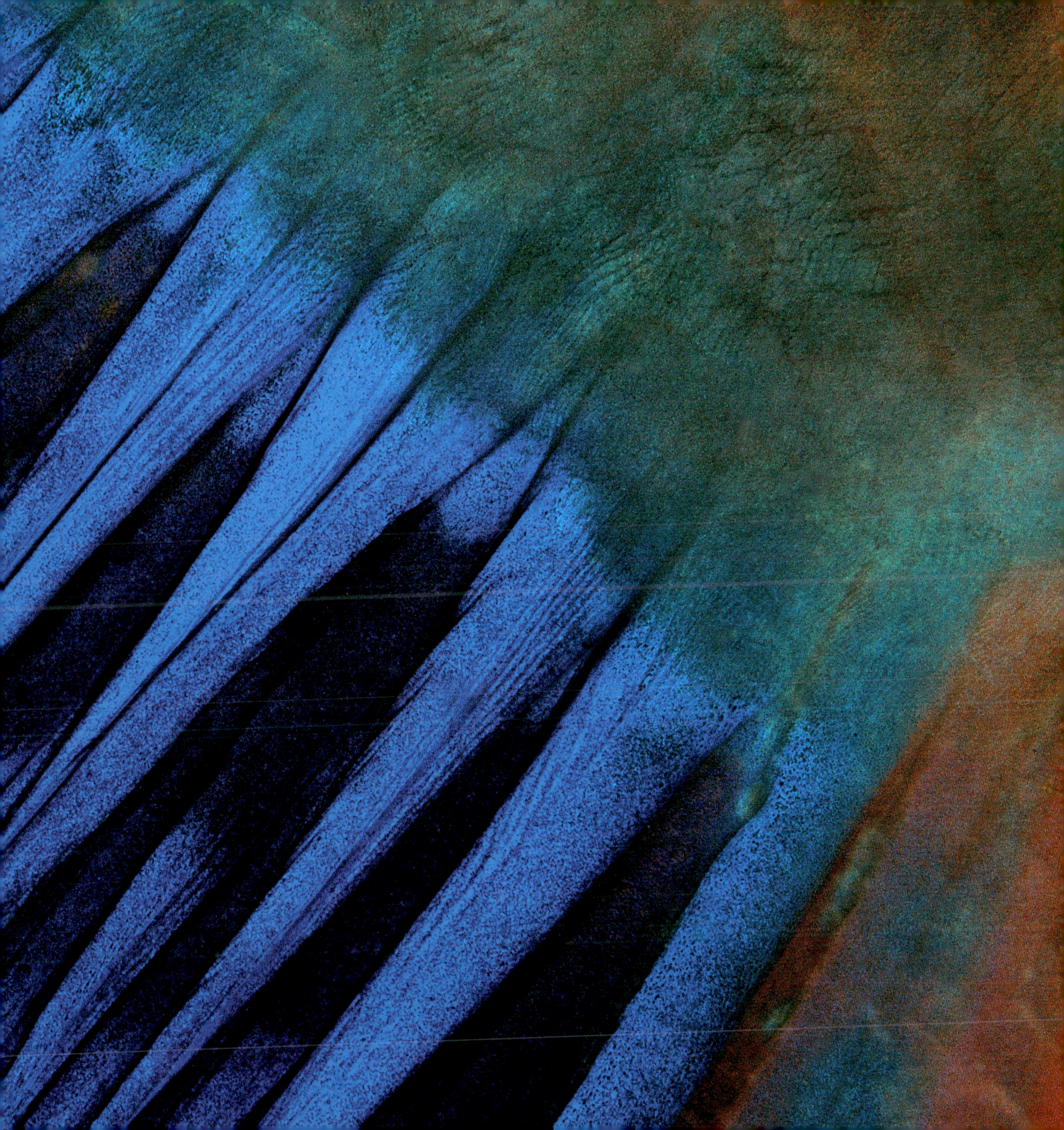

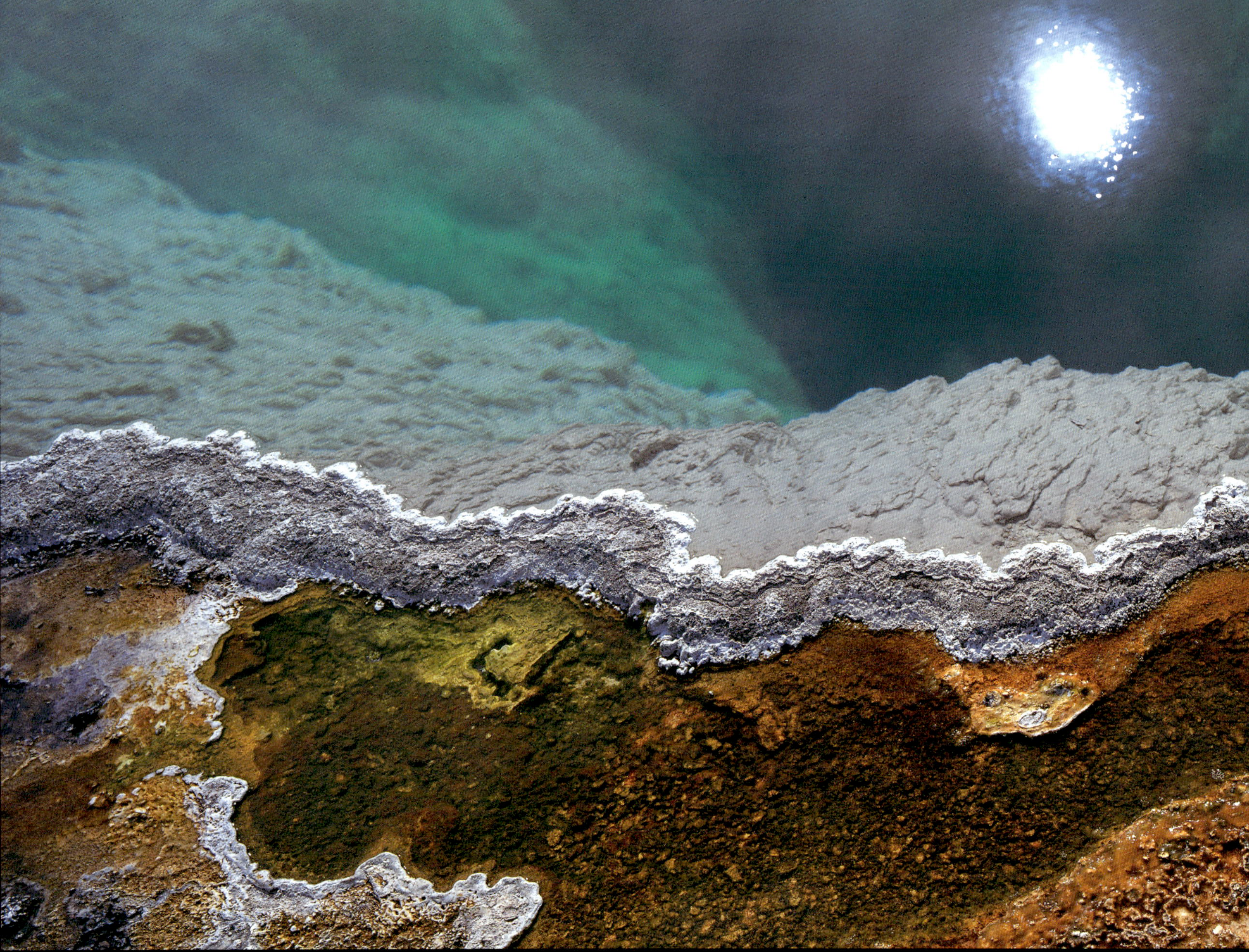

Elements

Benjamin D Walls

USA

'On first glance, this could be an abstract painting in a posh New York Studio,' says Benjamin, 'but even better, it is a portrayal of one of nature's wonders – a thermal pool in Yellowstone National Park.' The clear, hot water reflects the blue-greens, while at the cooler edges of the pool, yellow and orange bacteria and algae add colour to the palette. Having found the composition he wanted, Benjamin waited most of the day for the sun to be in just the right spot, 'hovering right about the blue depths of the pool' – an element that completes this striking composition.

Fuji GX617 with 90mm Fujinon lens and Fuji Focusing Screen; 1/4 sec at f45; Fujichrome Velvia 50; Bogen Carbon One tripod with Manfrotto Proball head; cable release.

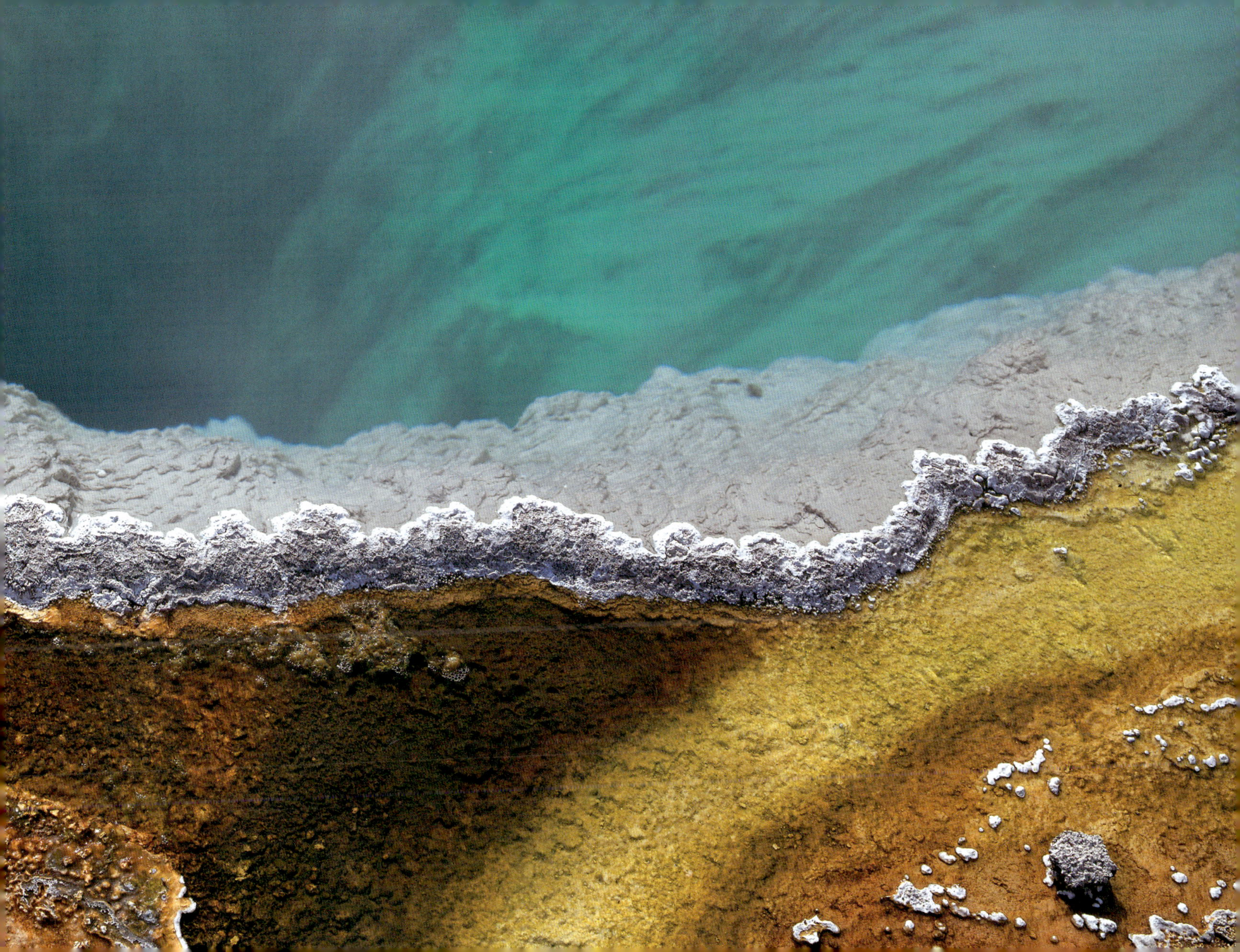

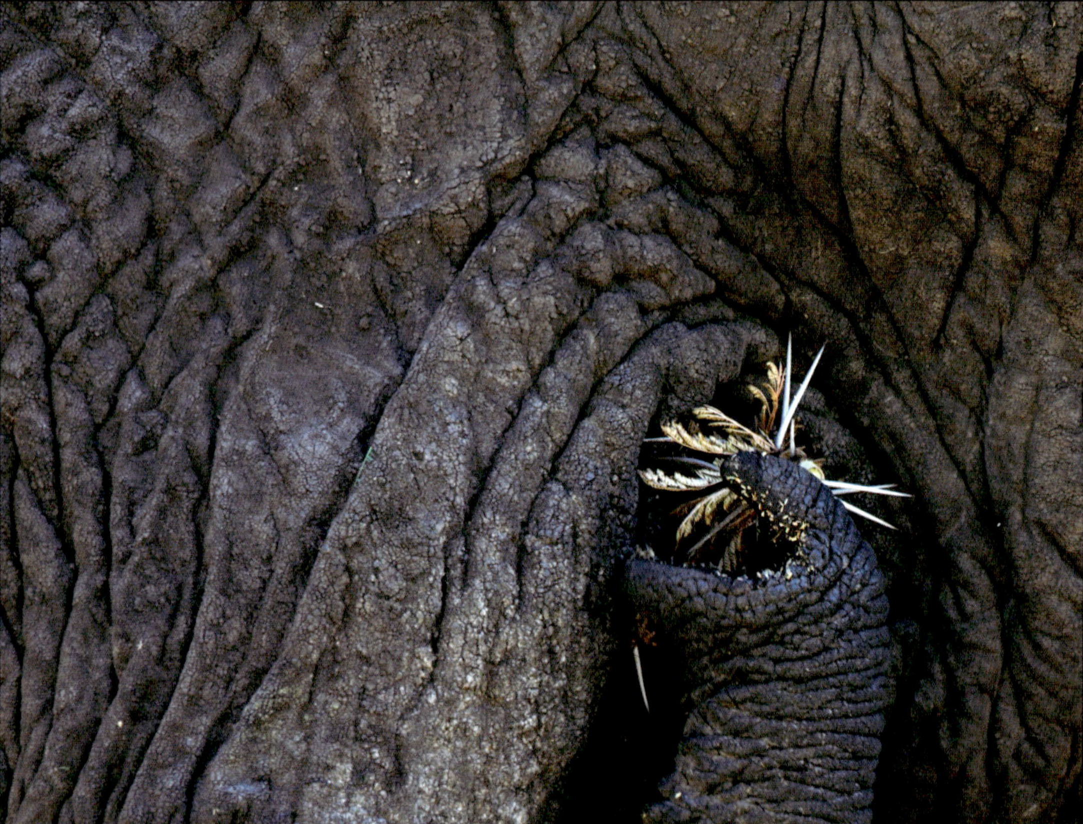

Tip of the trunk

Andy Biggs

USA

'What I set out to do was to present one of the most photographed animals in Africa in a fresh way,' explains Andy. The shot was taken early one morning in Tanzania and features the tip of the trunk of a large bull elephant browsing on acacia. 'The delicate dexterity of the tip contrasting with the thorns and fissured skin is what I particularly like about it,' says Andy.

Canon EOS 1D Mark II with EF 100-400mm lens; 1/100 sec at f6.3; 200 ISO.

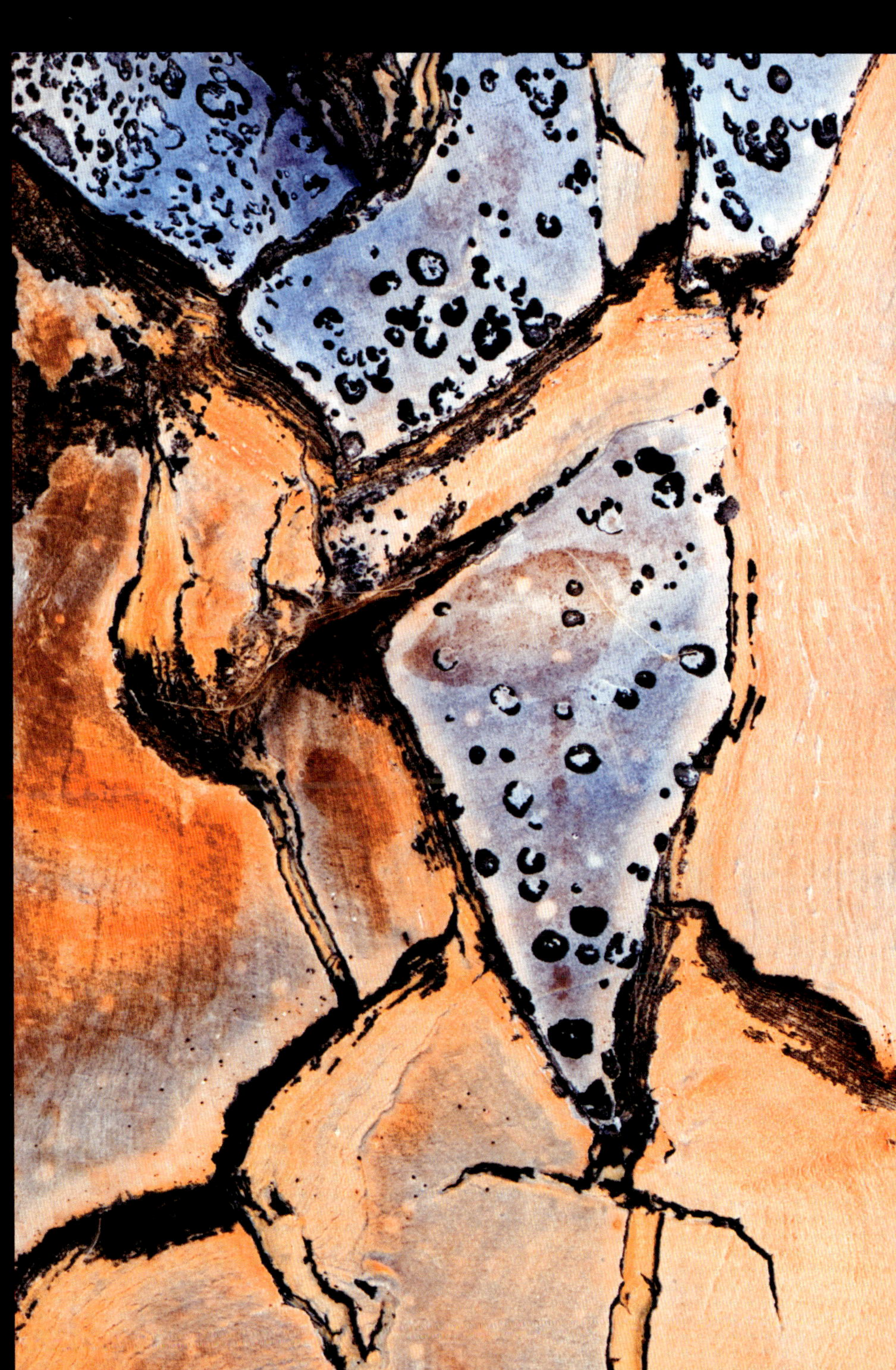

Bark as art

Katherine Keates

CANADA

Quiver trees – tough southern African aloes – are a constant source of photographic inspiration, whether as silhouettes or textured close-ups. 'As the trees age, the scales on the trunk become more defined, and in the dawn light, these golden-brown flakes create strong graphic patterns,' says Katherine, who was on a photographic trip to Namibia. 'I find the natural creation of such dramatic colour and design as stimulating and inspirational as any contemporary painting.'

Canon 20D with 28-135mm IS lens; 1/8 sec at f22; 100 ISO; extension tubes

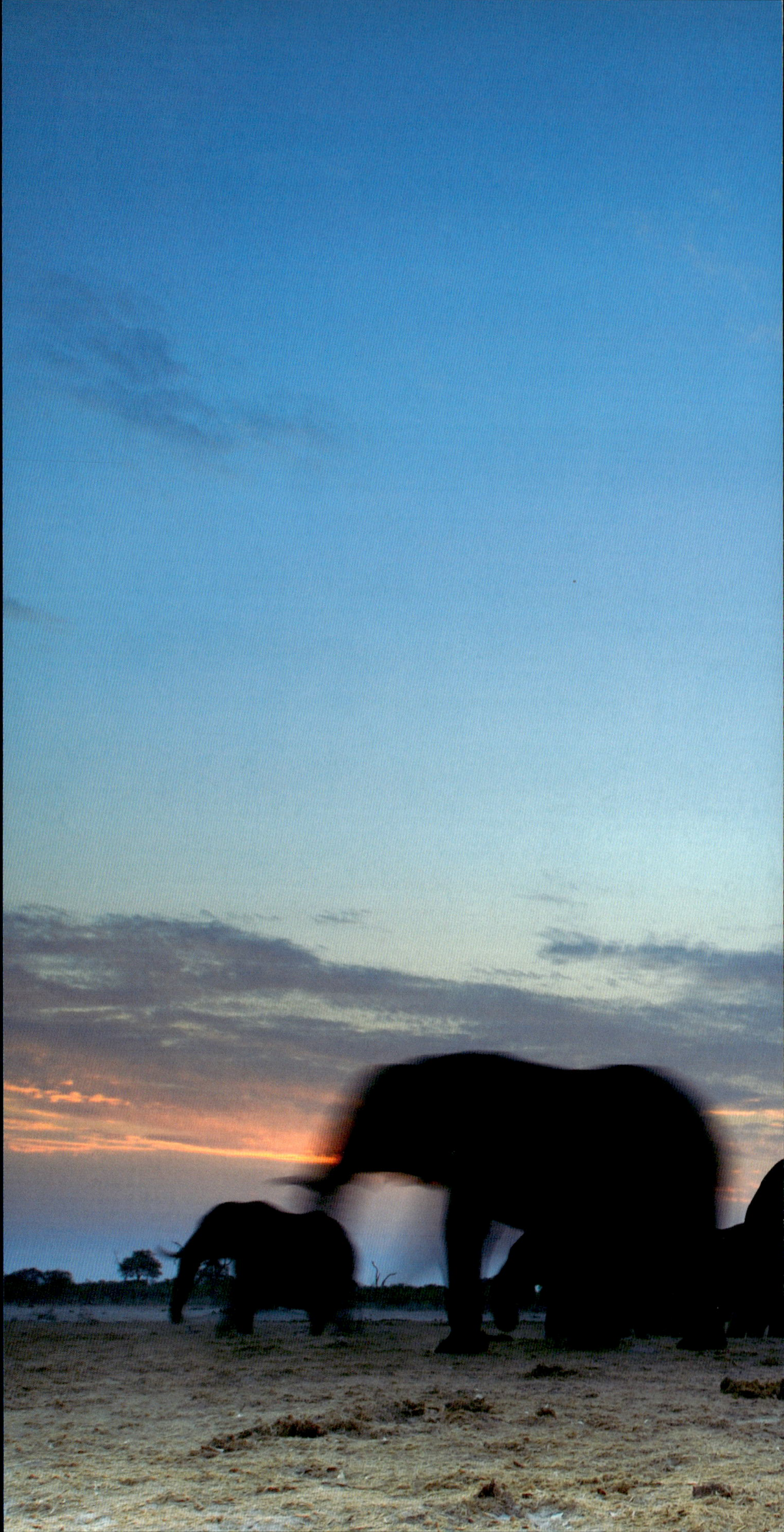

Bulls at twilight

Lorenz Andreas Fischer

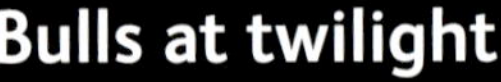

When bull elephants began to congregate peacefully for their evening drink, Lorenz was nearby, knowing that, as it was the dry season, these would be the only waterholes in a wide area of the Savuti region in Chobe National Park, Botswana. 'The twilight was so irresistible', he says, 'that I began to experiment for a while with long exposures, trying to conjure up the magic of the scene. When the huge bull passed close to my vehicle, I knew it was the final touch I needed.'

Nikon D2x with AF-S 17-35mm f2.8 lens; 1/1.3 sec at f7.1; 100 ISO; Singh-Ray hard grey graduation f2 filter; Gitzo Carbon 1227 tripod.

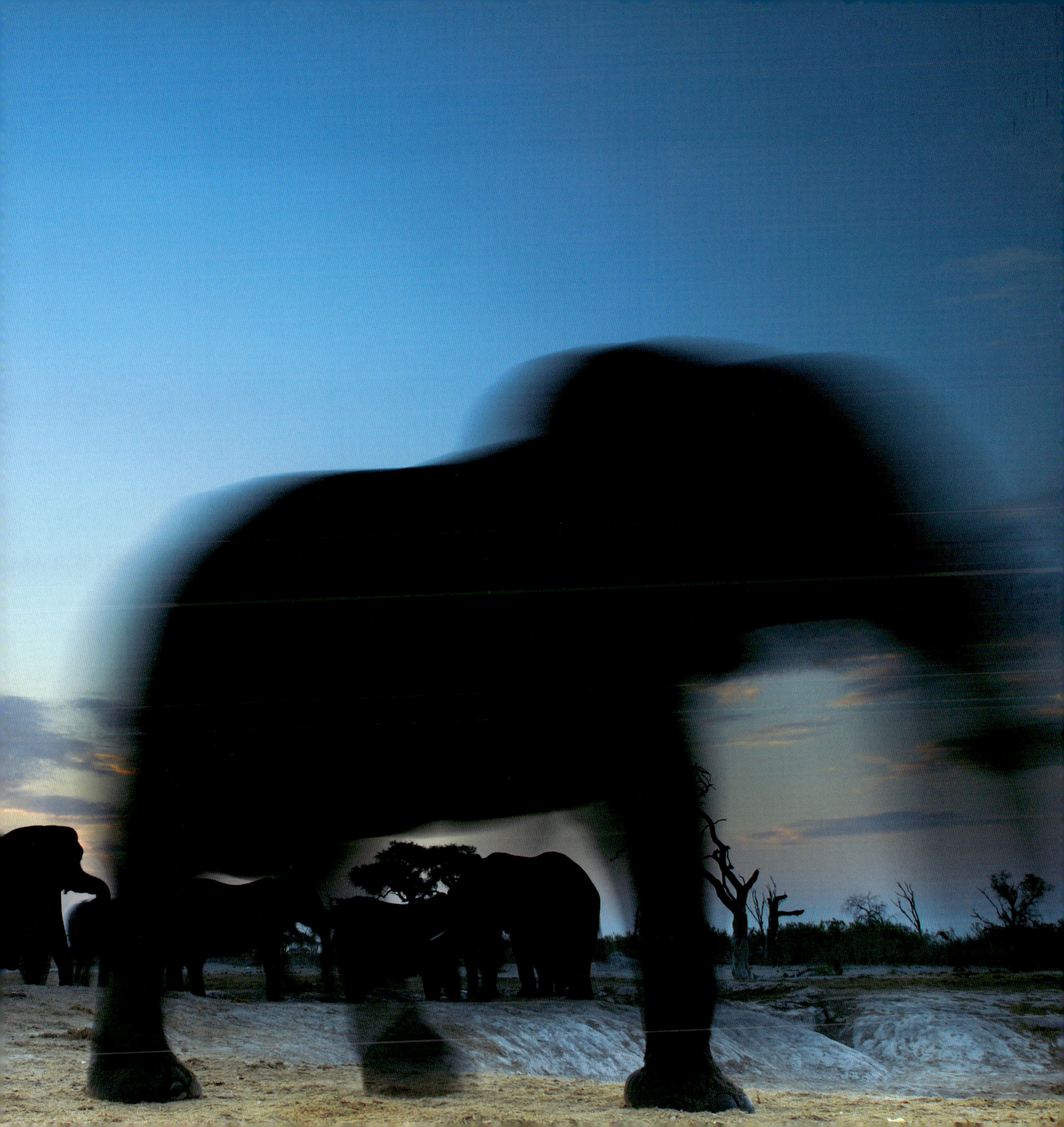

Wild Places

This is a category for landscape photographs, but ones that must convey a true feeling of wildness and create a sense of awe.

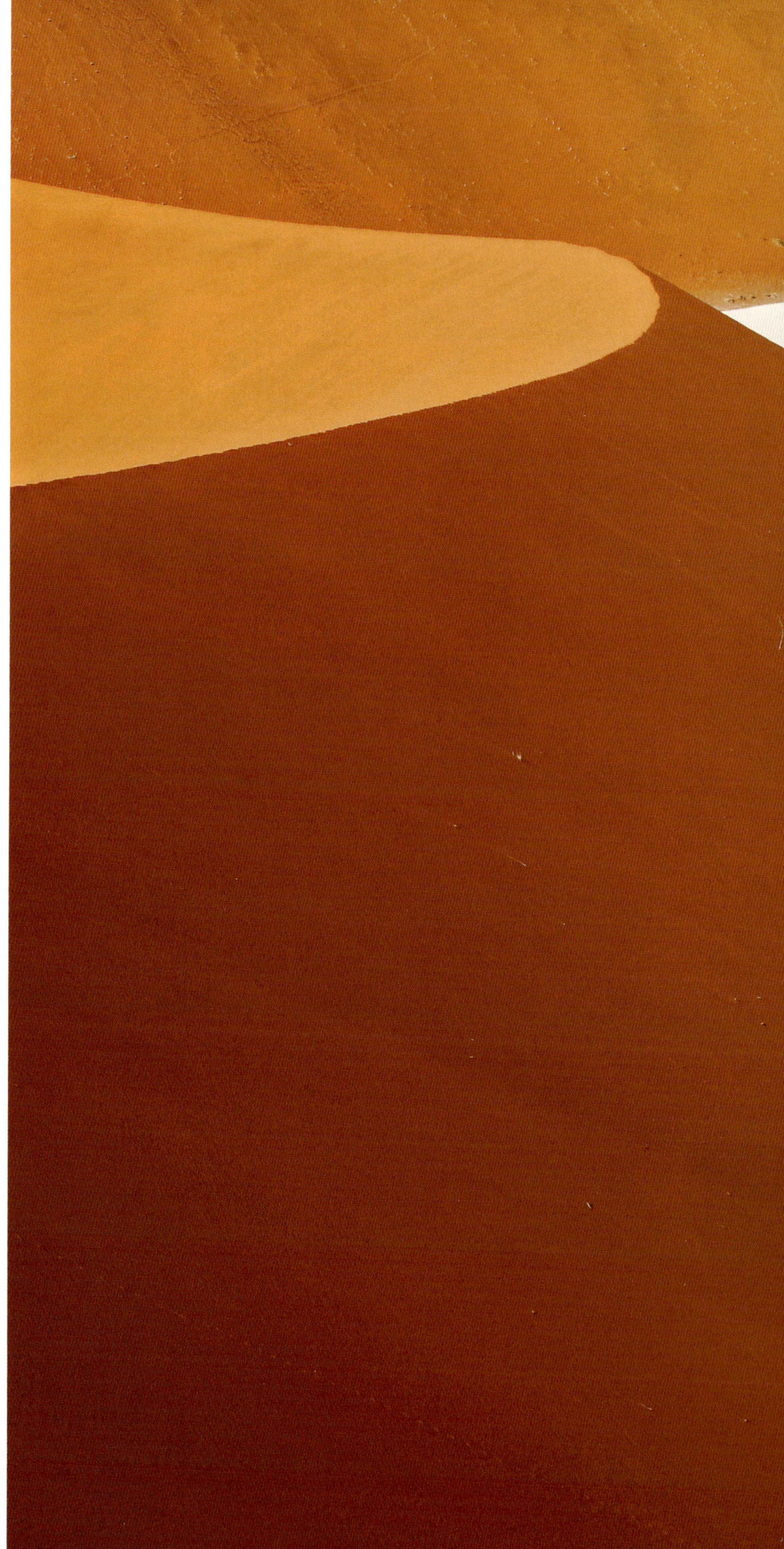

Dune

WINNER

Bernard van Dierendonck

THE NETHERLANDS

As the day lengthened at the Sossusvlei Dunes in Namibia, the light became harsh and the air hazy. It was then that Bernard, more used to the Alps, decided to scale Big Daddy. At 325m (1066 feet), this is Sossusvlei's tallest dune and one of the highest in the world. 'Halfway up', he observes, 'I was a tiny speck in a mineral world of giant lines sculpted by the wind – nature's architecture displayed at its best.' The dune's perfectly straight edge, its razor-sharp crest curving into the distance, contrasted against Deadvlei far below – a floodplain plastered with sun-baked mud. 'The shapes and colours were truly dramatic,' concludes Bernard. 'Nature organized to perfection.'

Canon EOS 1D Mark II with 24-70mm f2.8L USM lens; 1/125 sec at f11; 100 ISO.

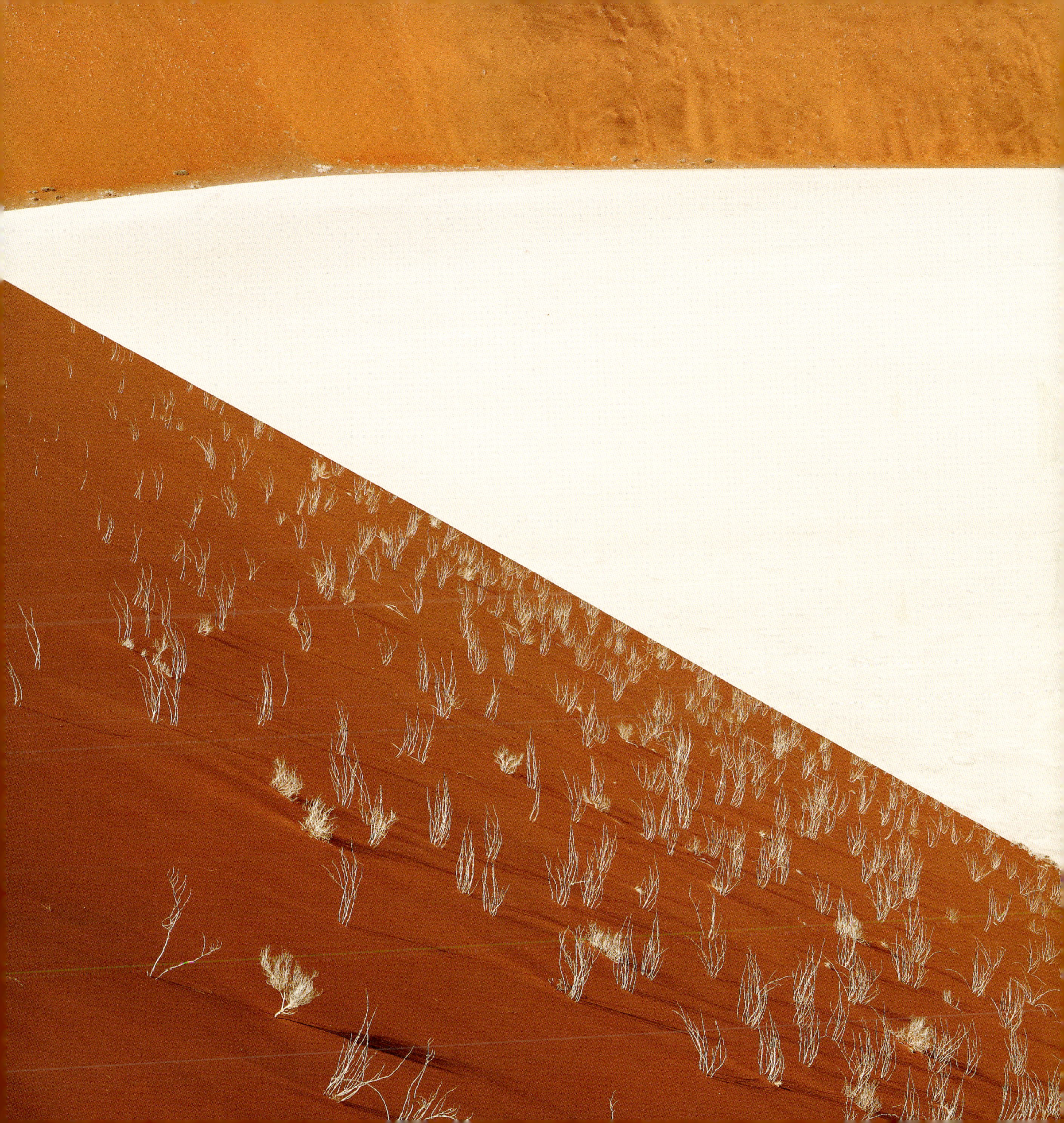

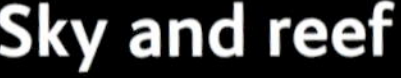

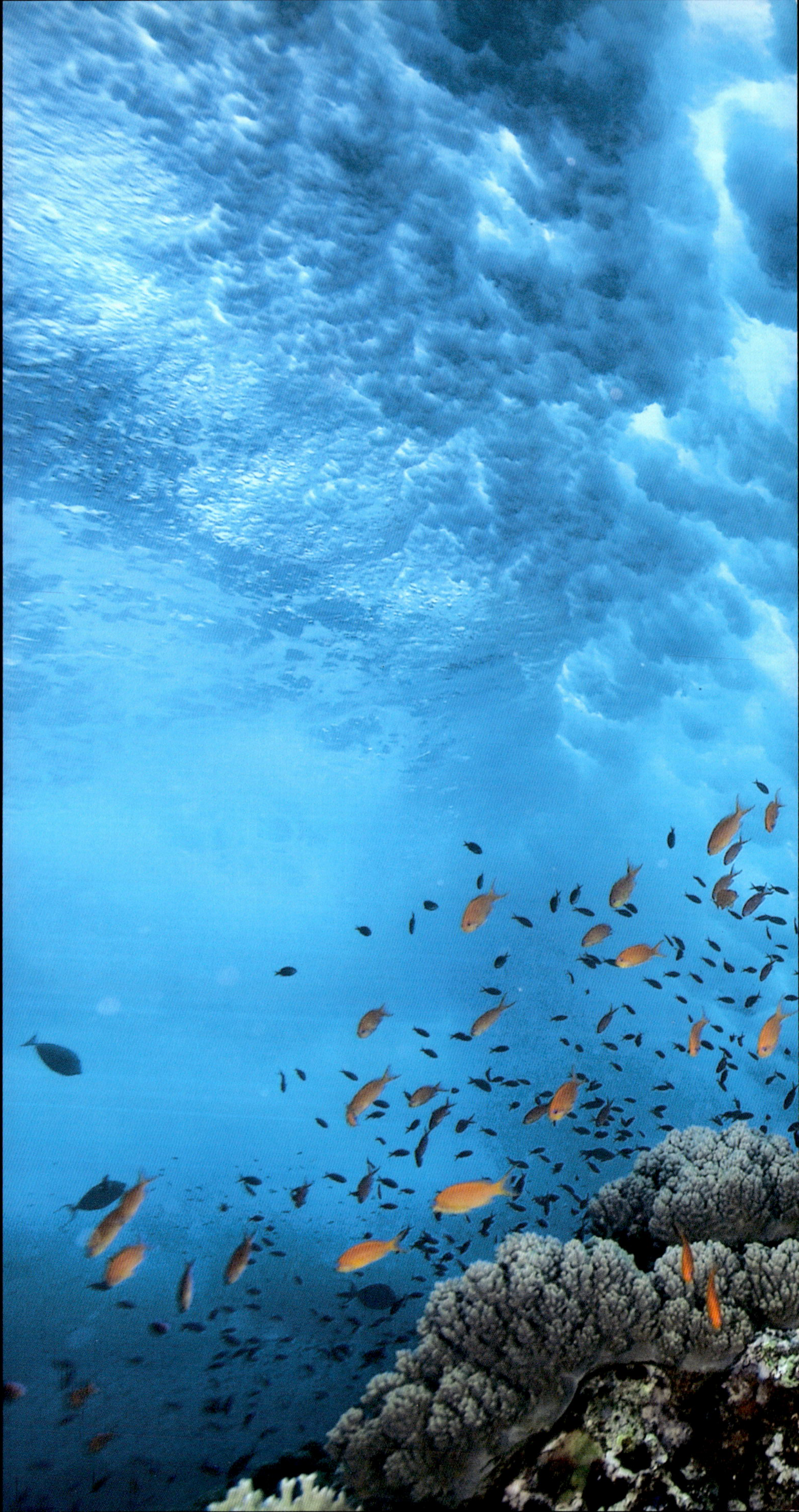

Sky and reef

RUNNER-UP

Jordi Chias

SPAIN

The sharks that Jordi was looking for on Elphinstone Reef in the Red Sea, Egypt, had departed to deeper water. So he decided to finish the dive but stay a short time to look at the breathtaking spectacle of waves crashing down above the beautiful reef. 'The rough water looked like banks of storm clouds stacked up on the horizon,' he says. 'It was as though we were in an upside-down world, preparing to climb out through the sky.' He took the picture just as a huge wave hit. The fish were obviously used to such 'windy' conditions and seemed unperturbed by the dramatic motion.

Nikon D70s with Nikkor 18-70mm ED-Dx lens; 1/160 sec at f6.3; 200 ISO; Hugyfot housing; Inon flashlights.

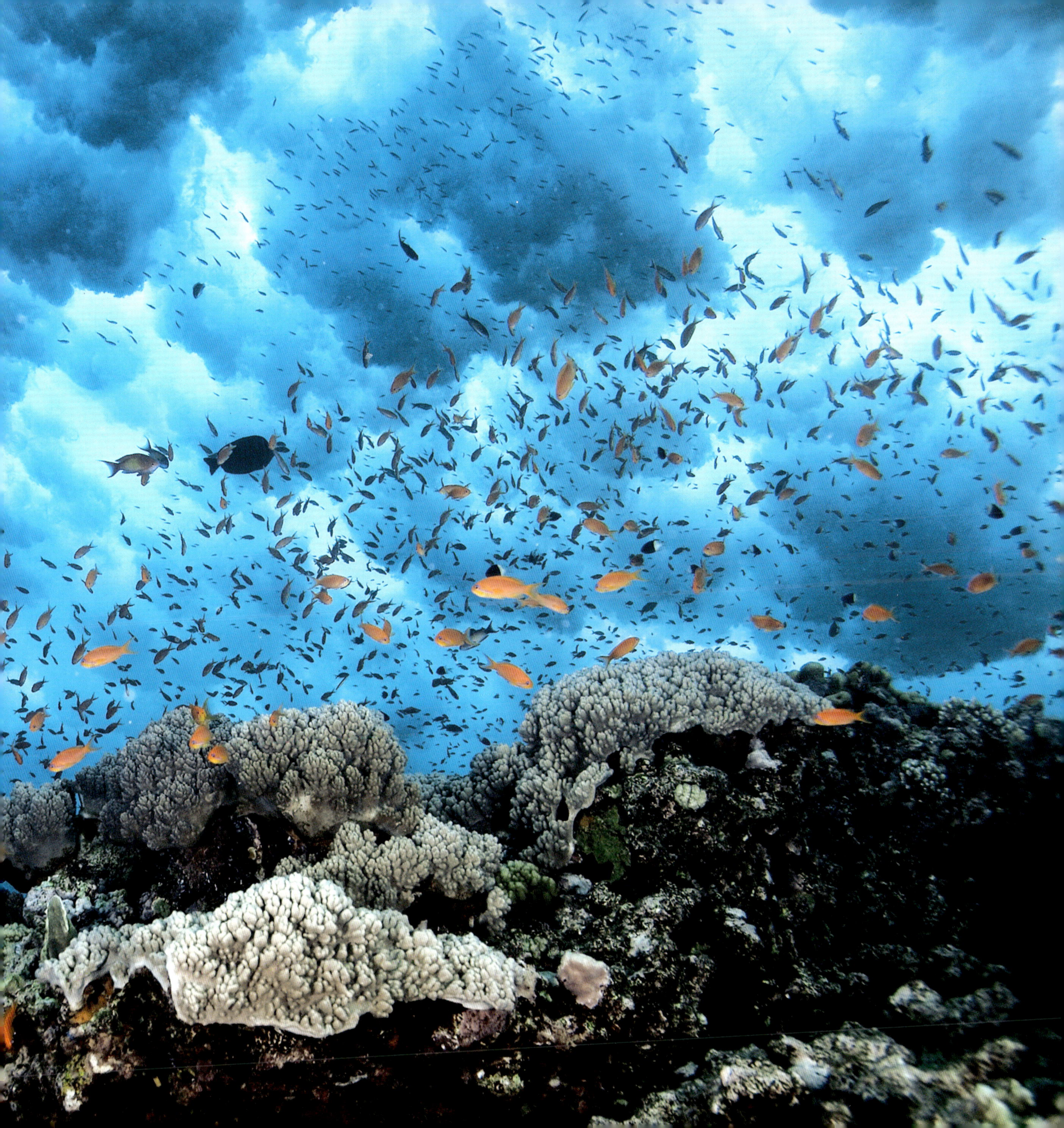

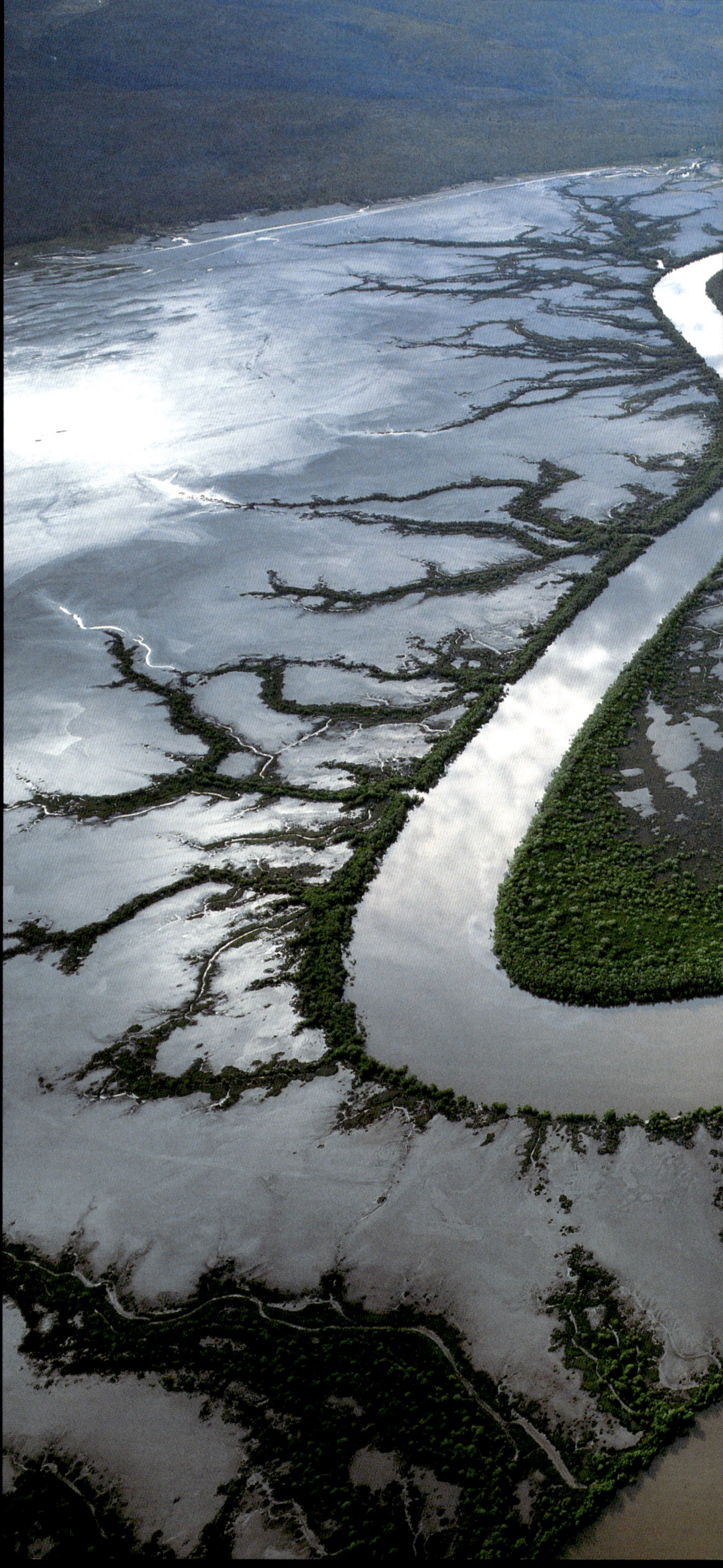

The great delta

SPECIALLY COMMENDED

Theo Allofs

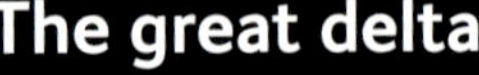

Australia is such a huge country that sometimes the only way to convey an impression of its vast landforms is to photograph them from the air. Theo wanted to show the scale of northern Australia's great Kimberleys wilderness coastal area, choosing to shoot a classic floodplain landscape in the rainy season, when the trees lining the river are lush and the land is flooded and almost impenetrable. 'I was also hoping', he says, 'that I wouldn't fall out of the plane when it banked steeply, so that I could photograph looking directly down.' To get in the perfect position for the composition he had in mind, the plane had to circle many times. The result was a vista of enormous proportions.

Mamiya 7 II (6x7 format) with 45mm lens; Fujichrome RVP.

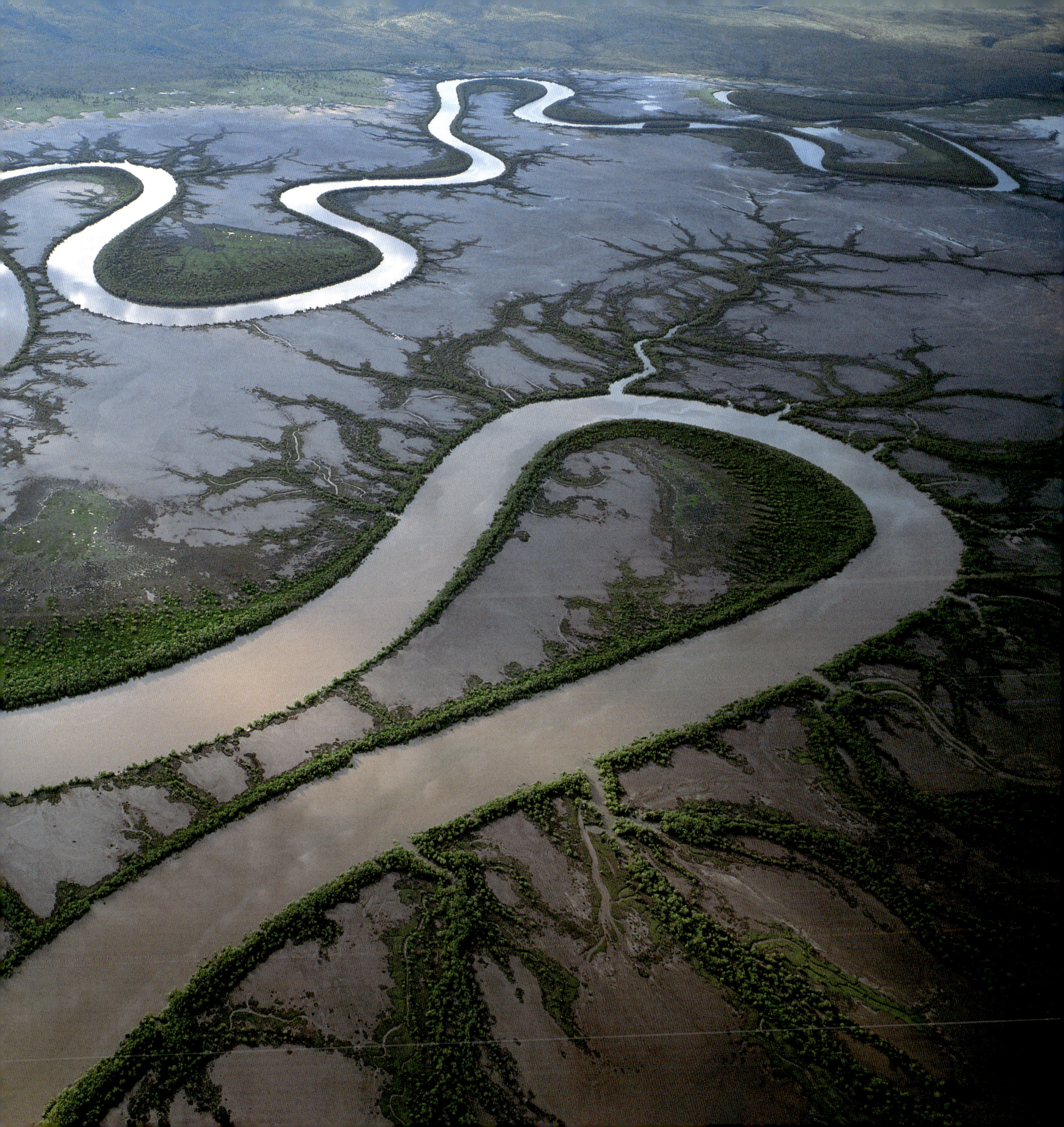

Antarctica sunrise

Daisy Gilardini
SWITZERLAND

Taken at three in the morning, this is the dawning of a spring day in the Antarctic. 'When I woke and saw this beautiful sunrise,' says Daisy, 'I quickly dressed and rushed on deck to enjoy the perfect moment.' Her first visit to Antarctica was in 1997, when she fell in love with the place. Since then she has regularly visited the polar regions – 'a passion that has become my photographic speciality'. On every trip, she wakes several times a night to check on the light. 'You simply can't describe how beautiful it is at the bottom of the world,' she says, 'but maybe this photo goes a little way to convey the magic of the place.'

Nikon D2x with Nikkor 80-200mm f2.8 lens; 1/160 sec at f5; 500 ISO.

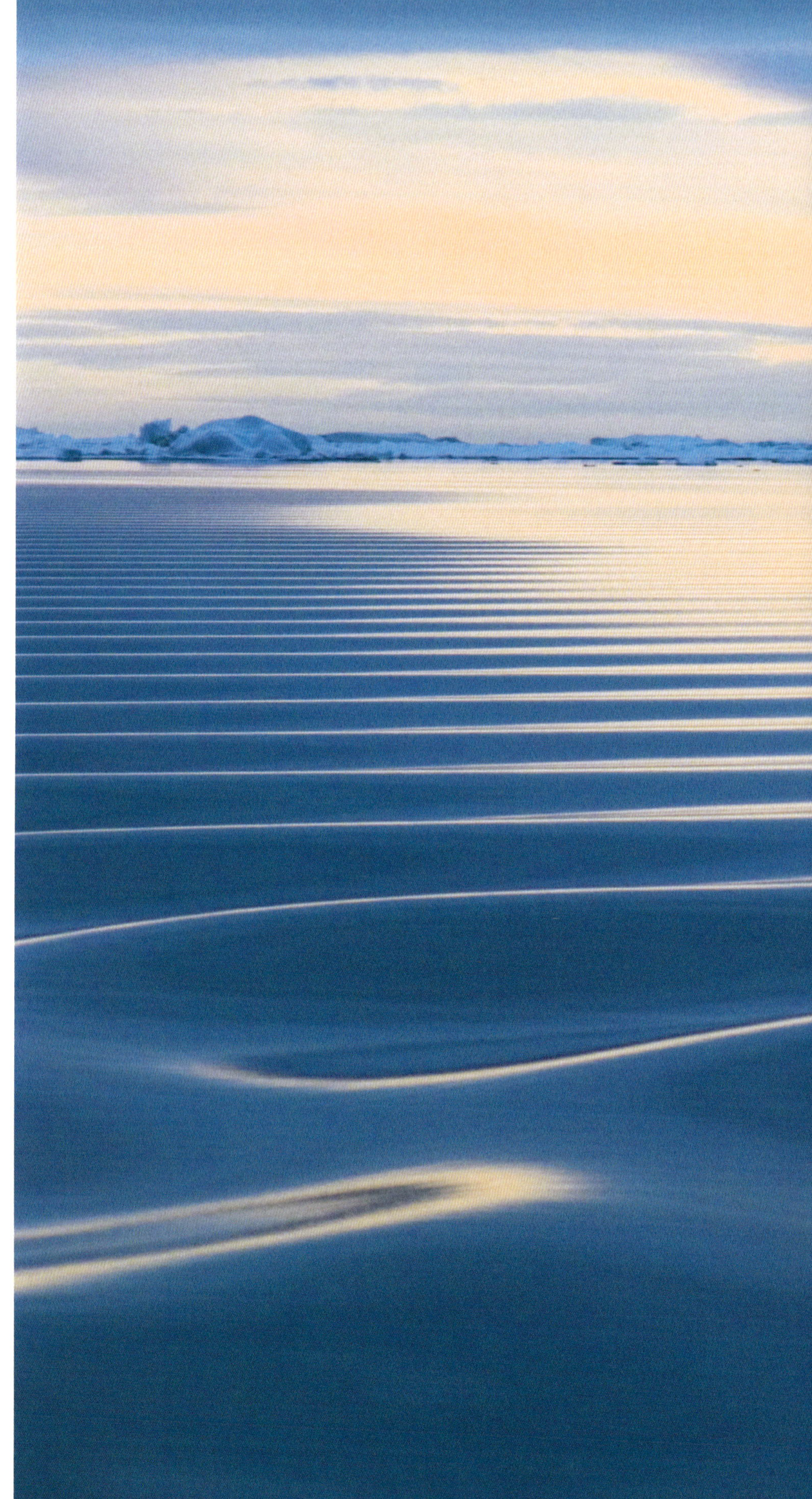

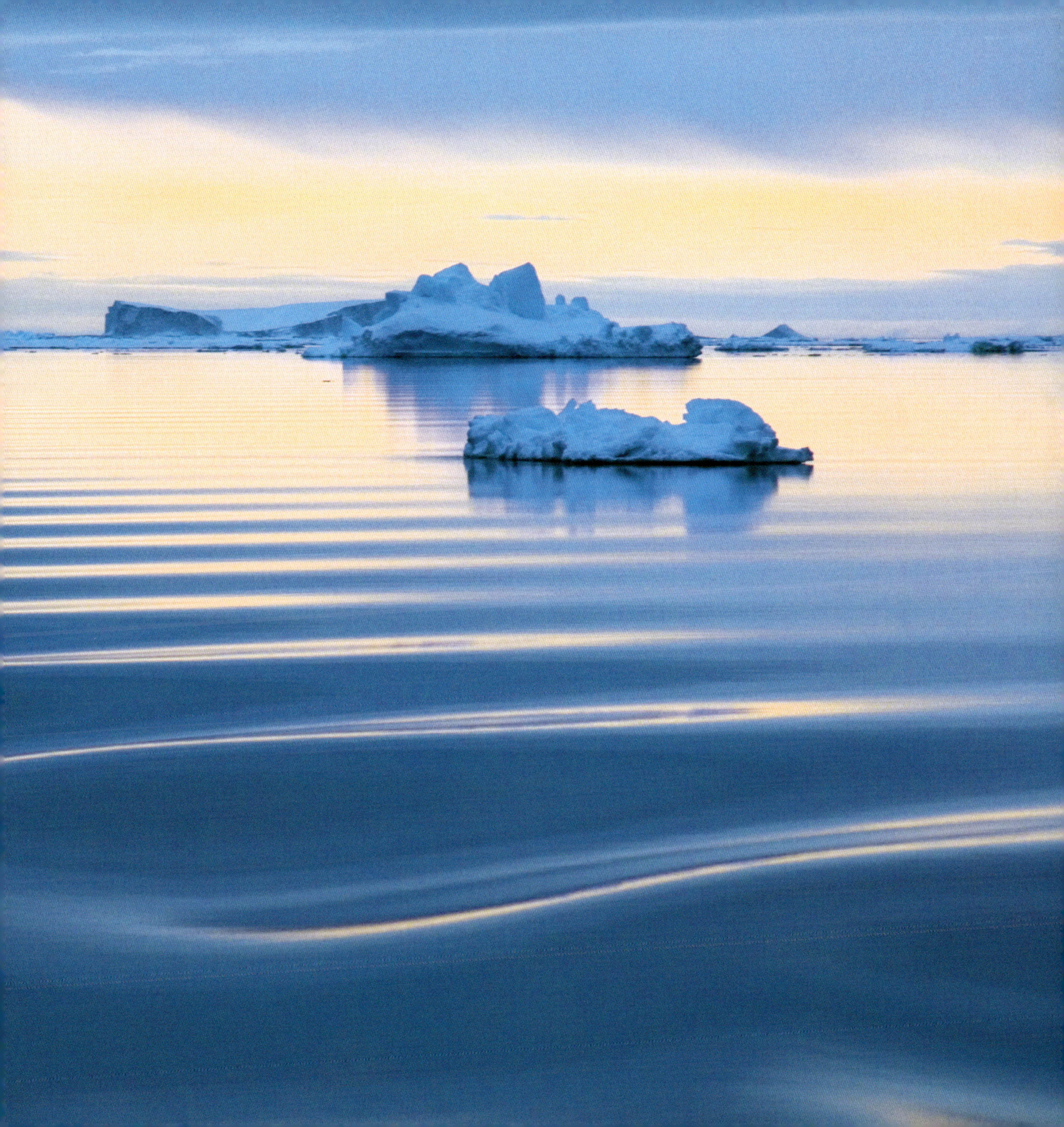

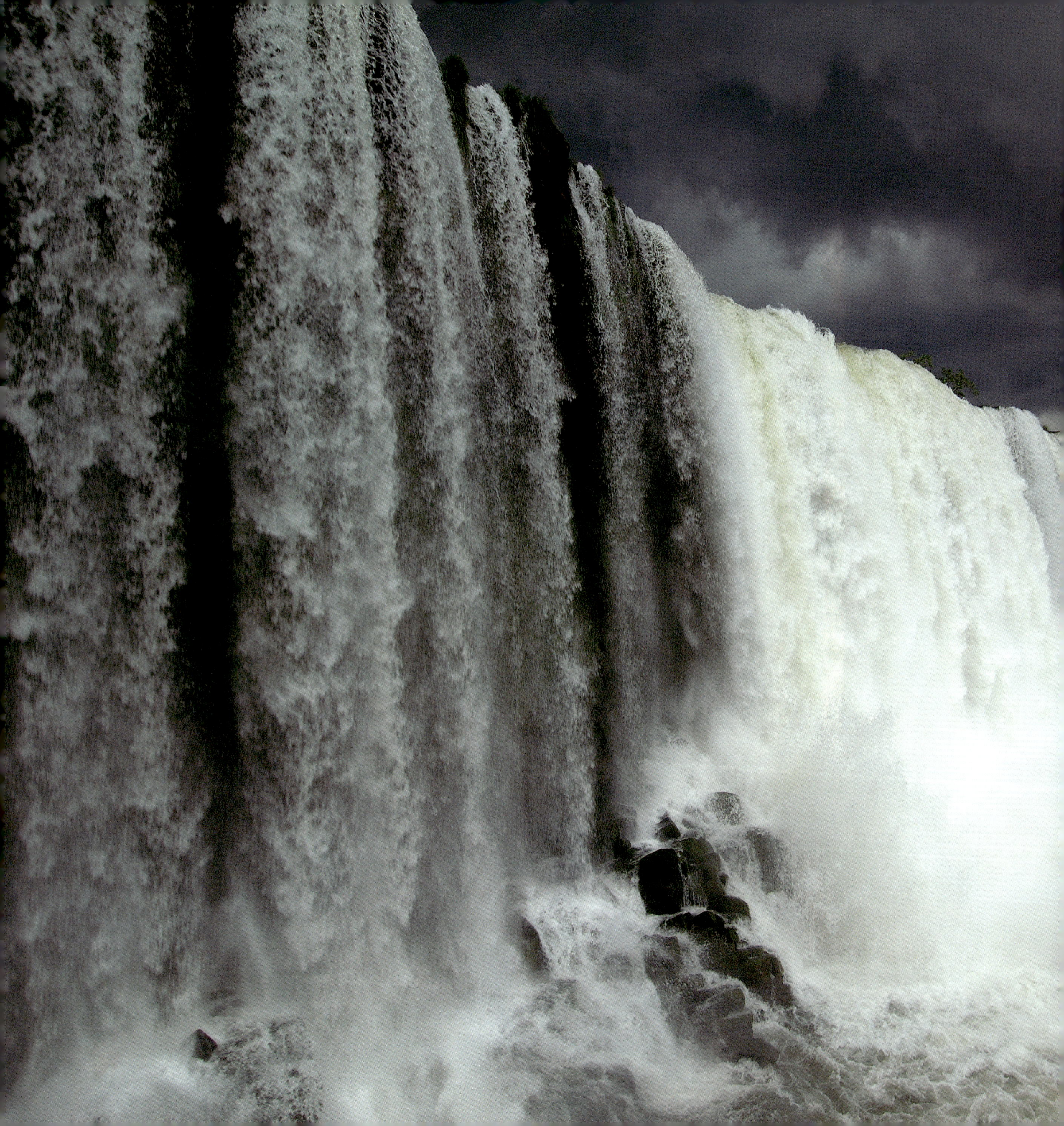

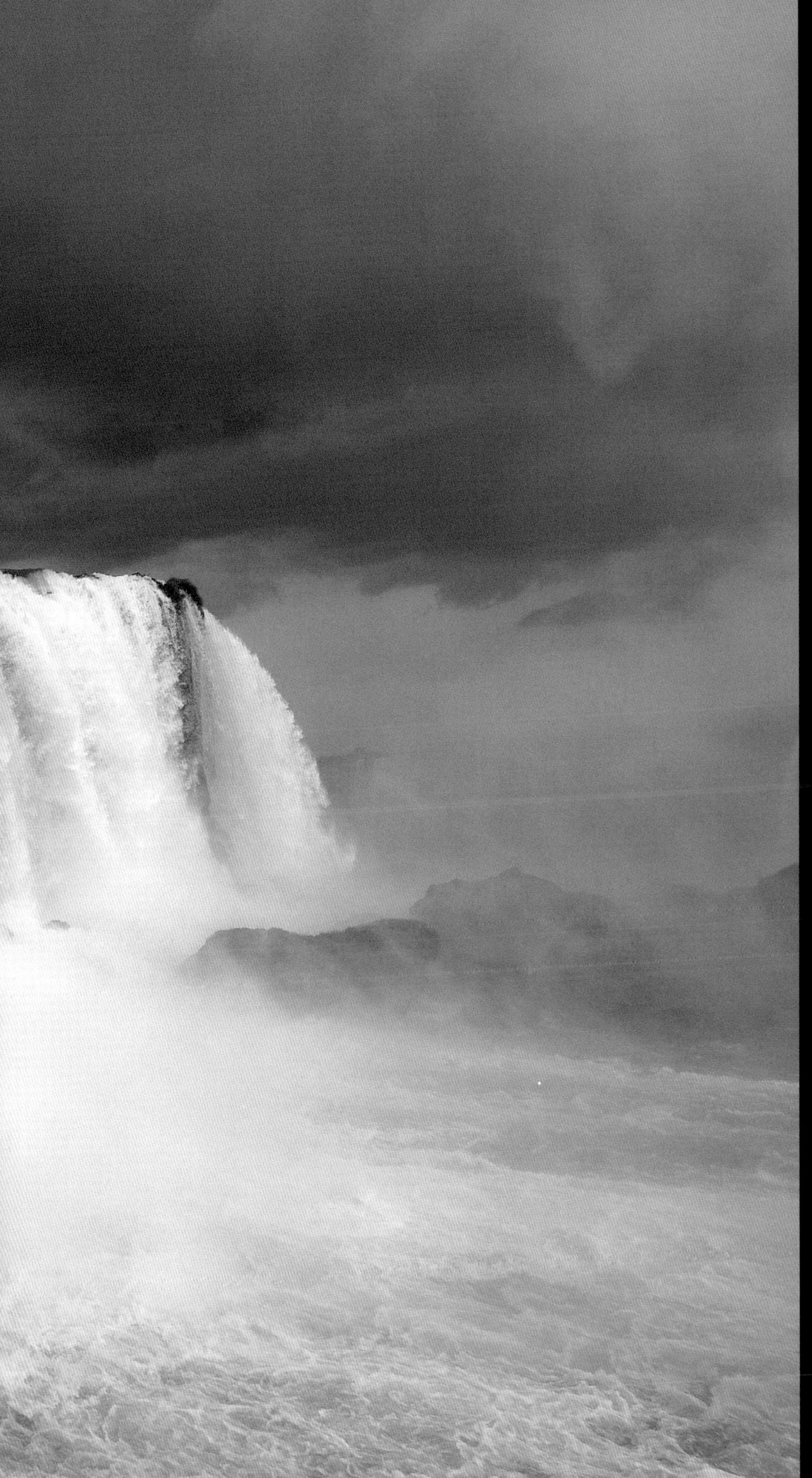

Great Water, Devil's Throat

Jan Baks

THE NETHERLANDS

The glare off the water on a hot February day made it difficult to photograph the spectacular Iguaçu Falls on the border of Brazil and Argentina. But then the weather suddenly changed – 'lots of wind and a gloriously inky sky preceding rain. With such a contrast between sky and water,' says Jan, 'you could at last begin to appreciate the scale and wildness of the place. The thunderous roar was deafening.' After an hour of dramatic thunderstorm, 'the sky cleared and the oppressive heat returned', he adds. These falls have spray that, in the right conditions, can reach heights of 90m (300 feet) as the river plunges into the chasm known as the Devil's Throat. Iguaçu comes from an Indian word meaning 'great water', and today these 2.5km- (1.6-mile-) wide falls have been honoured with UNESCO World Heritage status.

Nikon D2x with AF-S Nikkor 12-24mm 1:4G ED lens; 1/180 sec at f6.3; 160 ISO; tripod.

The World in Our Hands

A picture in this category must be thought-provoking and must convey our relationship with the environment, whether our connection with it, effects on it or dependence on it. The image must also be memorable, whether graphic, symbolic or poignant.

Hurricane tree

WINNER

Jocke Berglund

SWEDEN

When Hurricane Gudrun thundered across southern Sweden in January 2005, it left around 100,000 people isolated and without electricity. Deep snow, fallen trees and severe temperatures resulted in several people dying before help could reach them. Flying over Småland photographing the devastation, Jocke – who specializes in aerial photography – saw this 'remarkable oak tree print', formed partly by the storm brush of nature and partly by the impact on the soil of the forestry machines retrieving logs. 'It's as if the heavens had sent a message to the forest industry reminding them that, in this area, deciduous trees would have withstood the winds much better than pine – as well as being yet another stark reminder that global warming will lead to regular and stronger storm winds.'

Canon EOS-1Ds Mark II with 28-70mm f2.8 lens; 1/800 sec; 200 ISO; Cessna aircraft.

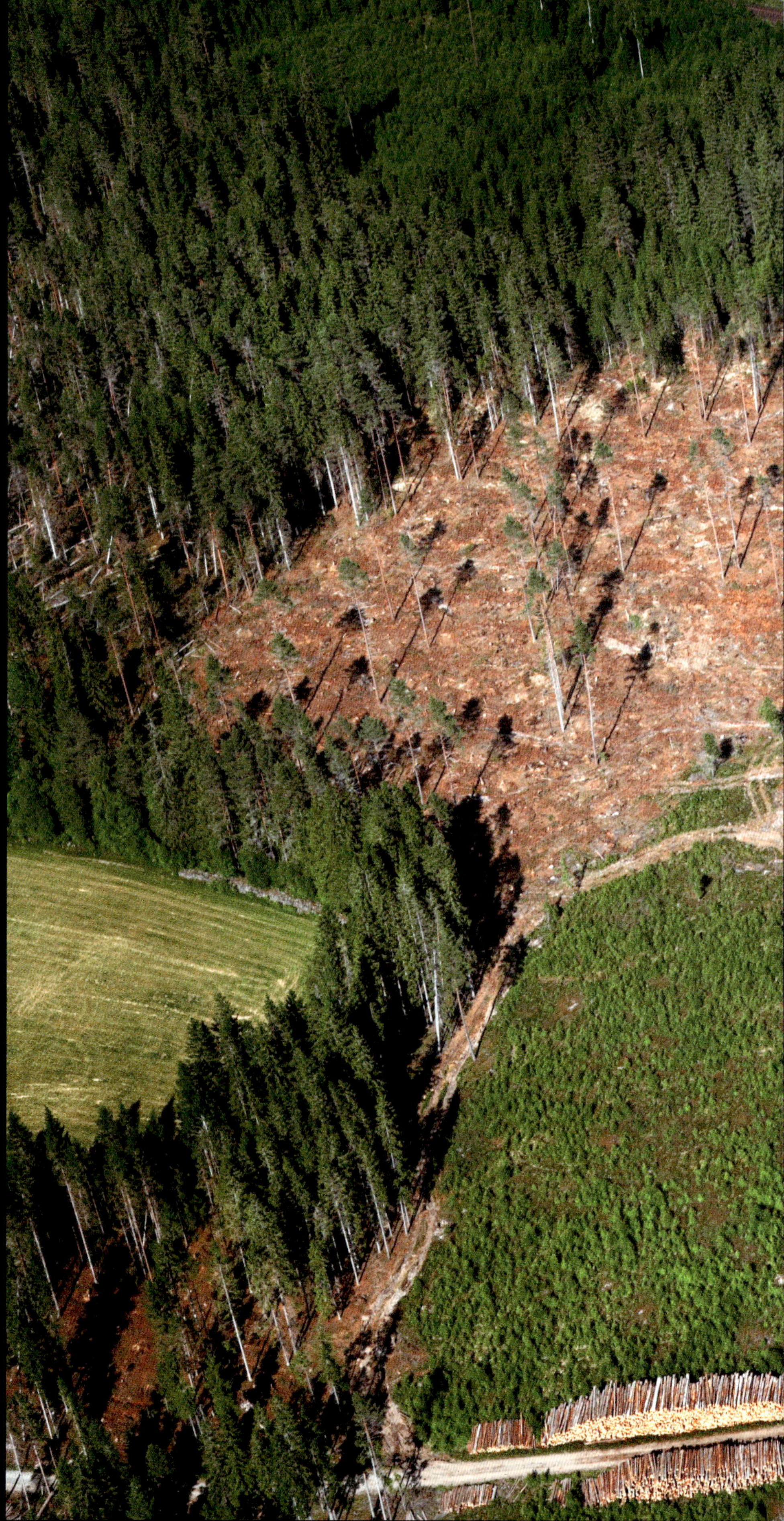

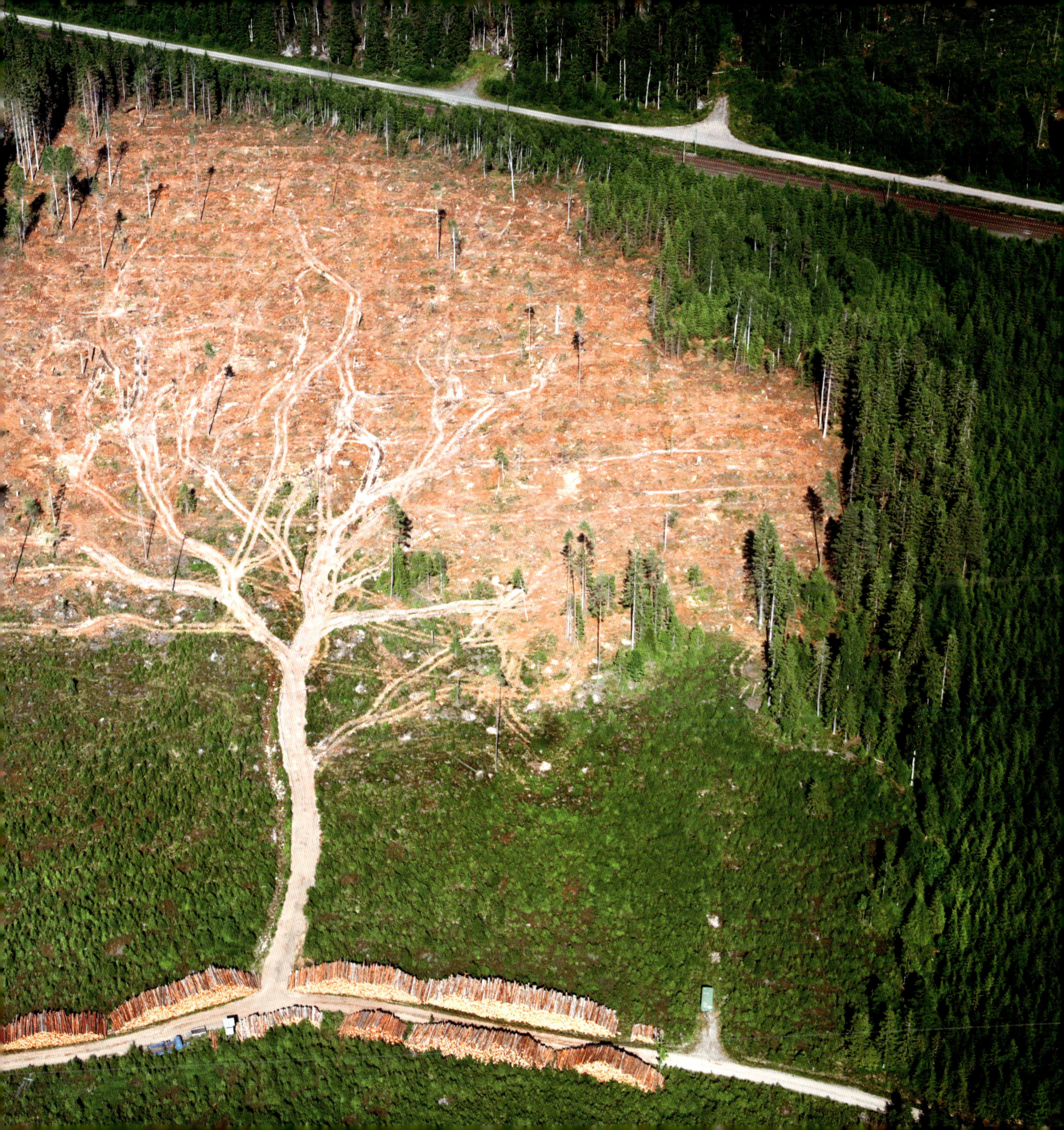

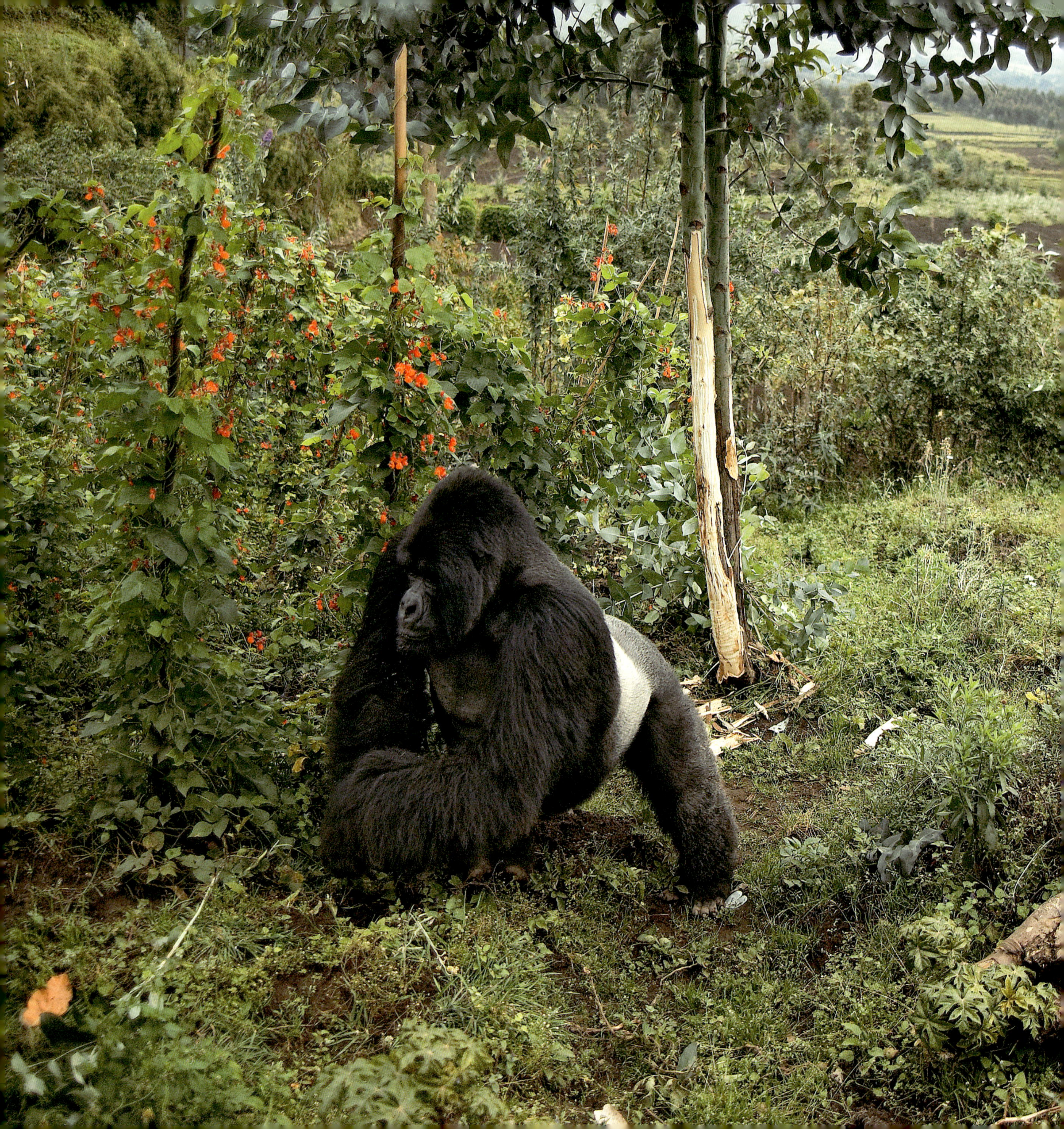

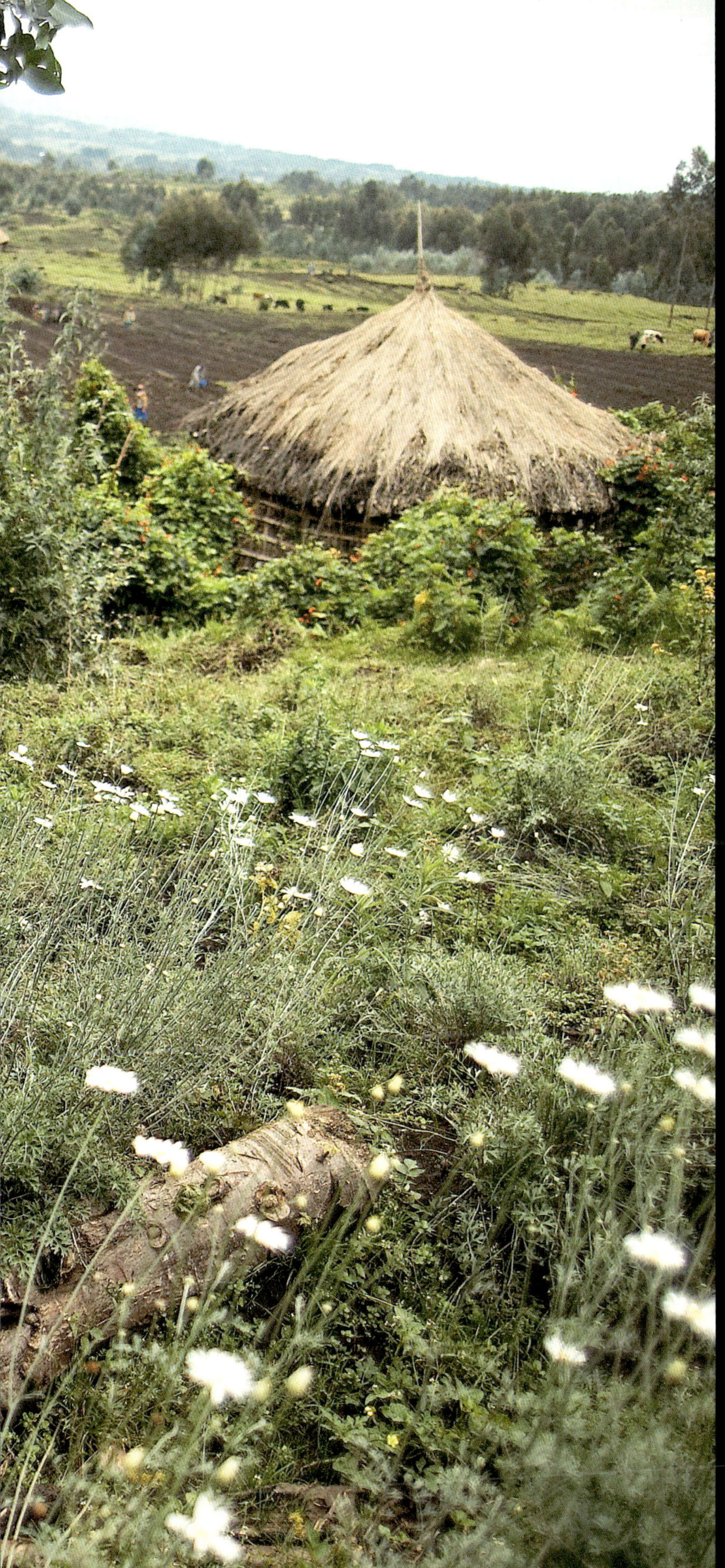

Silverback on the edge

RUNNER-UP

Joe McDonald

USA

Joe has made many treks to see the endangered mountain gorillas in the Volcanoes National Park in Rwanda, and most have involved jungle hikes for up to four hours. On this occasion, though, he encountered a troop of gorillas before even starting up the mountain. The farm fields go right up to the park boundary, and feeding in the papaya trees and among the bean rows were about 15 gorillas of all ages, some fairly close to the village huts. 'I was immediately struck by the symbolism of this image,' says Joe, 'illustrating not only the loss of the gorillas' habitat but also how their future depends on their relationship with the local people.' Fortunately, the locals are very tolerant of the occasional visits – though it must be quite a surprise to encounter the world's largest ape among your beans.

Canon 1Ds with Tamron 28-105mm f2.8 lens; 1/2000 sec at f2.8; 200 ISO.

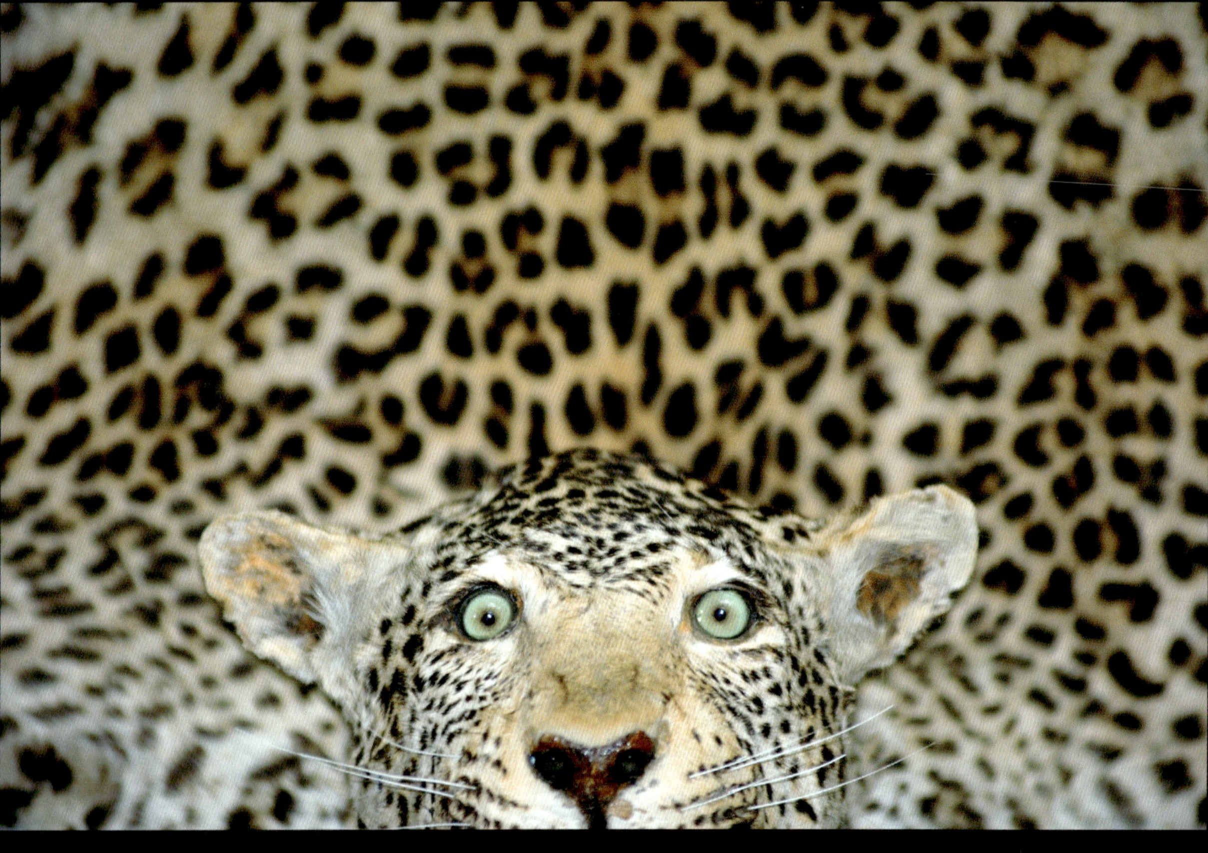

Leopard shot

Alessandro Bee

ITALY

While travelling in Tanzania, Alessandro stopped for a drink in a tourist shop. On the walls were skins. Viewing them were tourists who had only recently been looking at live animals in the parks. It was the leopard that affected Alessandro most. 'Its glass eyes stared straight at me.' Leopards are protected, but

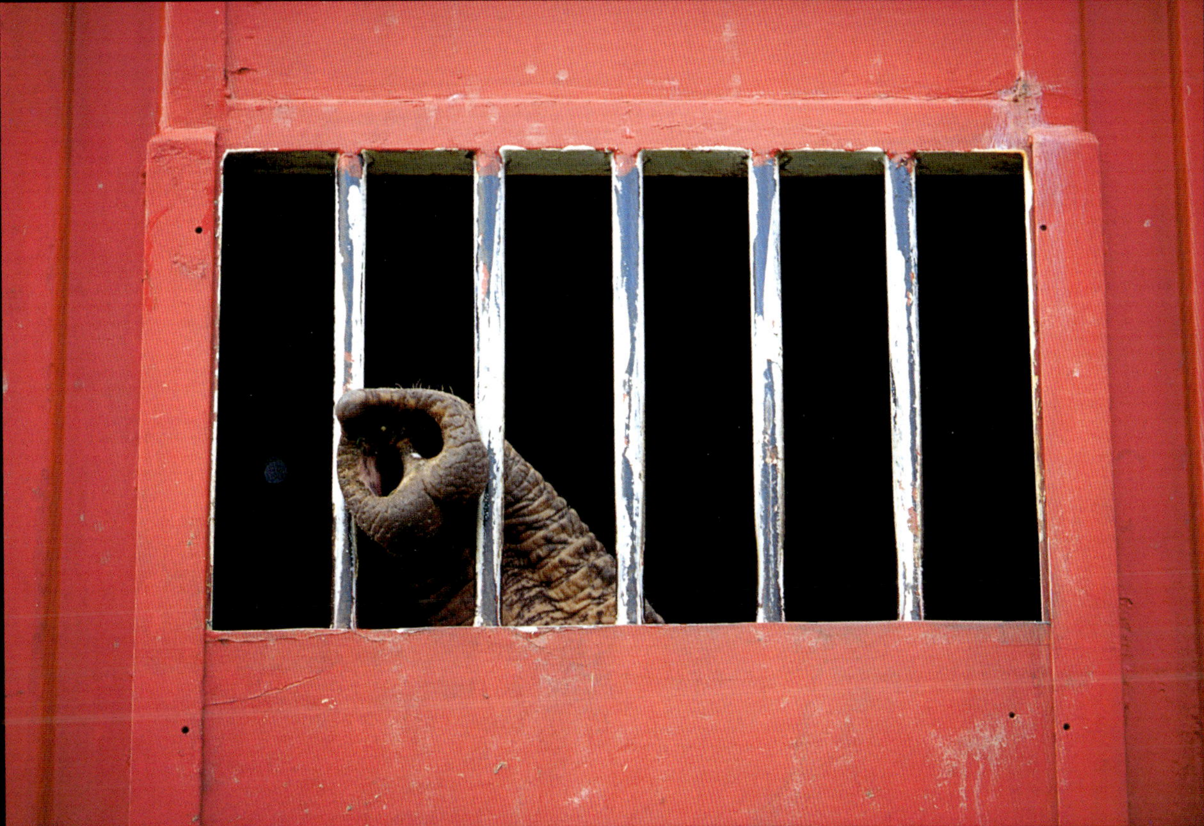

Circus life

Peter Lilja

SWEDEN

While passing through a village in northern Sweden, Peter saw a circus camped in a field and went to investigate the beast-wagons. Approaching a pink steel one, he noticed a small window with bars rubbed clean of paint. His curiosity was answered as the inmate – an Indian elephant – put its trunk tip up to the bars. 'I couldn't bear to think how long the elephant had to spend in such a dark, confined space and how far it had to travel in that container,' says Peter. Sweden has banned the use of some wild animals in circuses but not elephants. The UK has no ban on the use of wild animals in circuses or special welfare rules for their care.

Nikon F5 with 80-200mm f2.8 lens; 1/125 sec at f5.6; Kodak 100 ISO.

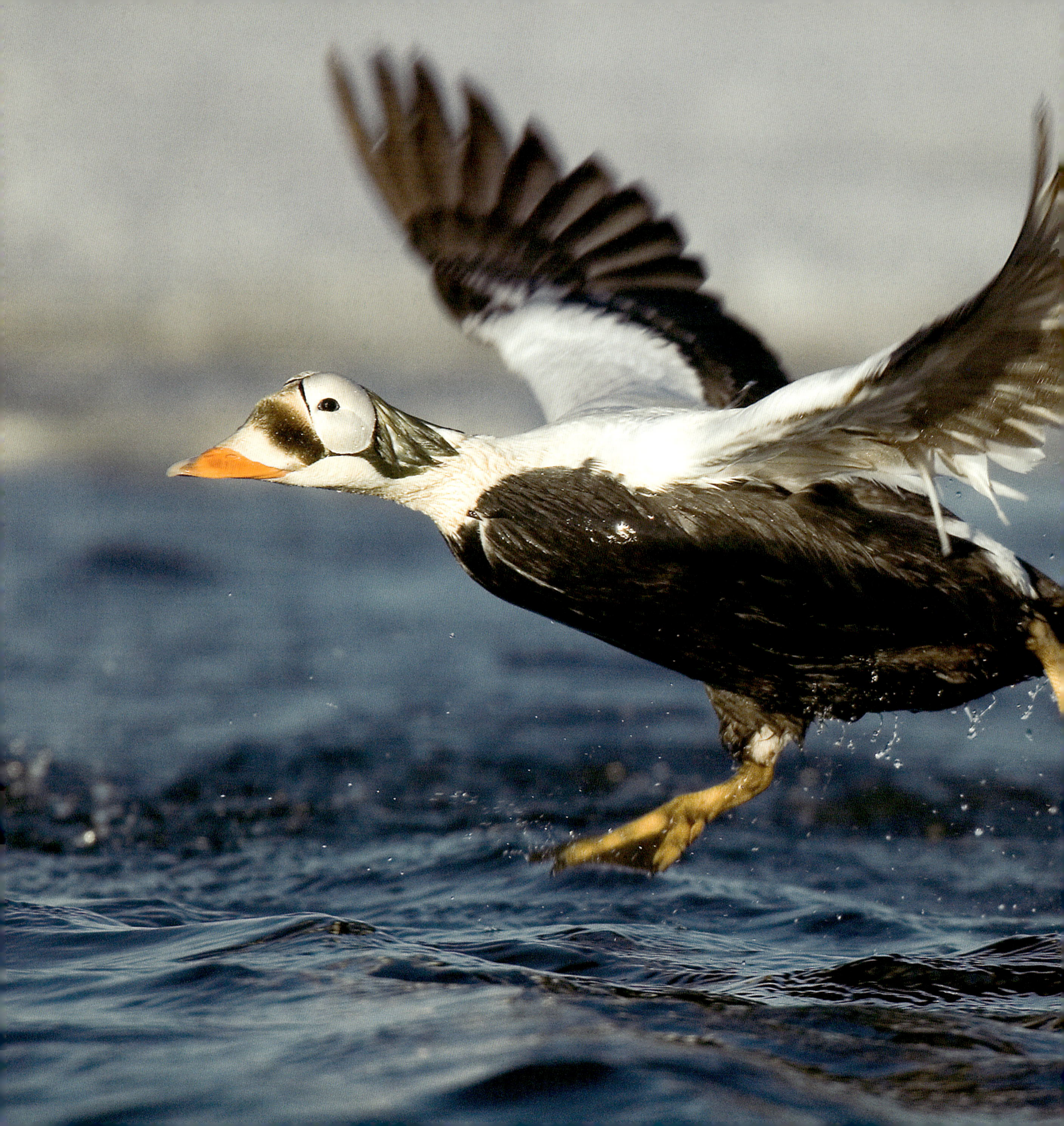

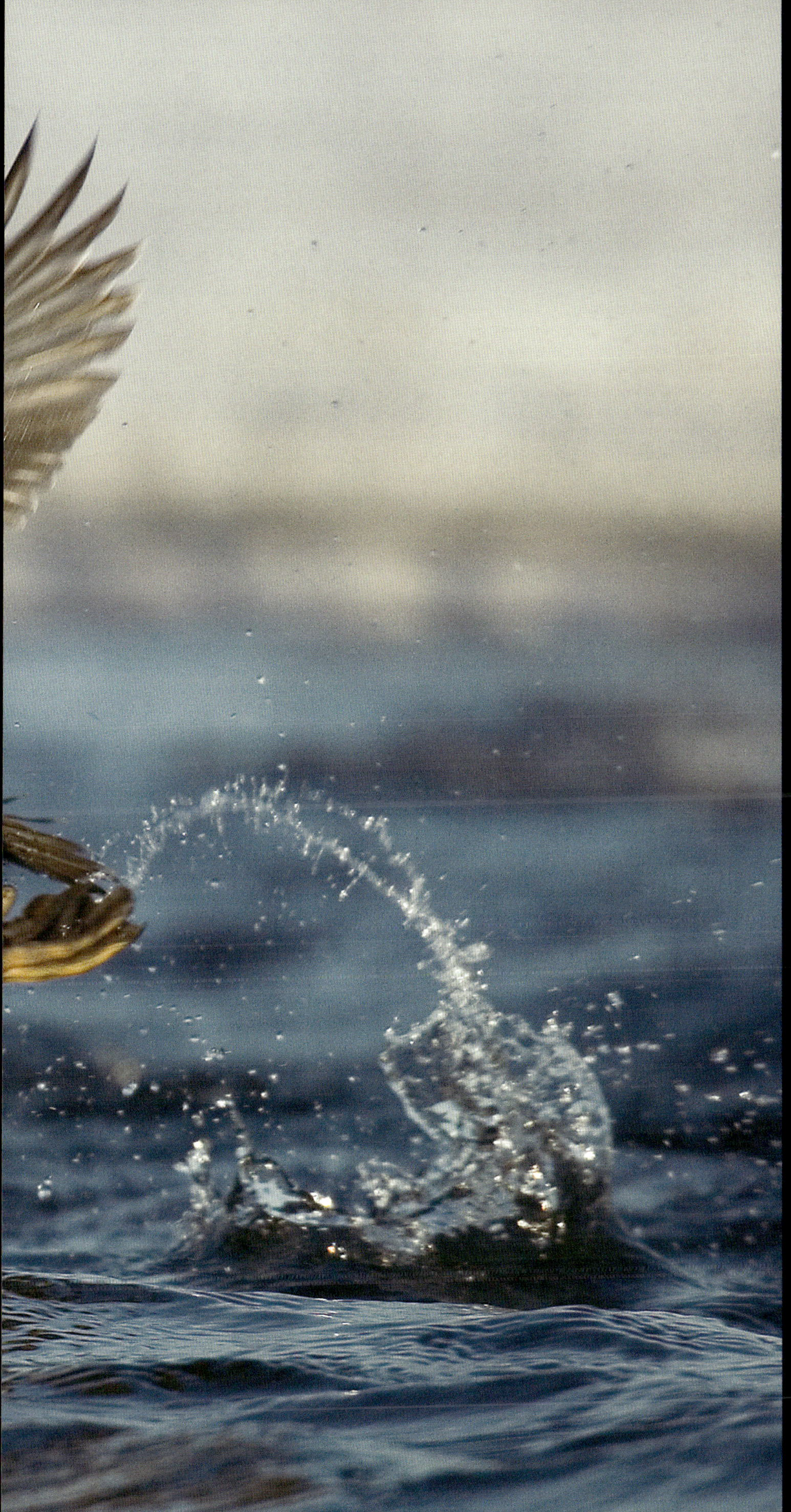

Gerald Durrell Award for Endangered Wildlife

Pictured here are species that are critically endangered, endangered, vulnerable or at risk (as officially listed in the IUCN Red List of Threatened Species).

Eider lift-off

WINNER

Stig Frode Olsen

NORWAY

Running on the surface, with much splashing and slapping of wings, the heavy male spectacled eider needed a 'runway' of several metres to achieve lift-off. He and his mate were feeding in an ice-free area of a lake in the far north of Alaska. Setting up his tripod beside the lake, Stig watched the pair as they fed in the open water. 'I noticed that they flew off several times a day to a nearby pond that was fairly ice-free,' says Stig, 'possibly because they had a nest site close by.' He was soon able to anticipate their departures and so was well prepared for this shot. Spectacled eiders breed mainly in three coastal areas of Alaska and Russia, and winter out in the Bering Sea. In Alaska, their numbers have dropped greatly over the past decades. Why is not known, but recent changes in the populations of prey, such as bottom-living molluscs and crustaceans in the Bering Sea, and disturbance by bottom-trawling fisheries may be major problems.

Canon 20D with 300mm f2.8 lens and 2x converter; 1/1600 sec at f5.6; 200 ISO; tripod.

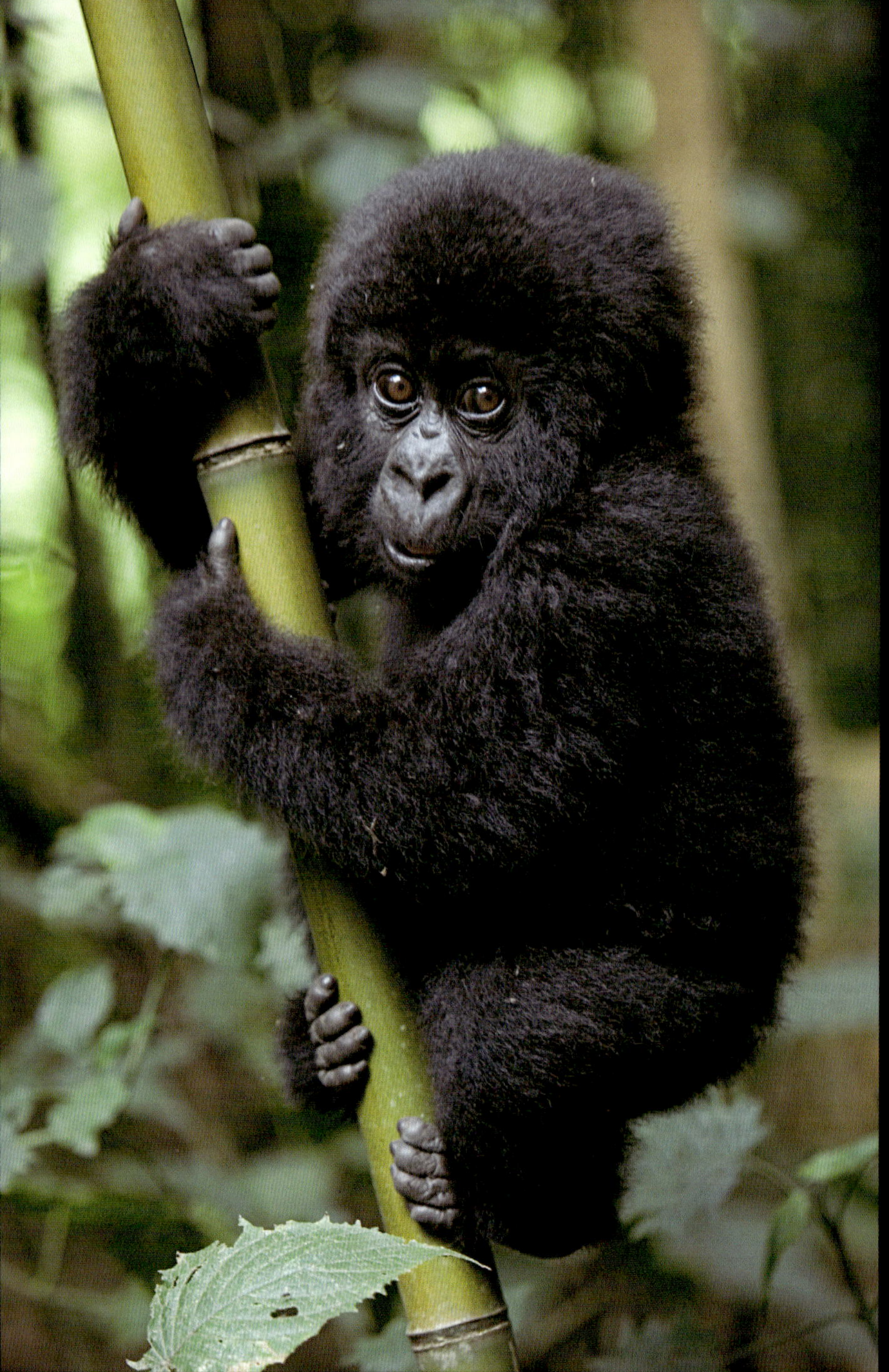

Human encounter

SPECIALLY COMMENDED

Suzi Eszterhas

USA

Mother mountain gorillas rarely let young babies wander out of arm's reach, but this ten-month-old was allowed to play on a bamboo stem while his mother gathered nettles in the Volcanoes National Park in Rwanda. He concentrated on climbing for several feet and then 'stopped to look at me', says Suzi. 'It was like looking into the eyes of a human – an adorable moment. He seemed so vulnerable.' He and his kin are vulnerable. With just 380 in the Virunga Mountain range in Rwanda, Uganda and the Democratic Republic of Congo, surrounded by a sea of agriculture, and only about 320 in Uganda's Bwindi Impenetrable Forest, mountain gorillas are highly endangered.

Canon EOS 1D Mark II, with 70-200mm f2.8 lens; 1/200 sec at f3.2; 800 ISO.

Golden-crowned sifaka

RUNNER-UP

Pete Oxford

UK

It took a week of patient fieldcraft before Pete was able to relax a group of five golden-crowned sifakas – among the world's most endangered primates. 'I watched them for a while,' he says, 'charmed by their deft leaps through the trees and their stunning looks.' This individual came to a sudden halt and peered from behind the tree trunk – 'a wonderful moment of contact'. Discovered for science in 1988, this lemur gets its name from its contact call – shee-fak. Confined to dry forest in the Daraina area of northern Madagascar, it is critically endangered, threatened largely by deforestation and artisanal gold-mining. Recently, though, a Malagasy conservation group, Fanamby, has started to work with the local people to find a way for them and the sifakas to survive together.

Nikon D2x with 300mm f2.8 lens and 1.4x teleconverter; 1/125 sec at f5.6; tripod; flash.

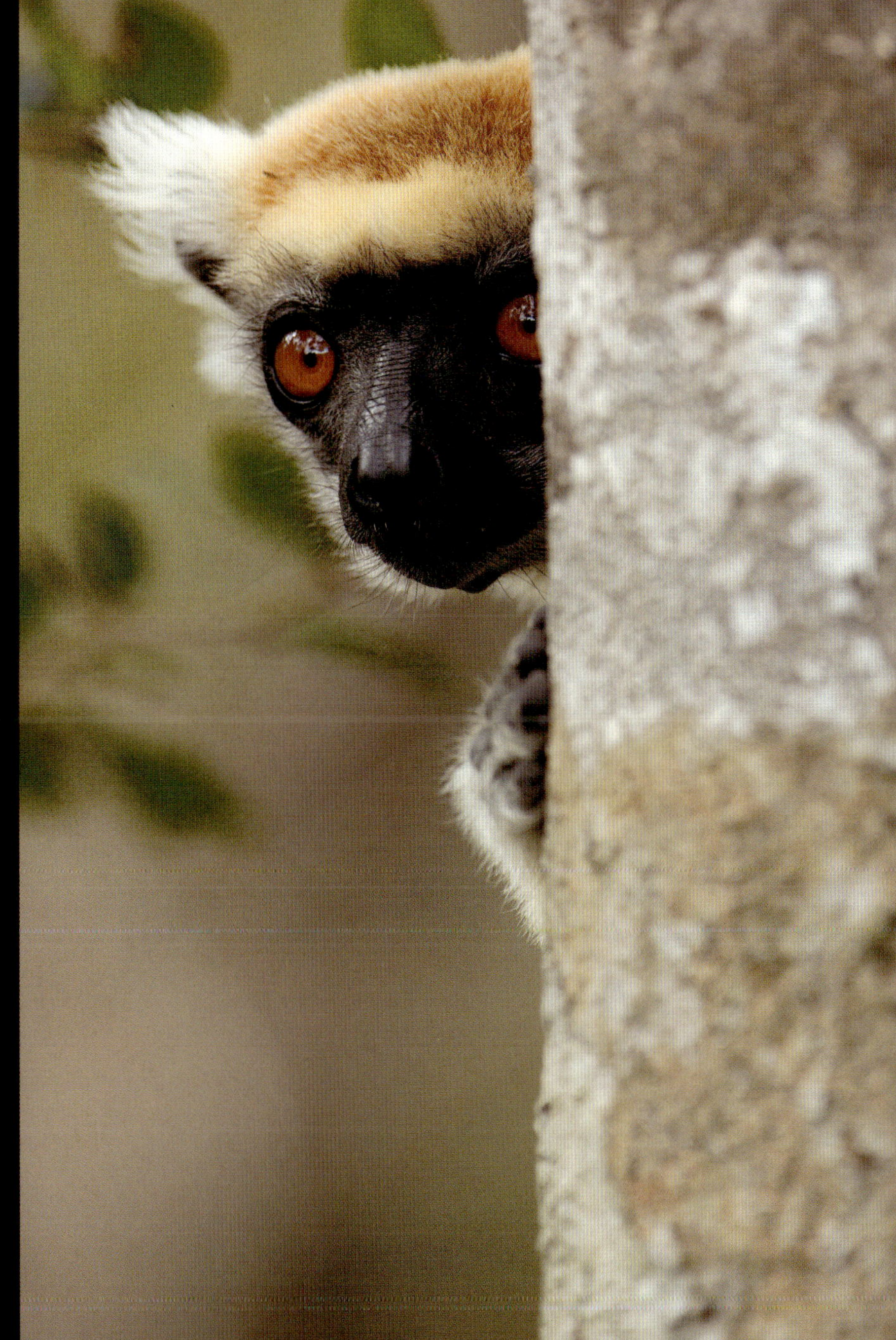

Napping manatees

Jun Kezuka

JAPAN

One January late afternoon, while snorkelling in Crystal River, Florida, Jun came across these napping manatees. 'They were in a quiet backwater,' says Jun, 'and the water was rather dark. I took this picture very carefully so as not to ripple the mirror-like surface or wake up the sleeping beauties.' Manatees are attracted in winter to the warm springs filtering up through the riverbed. You can be lulled into a false sense of security about the status of American manatees when you encounter so many of them in such a small area of river – Jun encountered up to 70 on one day. But in much of their range, they are threatened by hunting, fishing and pollution, and in Florida by development of their habitat (Jun was astonished to see such extraordinary, friendly animals so close to riverside houses) and by recreational boats – quite a few sported fresh wounds caused by outboard propellers.

Nikonos RS with 13mm fisheye lens; 1/8 sec at f5.6; Fujichrome Velvia 100.

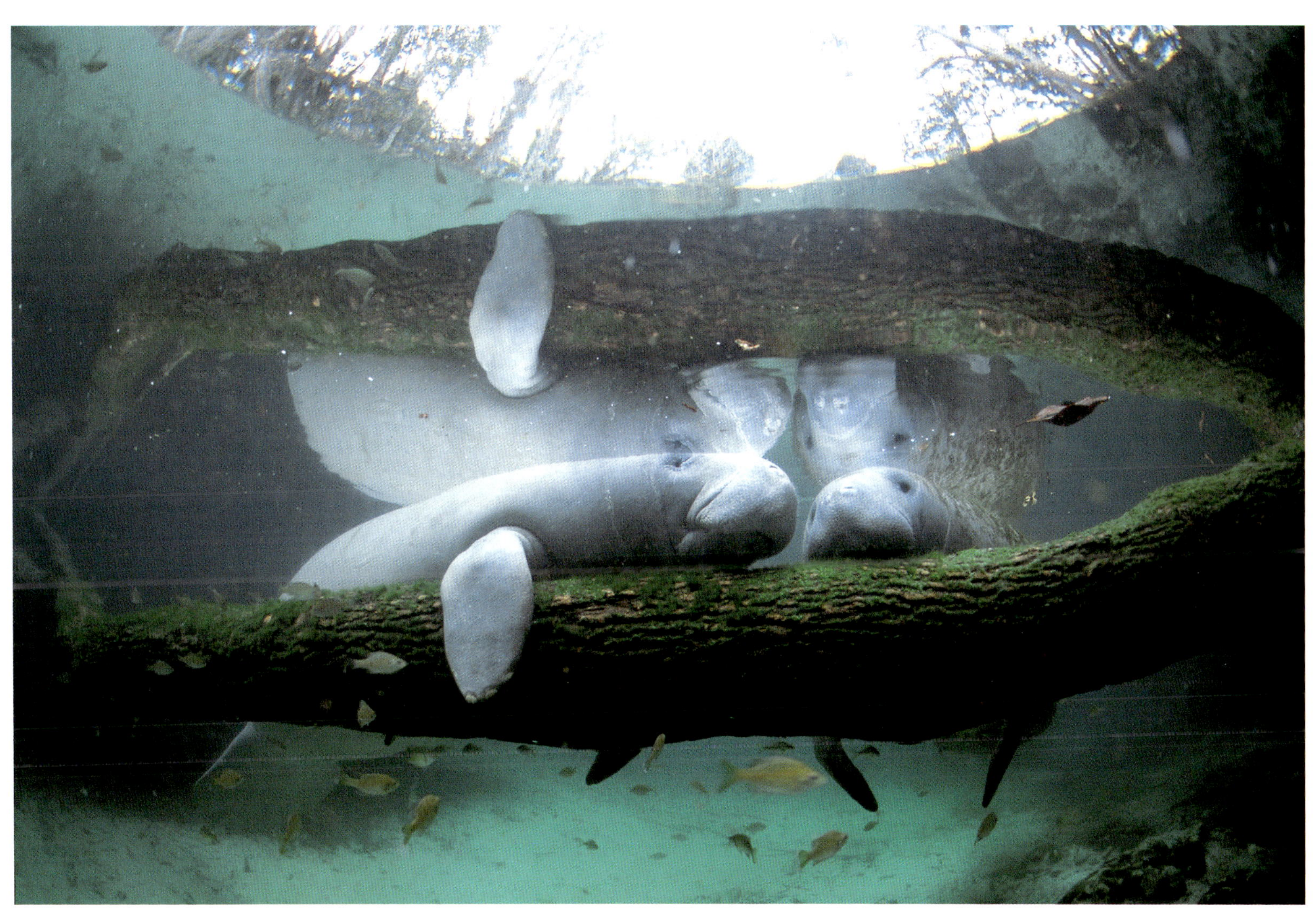

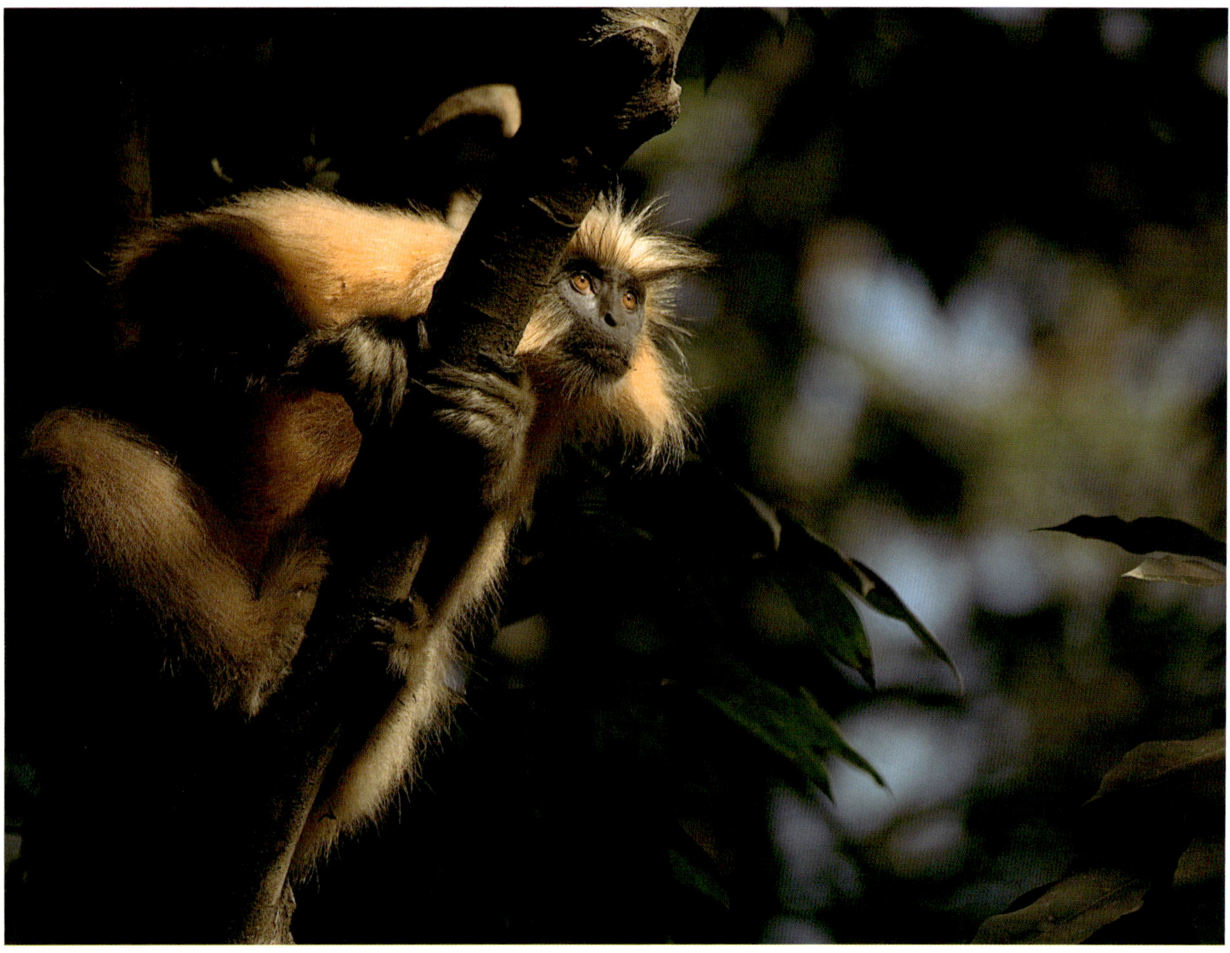

Golden leaf monkey

Bernard Castelein

BELGIUM

This wary individual, its beautiful coat spotlit, fulfilled Bernard's ambition to photograph a golden leaf monkey in the wild – a species known to science only since 1956. 'But to get the shot took five trips to Assam,' he says. These highly endangered langurs, threatened by logging, are confined to forest remnants in the Himalayan foothills on the border of Assam (India) and Bhutan. They live in the treetops and so are extremely difficult to photograph. 'I finally found a group that would allow me close enough to use a long lens,' says Bernard, 'but even then they were very nervous.'

Nikon D2x with Nikkor AFS 500mm f4 lens; 1/500 sec at f4; 200 ISO.

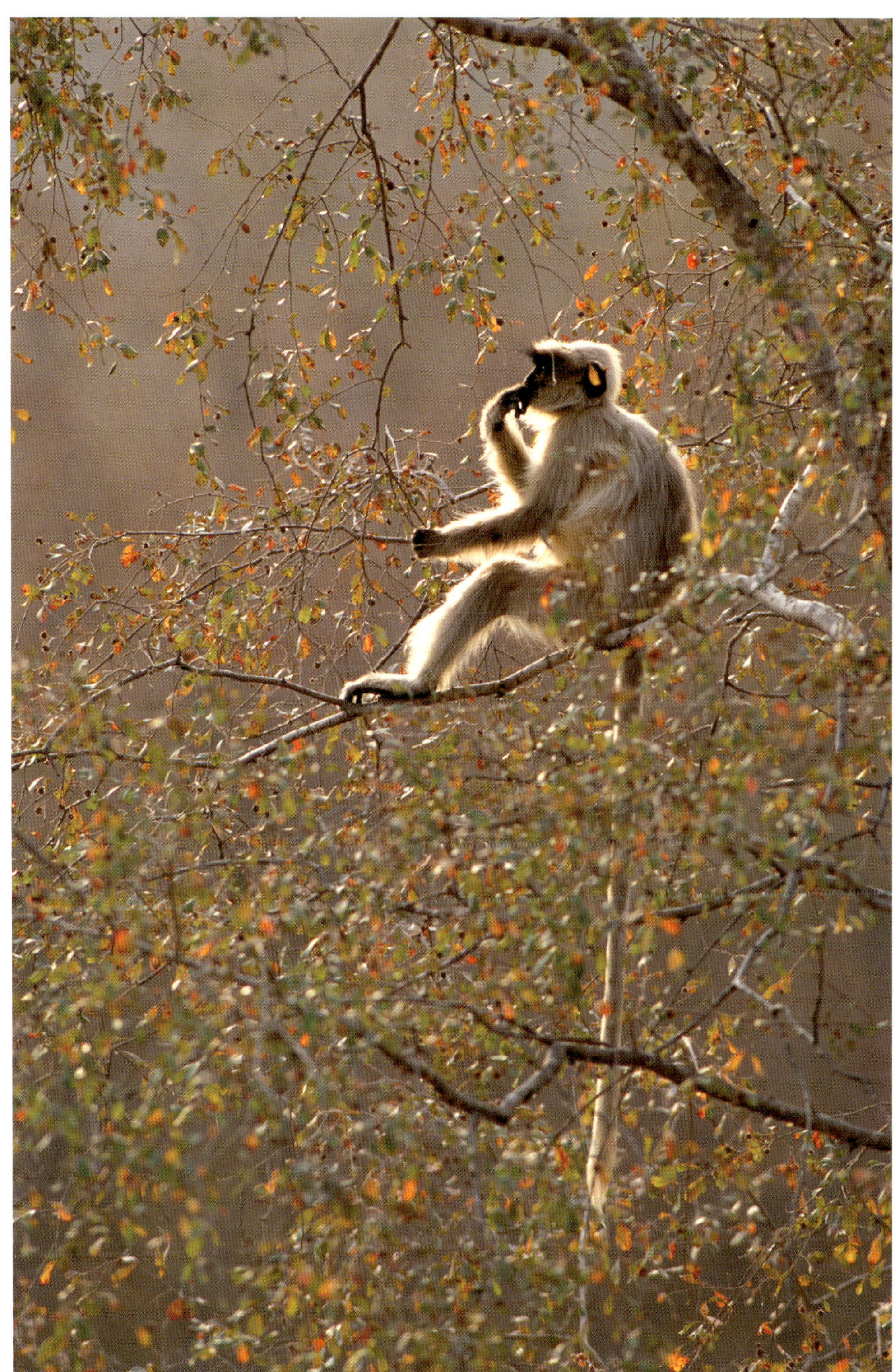

Sunlit langur

Jean-Pierre Zwaenepoel

BELGIUM

The most remarkable thing about this pensive Hanuman langur (aside from its human-like posture) is the extreme length of its tail – more normally seen being used as a balancing extension during the monkey's often acrobatic manoeuvres. Jean-Pierre was following a troop of some 90 monkeys in the Kumbhalgarh Wildlife Sanctuary in Rajasthan, India, when he spotted this adolescent, slightly isolated from the rest, 'possibly keeping guard but more likely just basking in the wonderful morning light'. Hanuman langurs are spread across the Indian subcontinent, often occurring within city limits. Yet even a species as adaptable as this is now considered vulnerable (albeit at a 'lower risk' level), mainly because of habitat loss.

Nikon F-100 with 500mm lens; f5.6; Fujichrome Velvia 100; tripod.

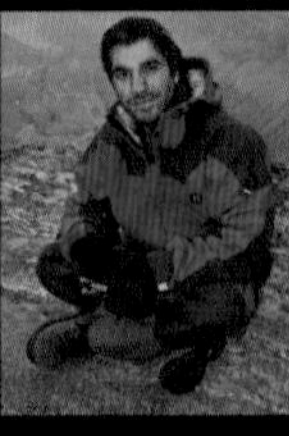

Serkan lives in Sweden but was born in Turkey. His interest in photography started when he was given a compact camera, but he has always loved nature. It was only on his twenty-second birthday, though, that he got his first SLR camera – a present from his wife. He became more and more interested in nature photography, but he really began to learn when he found a mentor – a professional nature photographer, also Turkish – who allowed Serkan to accompany him on trips. Today, Serkan is represented by two photographic agencies in Sweden.

Moon crow

When Serkan finished photographing a particularly beautiful sunset from his backyard, he suddenly realized that a full moon was rising. 'I already had plenty of classic moon shots,' he says, 'and wanted to make a different picture by having something in front of the moon.' Packing up 30kg of photographic equipment, he raced off into the woods to where he knew hooded crows would be roosting. 'There were dozens around in the trees, but none on the right branch.' Suddenly this individual obligingly landed just in front of the moon. Serkan had time to take only two pictures – one focused on the moon and the other on the bird (which he liked best) – before it flew off.

Canon EOS 20D with 300mm f4 lens and 2x converter; 1/20 sec at f16; 100 ISO; tripod.

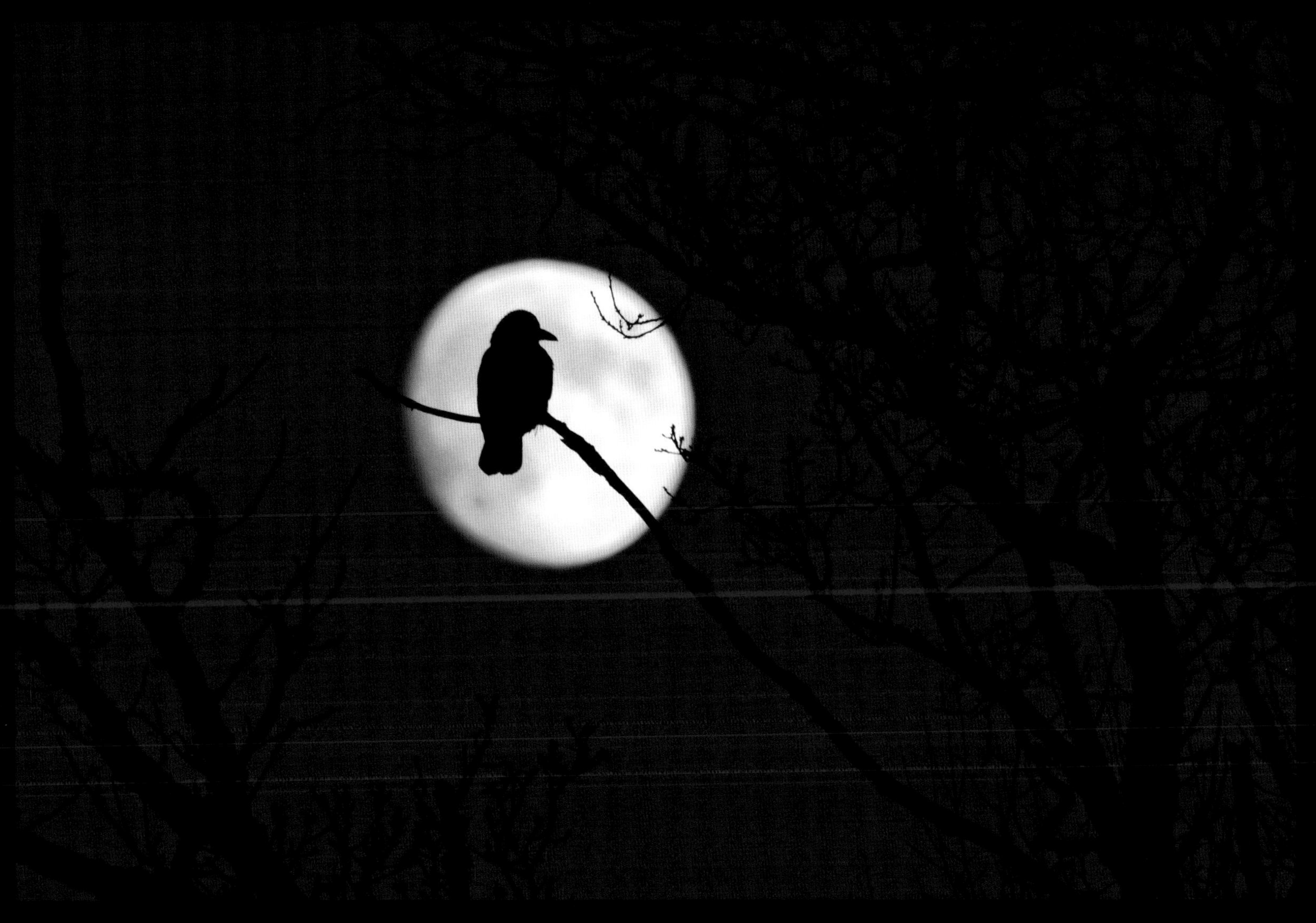

Hepatica blue

Swedish plants have a very short season in which to reproduce, and the forest floors burst into bloom as soon as the days are long enough. When Serkan heard about a particularly beautiful floral display in a forest in Uppland, central Sweden, he set off at once. He was not disappointed. 'There was a carpet of flowers,' he says. 'The difficulty was singling out just one.' Using his macro lens, he focused on one hepatica bloom, allowing the blur of flowers behind it to generate the electric-blue effect he was after.

Canon EOS 20D with 100mm f2.8 macro lens and +3 close-up lens; 1/125 sec at f2.8; 100 ISO; tripod.

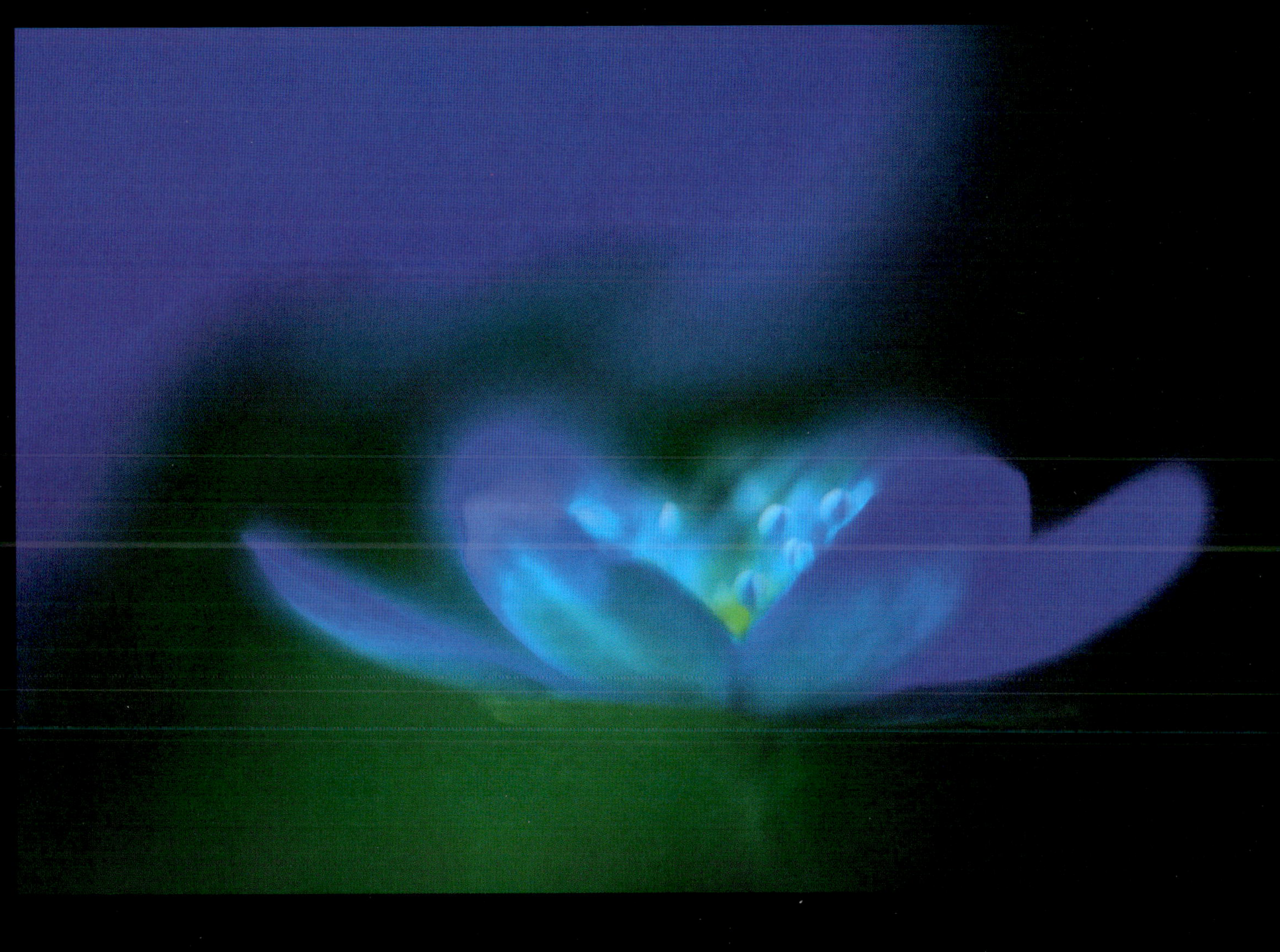

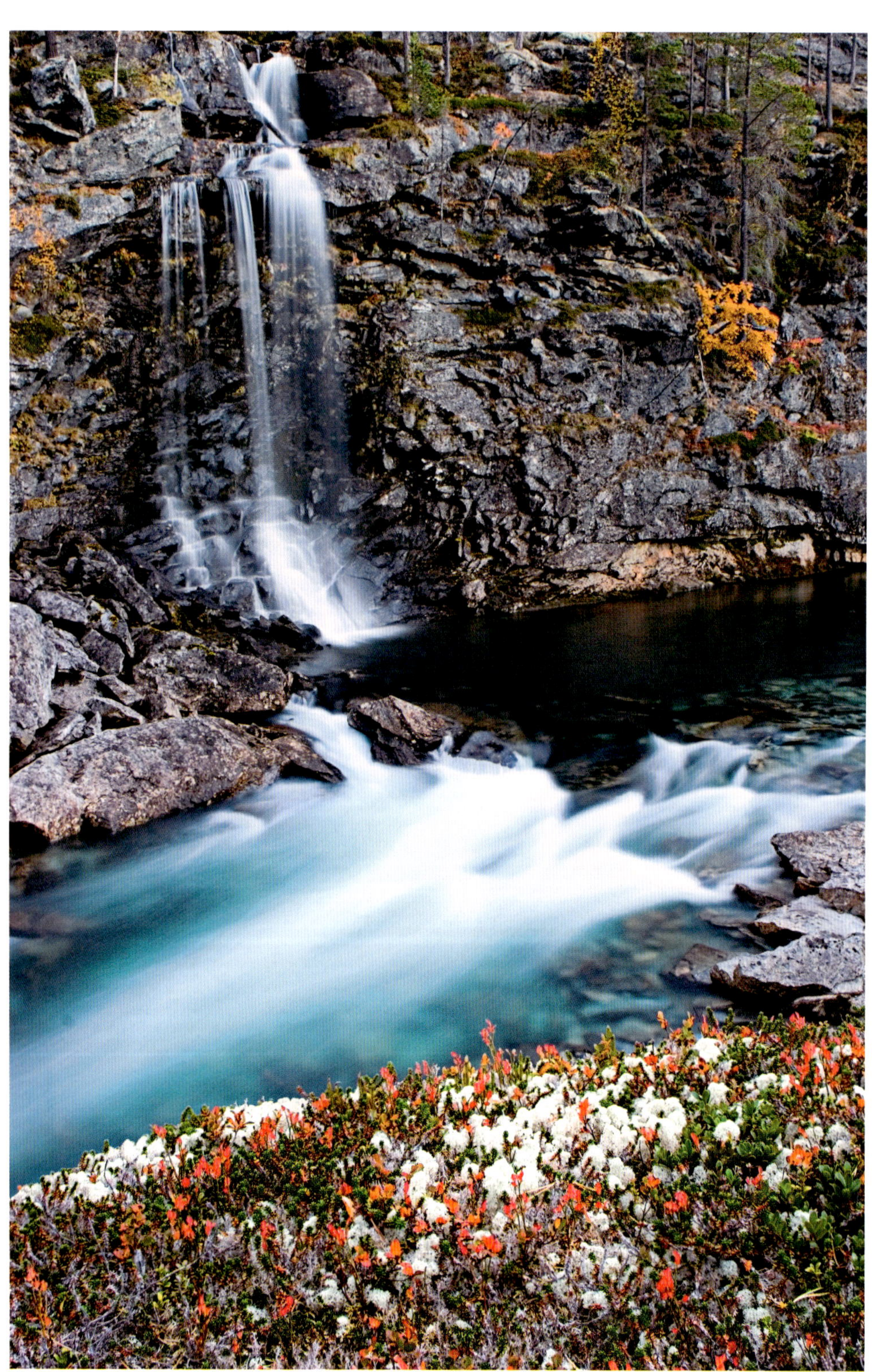

Autumn waterfall

It was Serkan's last day in Norway, and he had already taken hundreds upon hundreds of scenics and filled up all his memory cards. Then, in the southwest county of Møre og Romsdal, he was faced with the most beautiful autumn scene of all. He had no choice but to delete pictures from a memory card to take advantage of this mouth-watering sight. The rapids far below were a wonderful turquoise colour. 'When I found the perfect foreground – a carpet of autumn colour sprinkled with lichen,' he adds, 'I knew I could sit back and let the scenery speak for itself.'

Canon EOS 20D with 24mm f2.8 lens; 10 sec at f16; 100 ISO; tripod.

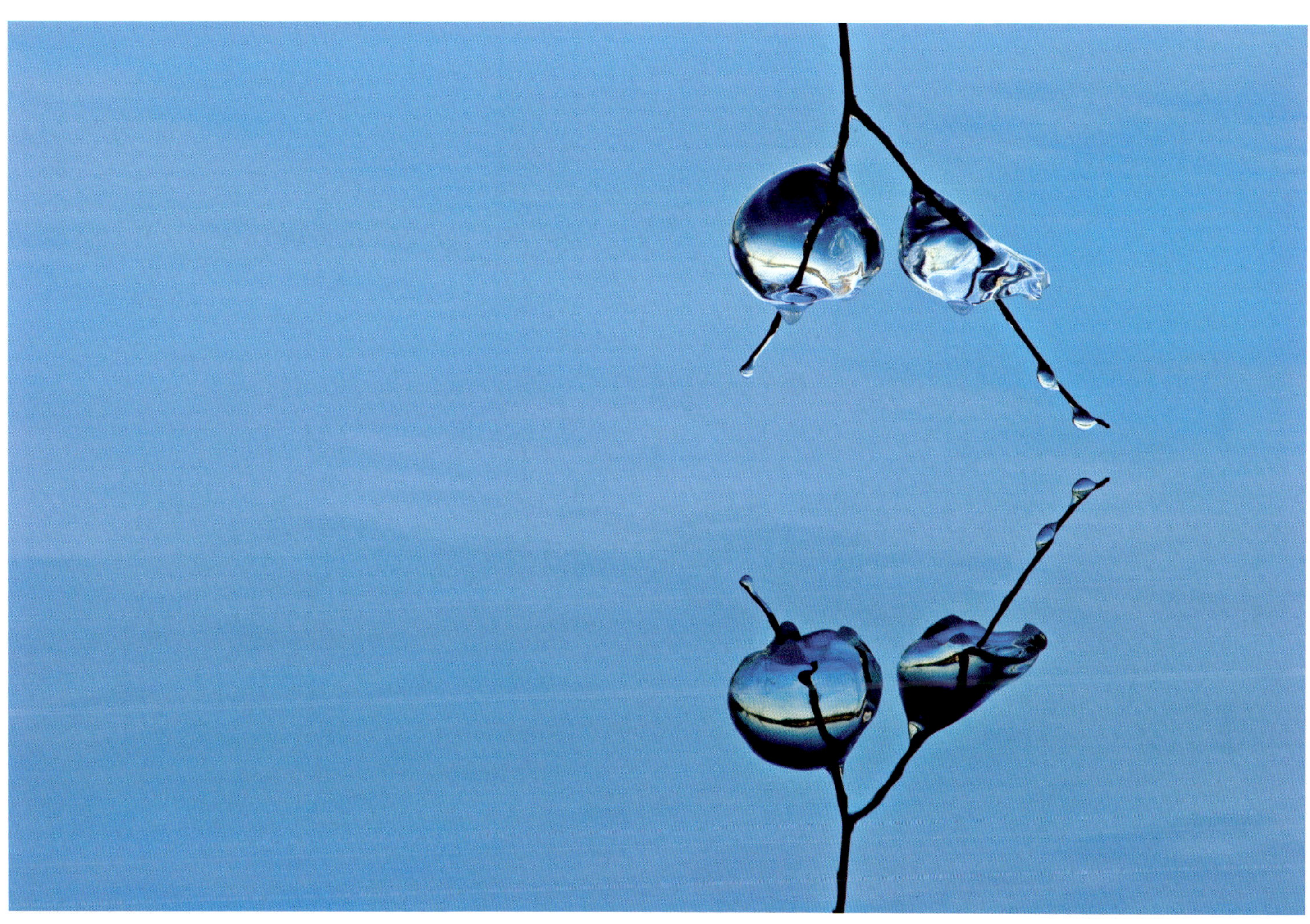

Ice baubles

There is a lake near his home that Serkan visits regularly. 'On this day, the lake was dead still,' he says, 'and reflected in it was the sunlit winter wood.' Instead of taking the obvious, classic shot of a reflection in the lake, he decided to create something more abstract to represent the scene's tranquillity. 'The diamond-like ice-drops on the delicate twig are reflecting both the calm water', he says, 'and also the landscape reflection in the water,' and, in turn, they are reflected in the mirror-still water. 'The overall impression is one of utter calm.'

Canon EOS 20D with 300mm f4 lens; 1/160 sec at f8; 100 ISO; tripod.

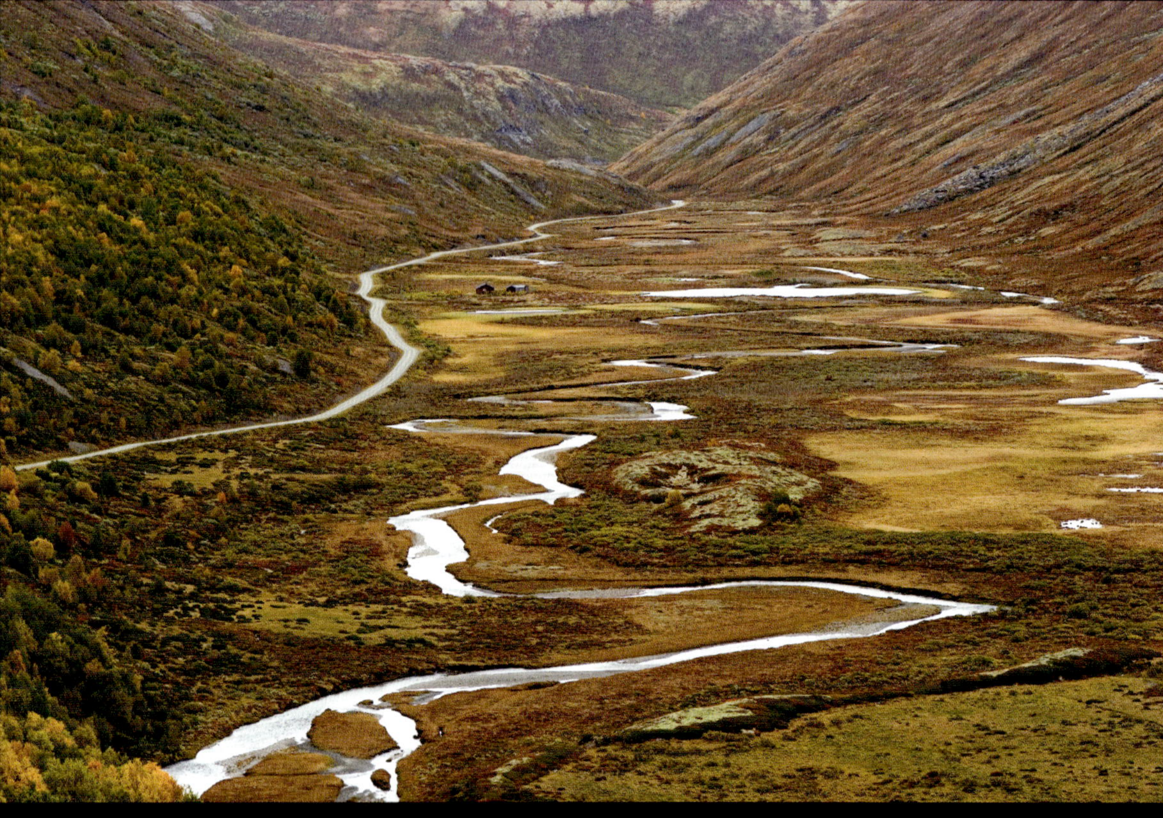

The great valley

This is Grimsdalen, in Oppland, Norway, photographed in September while Serkan was on a trip in search of autumn colour. 'I drove up the valley till I got a view that showed the whole great vista, with its beautiful colours and shapes. I love the patterns that the river makes where the water reflects the sky.'

Canon EOS 20D with 100mm f2.8 lens; 1/15 sec at f8; 100 ISO; tripod.

River of birches

'As well as looking for beautiful colours,' says Serkan, 'I am always searching for lines and shapes in the landscape.' While travelling one autumn in Jotunheimen National Park, Norway, all these elements came together in the form of this river of birch trees zig-zagging down the mountainside. The afternoon light was bright, but the harsh shadows worked in his favour, emphasizing the lines and highlighting the golden trees.

Canon EOS 20D with 300mm f2.8 lens; 1/200 sec at f8; 100 ISO; tripod.

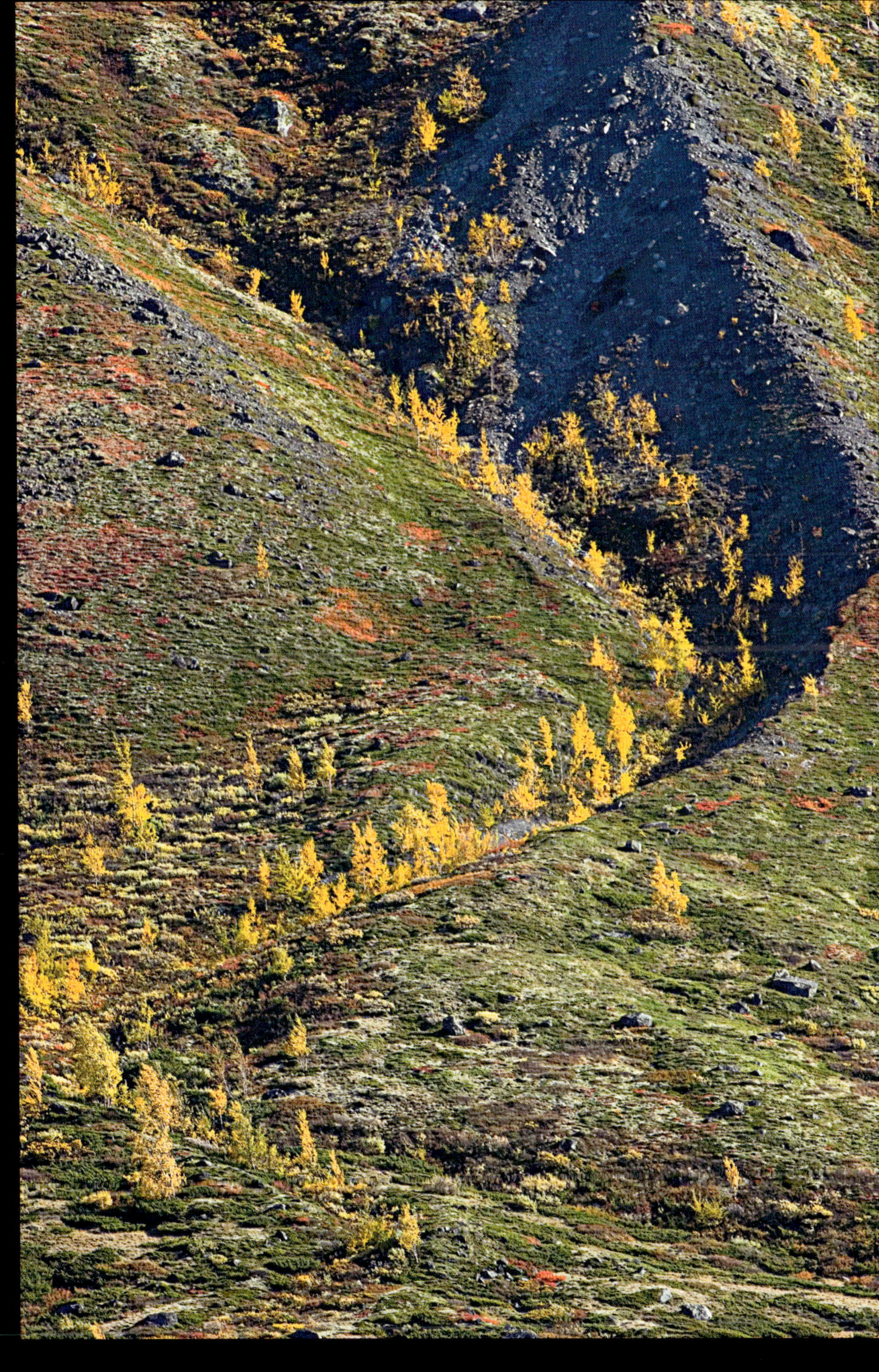

The Shell Young Wildlife Photographer of the Year Award

'his award, a big cash prize and the title Shell Young Wildlife Photographer of the Year 2006 s given to the photographer whose single image s judged to be the most striking and memorable of all he pictures by young photographers aged 17 or under.

Rick Stanley

USA

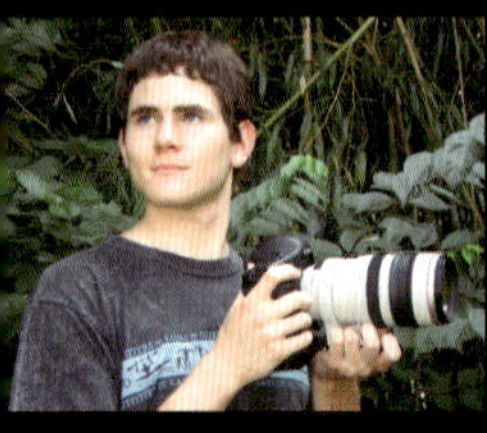

Rick has been interested in nature as long as he can remember and has been taking photographs since he was eight. He has already had two pictures published in books, the first when he was twelve. Rick's grandfather has ties with the Dominican Republic and has helped establish an ecological reserve there, which is where Rick took his winning shot, while on an expedition with scientists from the Smithsonian Institution documenting insect life. Now 17, Rick intends to go to university and major in biology, focusing on ecology and evolutionary biology, and then 'work as a biologist, travelling the world studying and photographing nature – and in the process, convincing people to save the environment'.

The dilemma

While on an expedition in the Dominican Republic with a group of naturalists, Rick wandered off with his Dominican friend Rubio to look for wildlife in the forest. 'Suddenly,' says Rick, 'we heard a loud squeaking.' Rubio was the first to discover its source – a distressed Hispaniolan treefrog, which had been caught by a green vine snake. 'I photographed the drama as the frog dangled in front of me, but Rubio was unable to resist helping the victim and gently touched the snake, which promptly dropped its meal and slithered away along the branches.' The frog, seemingly unaffected by the snake's mild venom, hopped off. Rick was left wondering whether it would have been morally better to let the snake have its meal – and, indeed, if it would have succeeded in swallowing such a large frog had it been left to try.

Canon EOS 1D Mark II with Canon EF 24-70mm f2.8L USM zoom lens; 1/400 sec at f8; 800 ISO.

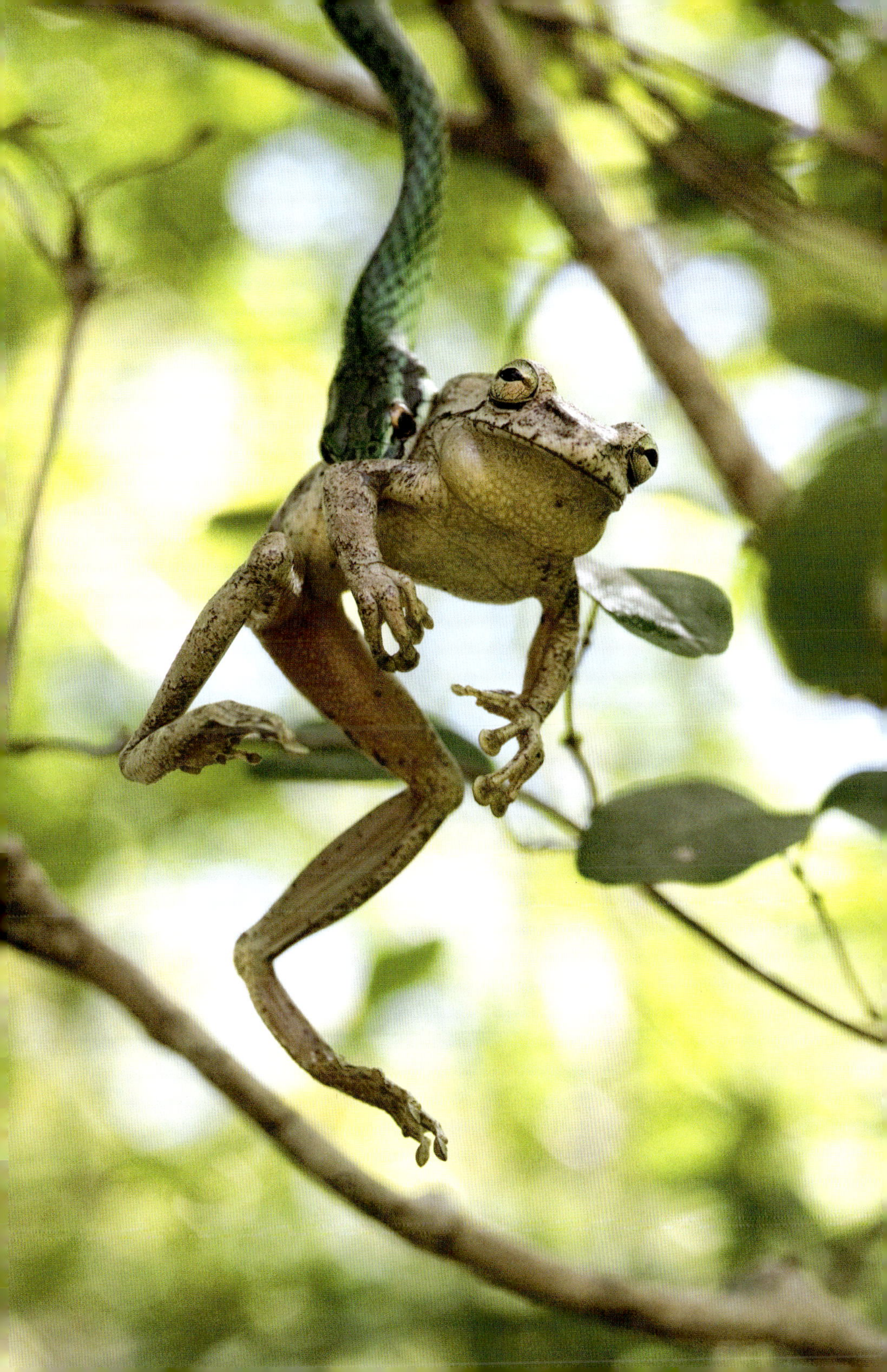

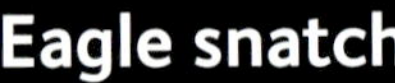

Eagle snatch

RUNNER-UP

Mart Smit

THE NETHERLANDS

This was the second time Mart had visited Lauvsnes, a village halfway up the coast of Norway, to try to photograph white-tailed eagles. 'I adore these magnificent birds,' he says, 'and was determined to get a decent picture.' Taking pictures from a boat in strong wind, rain and high waves without a tripod 'made things particularly tricky', says Mart. But then his luck changed. 'A calm sea, pleasant weather and, most important, a cooperative eagle' that plucked a fish from the sea in just the right spot gave him the shot he wanted.

Canon EOS 20D with Canon 400mm f5.6 lens; 1/3200 sec at f6.3; 400 ISO.

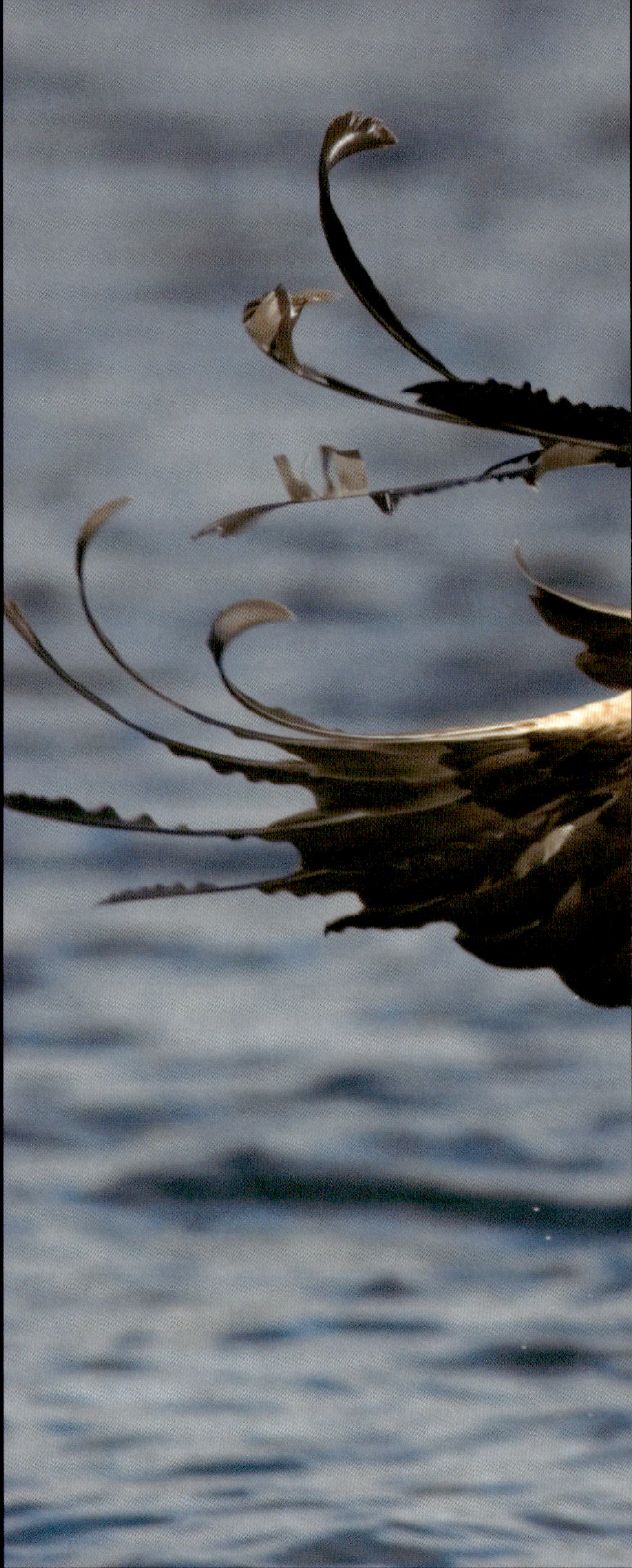

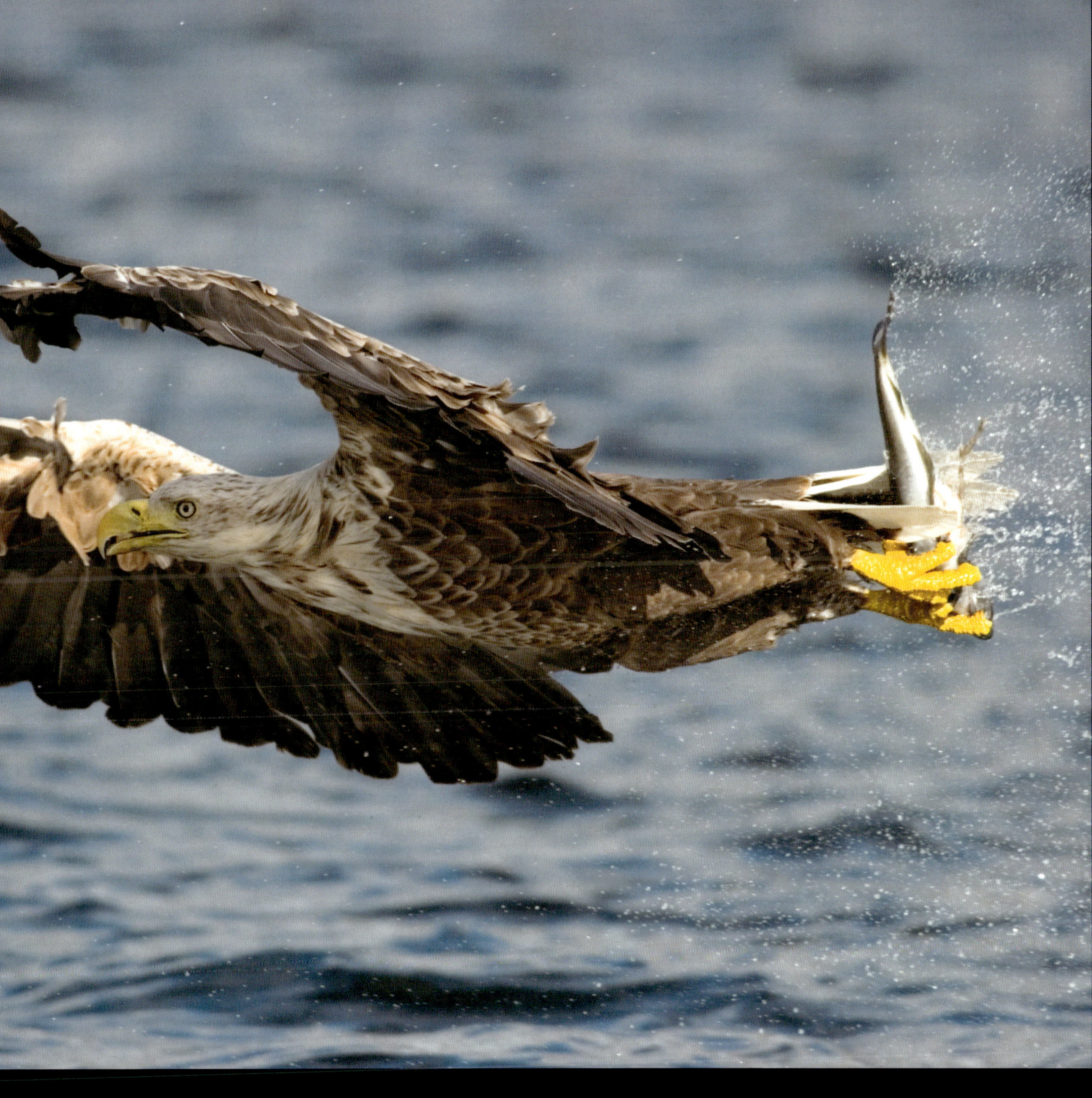

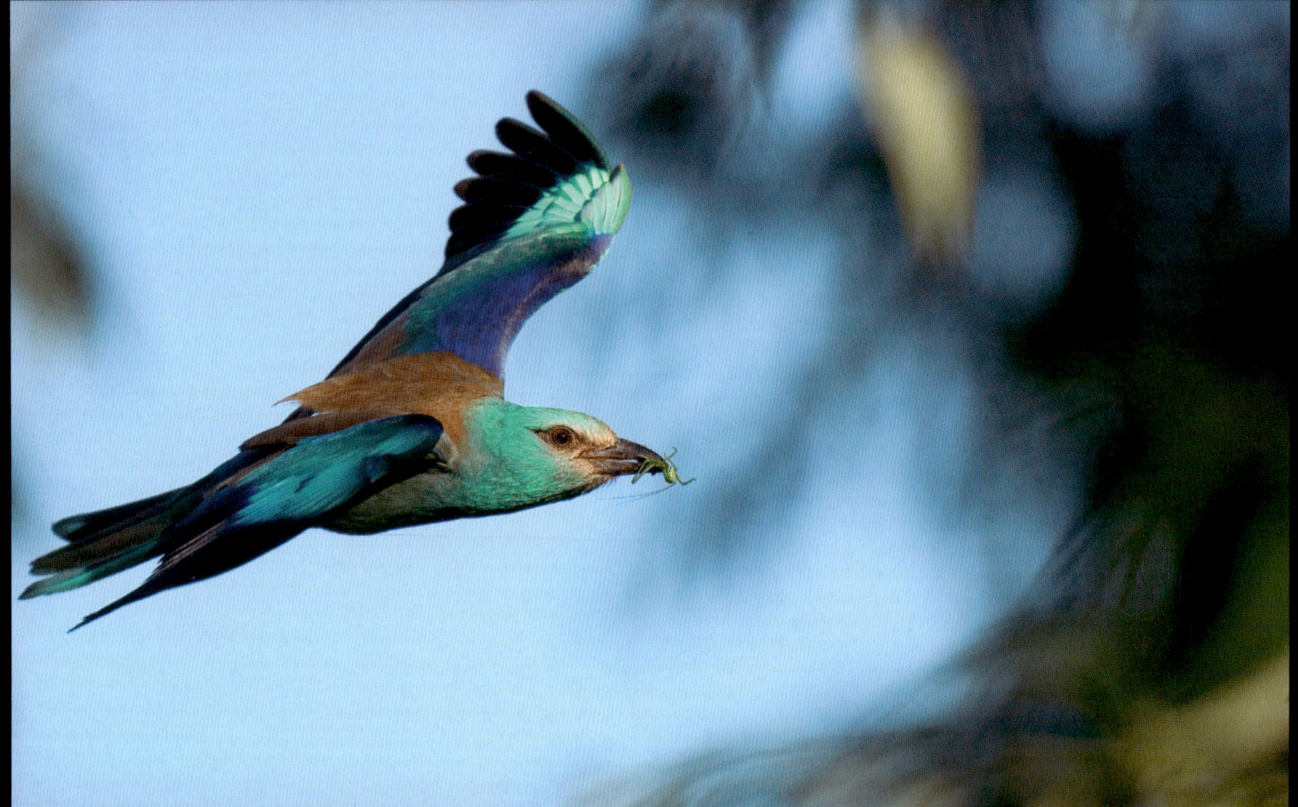

Roller catch

SPECIALLY COMMENDED

Mateusz Kowalski

POLAND

Sporting such beautiful plumage, rollers are always a treat to photograph. Mateusz located this roller's nest-hole in an old willow in Biebrzanski National Park, northern Poland. And as it returned with a bush cricket in its bill for the chicks, Mateusz was there to capture the moment. 'Photography was tricky because of the dense light,' he says. 'Also I didn't want to disturb such a hard-working bird by using flash at the nest-hole.' So he opted to take the picture as it was in flight – a good decision, as there was enough light to illuminate the iridescent plumage and create a sensational picture.

Canon EOS 1D with 300mm f2.8 IS lens; 1/2500 sec at f2.8; 500 ISO; 2x teleconverter.

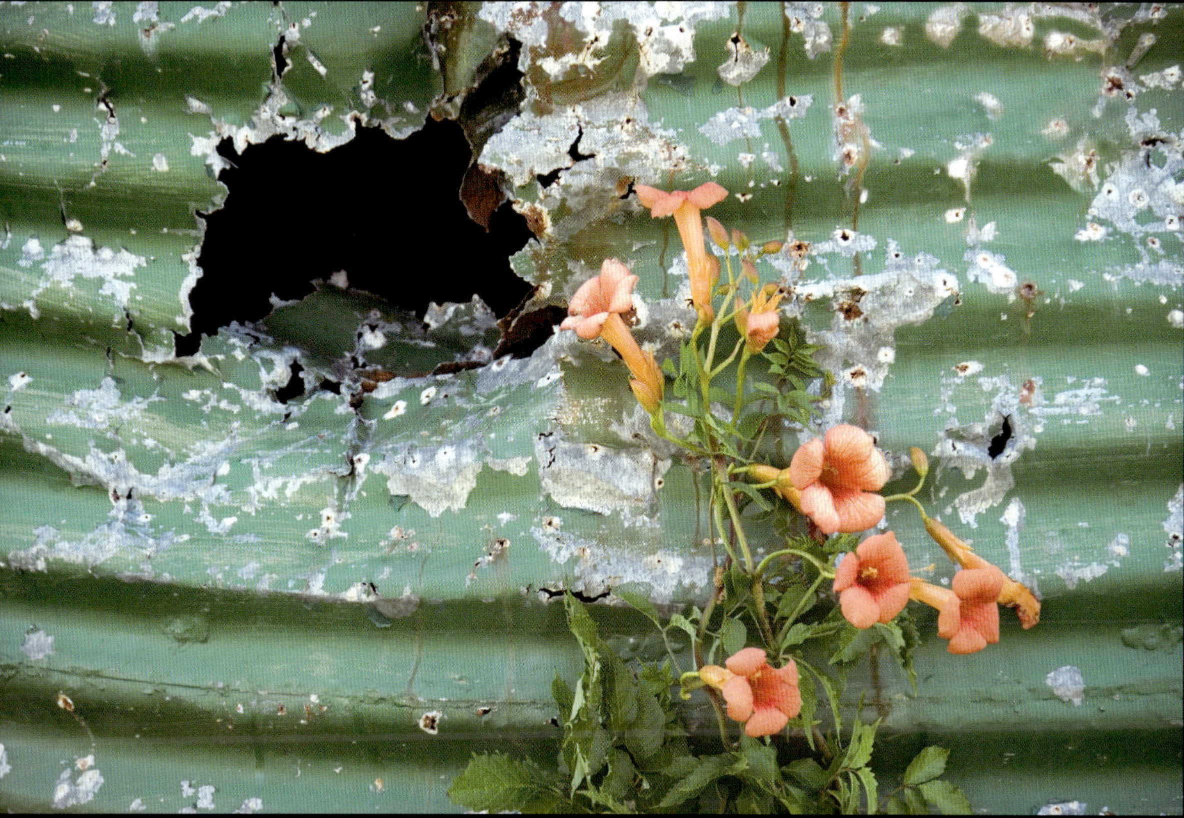

Survivor

Daniel Tregeagle

AUSTRALIA

The vegetation of the Myall Lakes National Park in New South Wales, Australia, is both fragile and unique. Daniel cycled off to explore, hoping to find some botanical treasures to photograph. But it was extremely hot and dry, and the only flowering plant he could find worth photographing was this trumpet vine scrambling over an old sheet of corrugated iron. Its apricot flowers were a beautiful contrast against the green paint, but the plant's obvious success points to a more sinister aspect: it is an invasive alien from North America – one of many that are threatening Australia's vulnerable flora.

Canon EOS 20D with Tamron 18-200mm f3.5-6.5 lens; 1/200 sec at f8; 800 ISO.

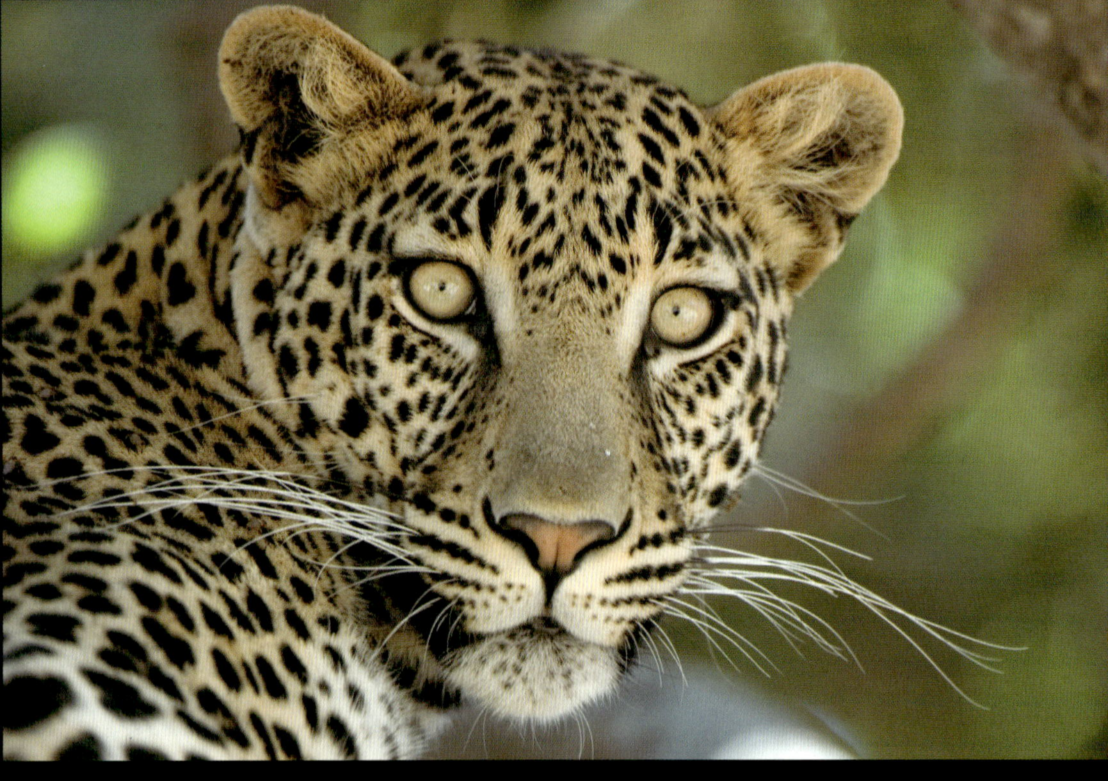

Leopard stare

Luke Marazzi

UK

Feather care

Evan Graff

USA

At sunrise, Evan went on the prowl along the boardwalks in the Everglades National Park, Florida, looking for subjects to photograph. 'This double-crested cormorant sat quietly for a long time', he says, 'until the sun rose and it started to warm up.' When it began to preen itself, Evan focused on its pristine breeding plumage. 'I had never seen one with such a large crest or such a vivid turquoise eye.'

Nikon D70 with Sigma 50-500mm f4-6.3 EX lens; 1/400 sec at f10; tripod.

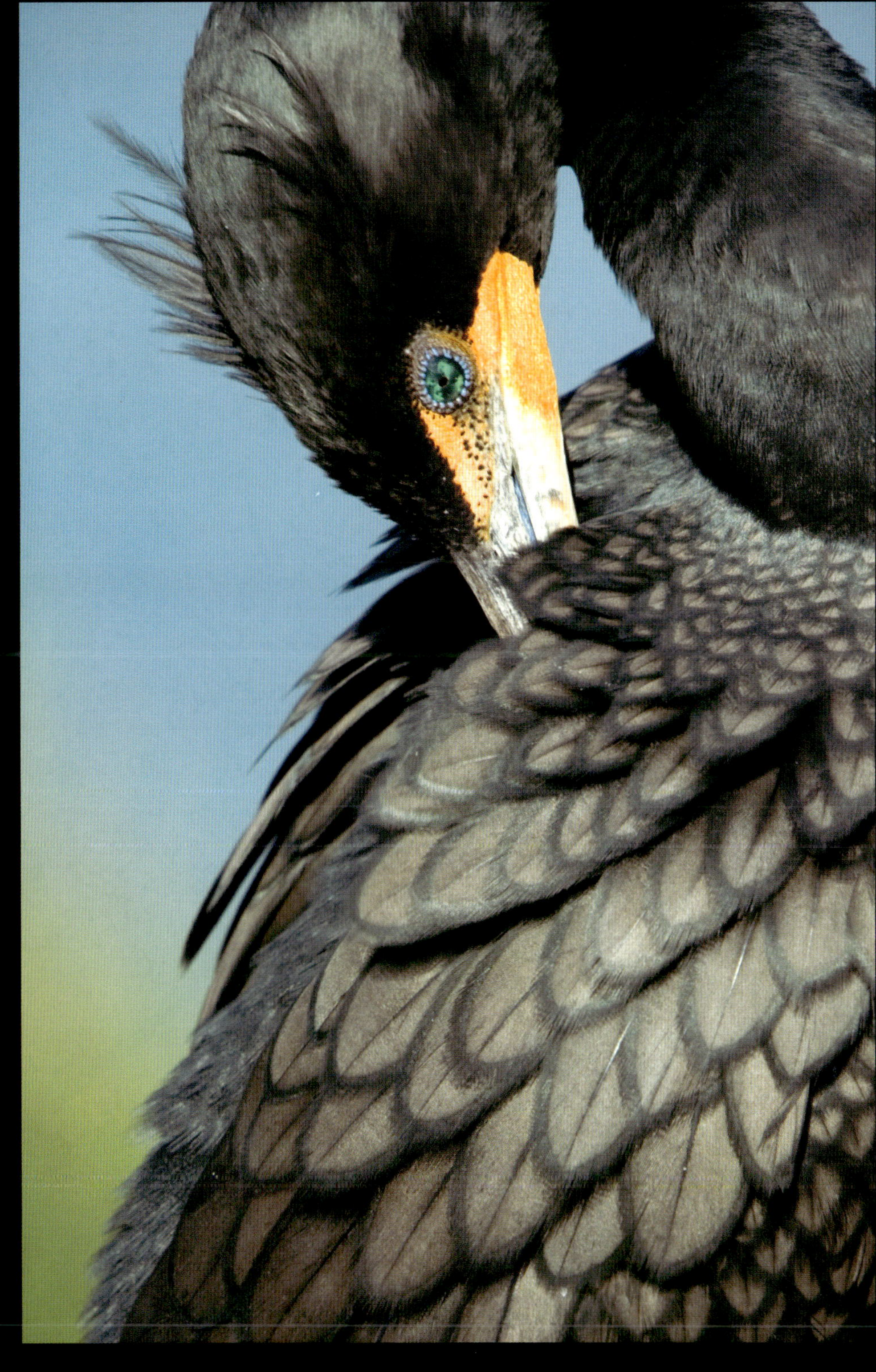

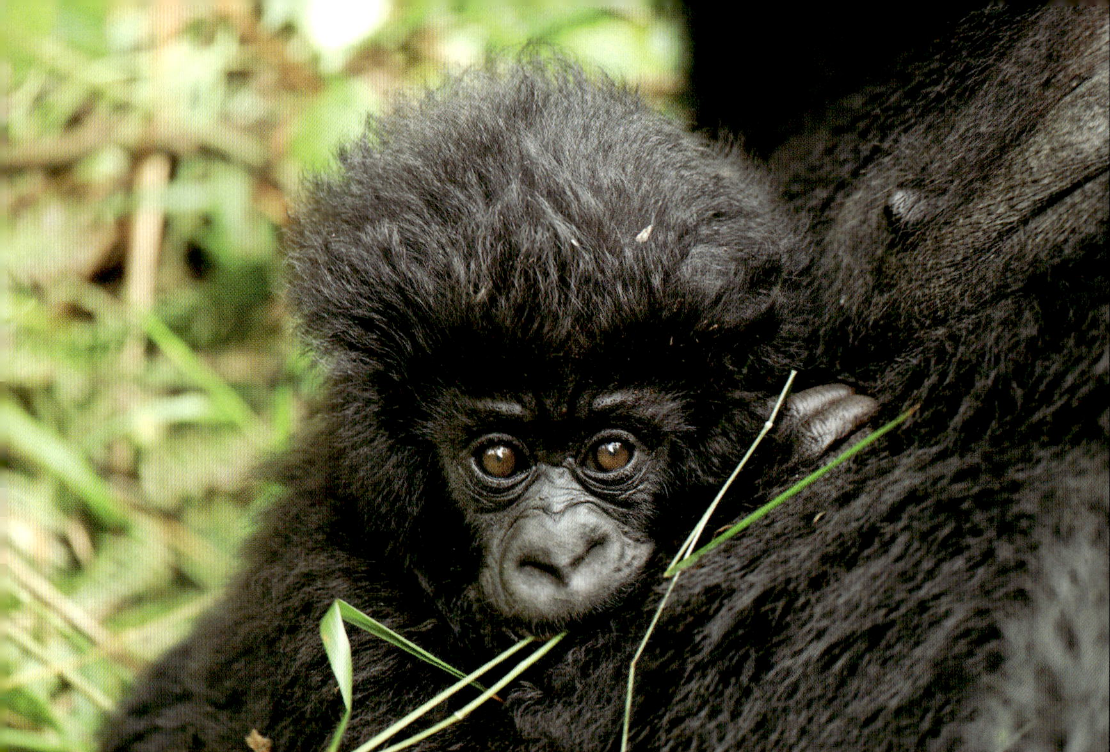

Mountain baby

Cameron Amadeus Myhrvold

USA

After hiking all morning through the misty rainforest in the mountains of the Volcanoes National Park in Rwanda, Cameron encountered a group of mountain gorillas. One had a tiny infant riding on her back. 'The baby was quite curious, and when it made eye contact, I quickly snapped several pictures.' The baby continued chewing grass in a nonchalant manner before climbing down and crawling off to play with some other babies.

Canon EOS-1Ds with 100-400mm f4.5-5.6 lens; 1/40 sec at f5.6; 800 ISO; monopod.

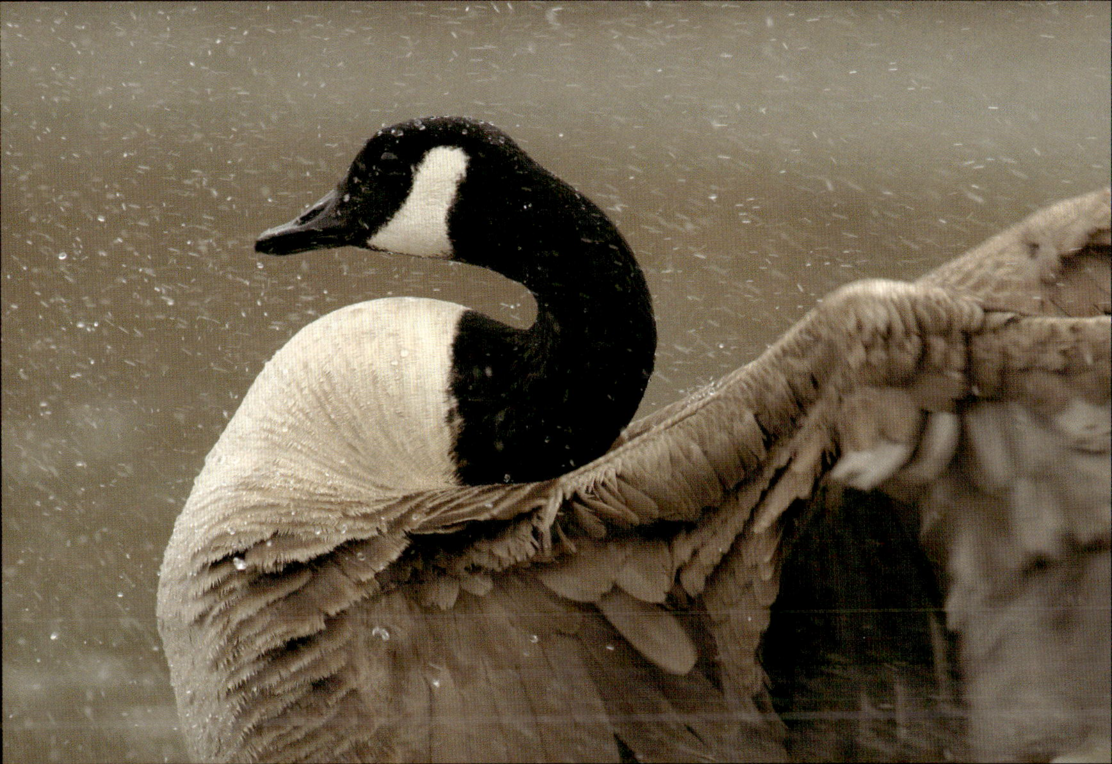

Goose bath

Avi Kenny

USA

Avi went down to his local lake to get some Canada goose action. He noticed that after bathing they flapped their wings vigorously to dry themselves off, and he decided to concentrate on this behaviour. As this individual flapped itself dry, he snapped one fast shot. 'I was lucky that the light was quite dull,' he says, 'bringing out the beautiful, subtle colours of the plumage against the water.'

Porcelain fungus

Mart Smit

THE NETHERLANDS

This young fungus is as shiny, translucent and exquisite as its name suggests. Mart found it on a rotting beech tree in a forest close to his home in northern Holland. 'The weather was so erratic,' he says, 'one moment cloud, the next sun.' Just as he had set up his tripod and fixed an extender to his lens, the sun burst through and bathed the fungus in light. The insect landing was the added bonus.'

Canon EOS 20D with 300mm f2.8 lens and 2x extender; 0.6 sec at f22; 200 ISO; tripod.

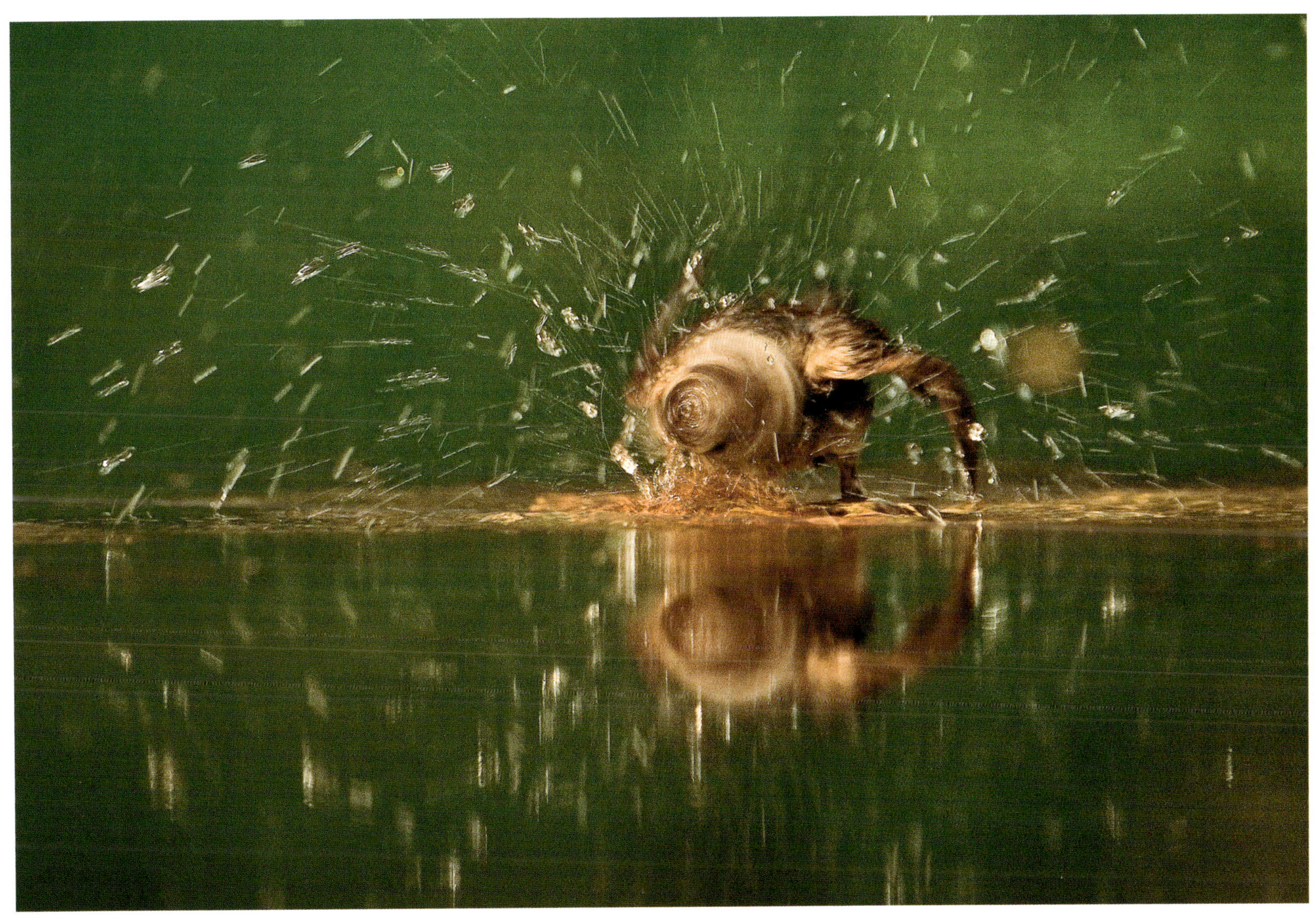

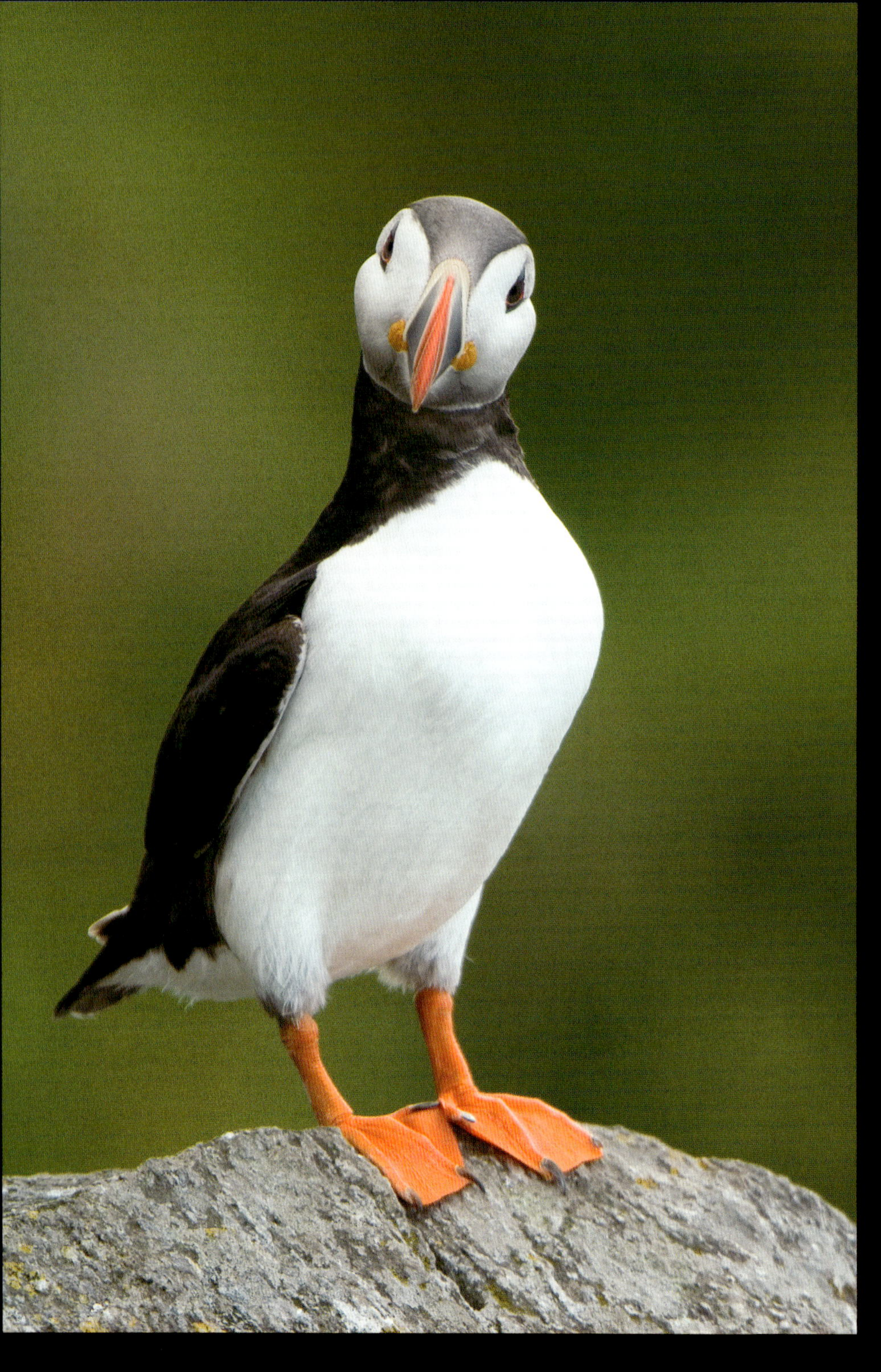

Puffin pose

RUNNER-UP

Adrien Imre

HUNGARY

One lovely, long, light evening on Runde, an island off the southwest coast of Norway, Adrien sat watching a rock. She was on a photo workshop and had chosen the rock because of the 'gorgeously green' background and hoped a puffin would choose it, too. 'My rock-watching paid off', she says, 'when this character landed and turned to look at me.' A photogenic bird, an 'intimate ambience' and beautiful light gave her the photograph she was after. In summer, thousands upon thousands of Atlantic puffins descend on Runde to breed on the rocky coast – sometimes up to 100,000 of them. Throughout the rest of the year, regardless of the weather, they ride the ocean.

Canon EOS 20D with EF 300mm f2.8 IS USM lens and Sigma EX 2x teleconverter; 1/640 sec at f5.6; 400 ISO; tripod.

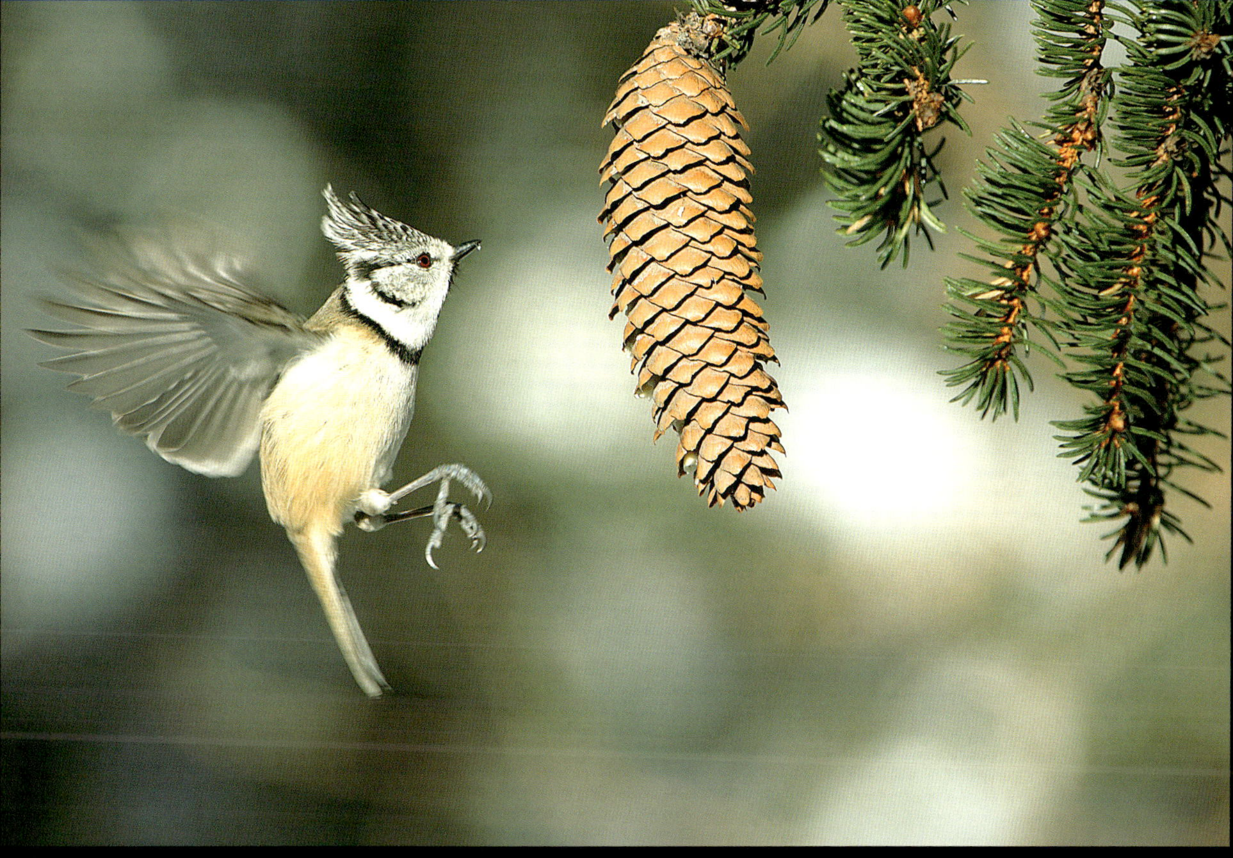

Tit acrobatics

SPECIALLY COMMENDED

Alberto Fantoni

ITALY

Alberto lives near the Alps of Lombardy, northern Italy, and often goes up there to photograph animals with his father and brother. Almost always he sees tits flying among the branches. On his last winter trip, he decided to put a birdfeeder on a fir tree, positioned so that there were cones in front, and wait to see

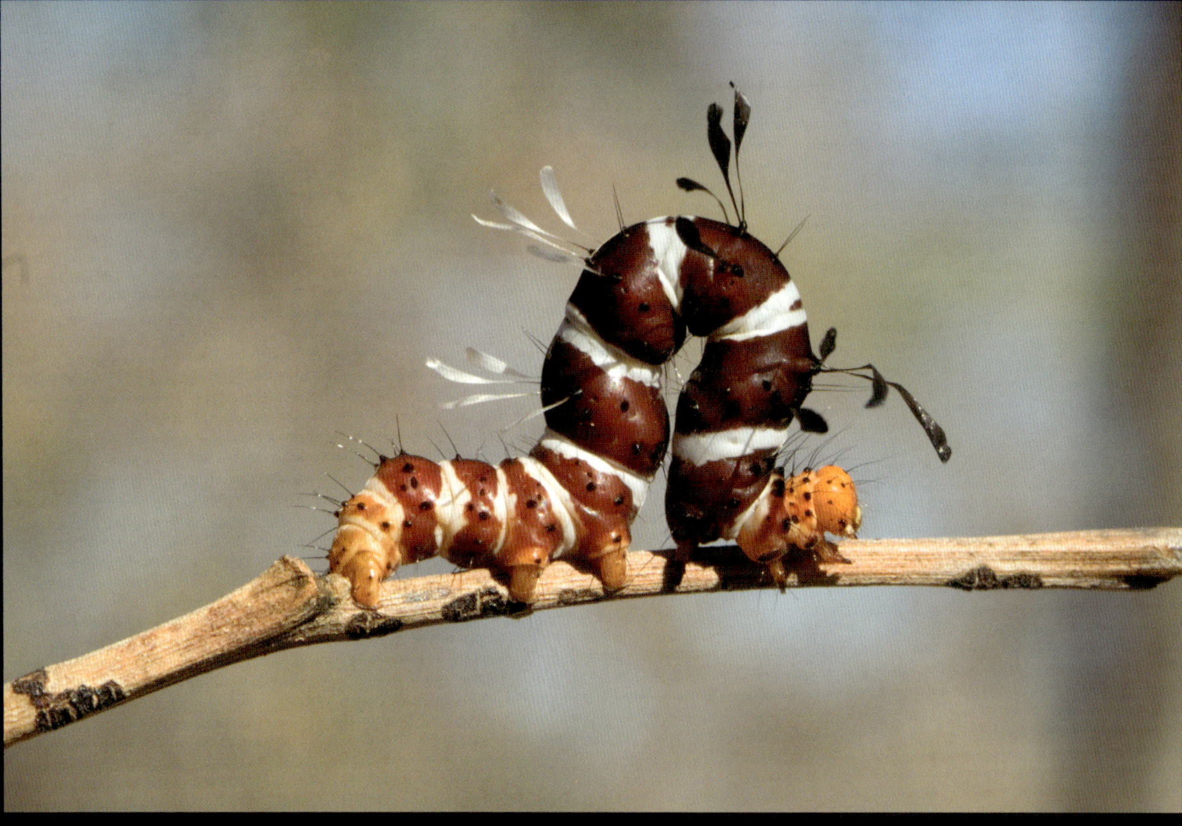

Looping looper

Kyle Dickerson

SOUTH AFRICA

Kyle was with his family in Sabi Sands Game Reserve, South Africa, when he spotted this dice-moth caterpillar on a stick right beside their vehicle. 'We had stopped because mum and dad were photographing a bee-eater,' he says, 'but I couldn't photograph it

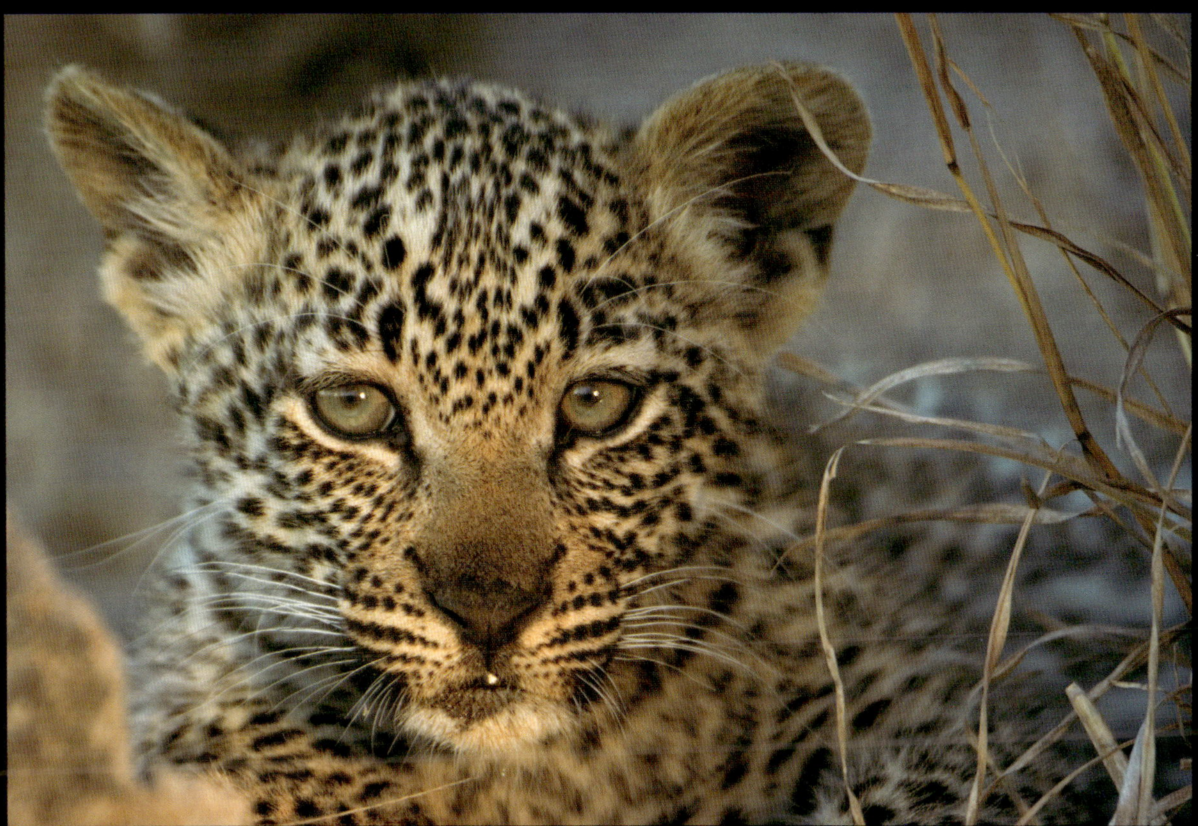

Shy baby

Kyle Dickerson

SOUTH AFRICA

Kyle and his parents came across this leopard cub hanging around an ant nest in South Africa's Sabi Sands Game Reserve. They all took photos, keeping as still as possible so as not to disturb it – it was shy and kept hiding behind the ant heap. 'His mother was close by in the bush feeding on an impala that she had caught,' says Kyle, 'so we obviously didn't want to disturb her either.' Every now and then the cub peeped over the mound, allowing Kyle to get this portrait.

Canon EOS 350D with 100-400mm lens; 1/60 sec at f5.6; 200 ISO; beanbag.

Plover at dusk

Fergus Gill

UK

While photographing one evening on a beach on the Isle of Luing, Argyll, Fergus encountered a ringed plover that seemed far more approachable than normal. 'I soon realized why,' says Fergus. 'It had a tiny chick, which couldn't have been more than three days old.' Watching from behind a large slate dyke, Fergus saw the plover parent gather the chick under its breast to keep it warm. 'Though a beautiful sight,' says Fergus, 'it didn't make a great photograph.' Then he saw the other parent posing on top of the slate stones, the setting sun behind it. 'This was what I was looking for,' he says. 'The bird had a lovely halo around it, and the black rocks were burnished with gold.'

Nikon D70 with 200-400mm f4 lens; 1/80 sec at f4; 200 ISO; beanbag.

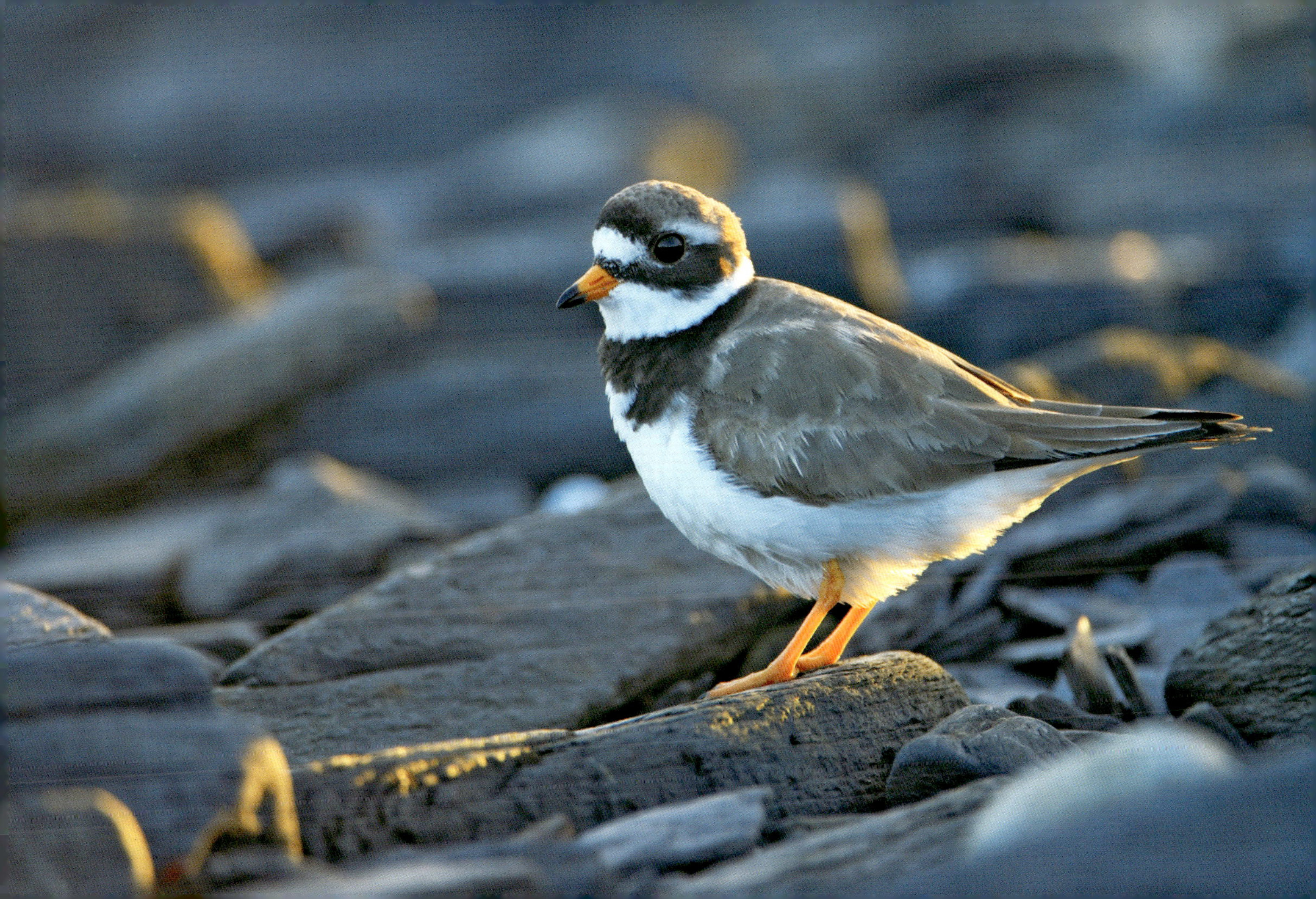

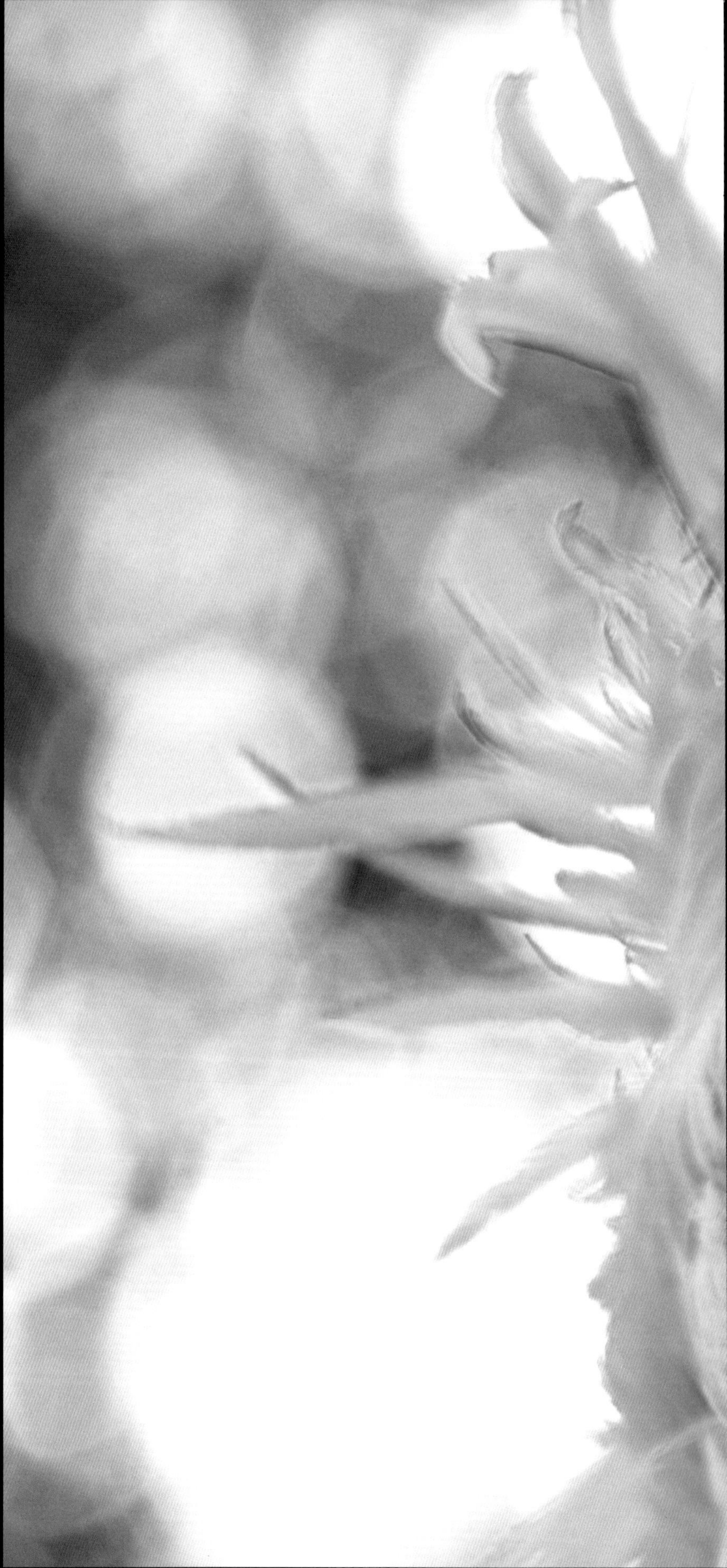

Pelican glare

WINNER

Nils Grundmann

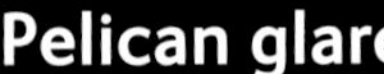
GERMANY

Nils went specially to the deer park in Berlin to watch the Dalmatian pelicans that live semi-free there. 'I was fascinated by their bathing antics in a fountain,' says Nils, 'and watched them for ages with my father.' After washing, they sat on a fence to preen their feathers, which is where Nils singled out this individual. 'I lay on the ground directly in front of it and focused on its head. The bird stared at me hard, curious about my behaviour,' adds Nils, 'which is when I took the shot.'

Canon EOS 10D with EF 100-400mm f4.5-5.6L IS lens; 1/60 sec at f4.5.

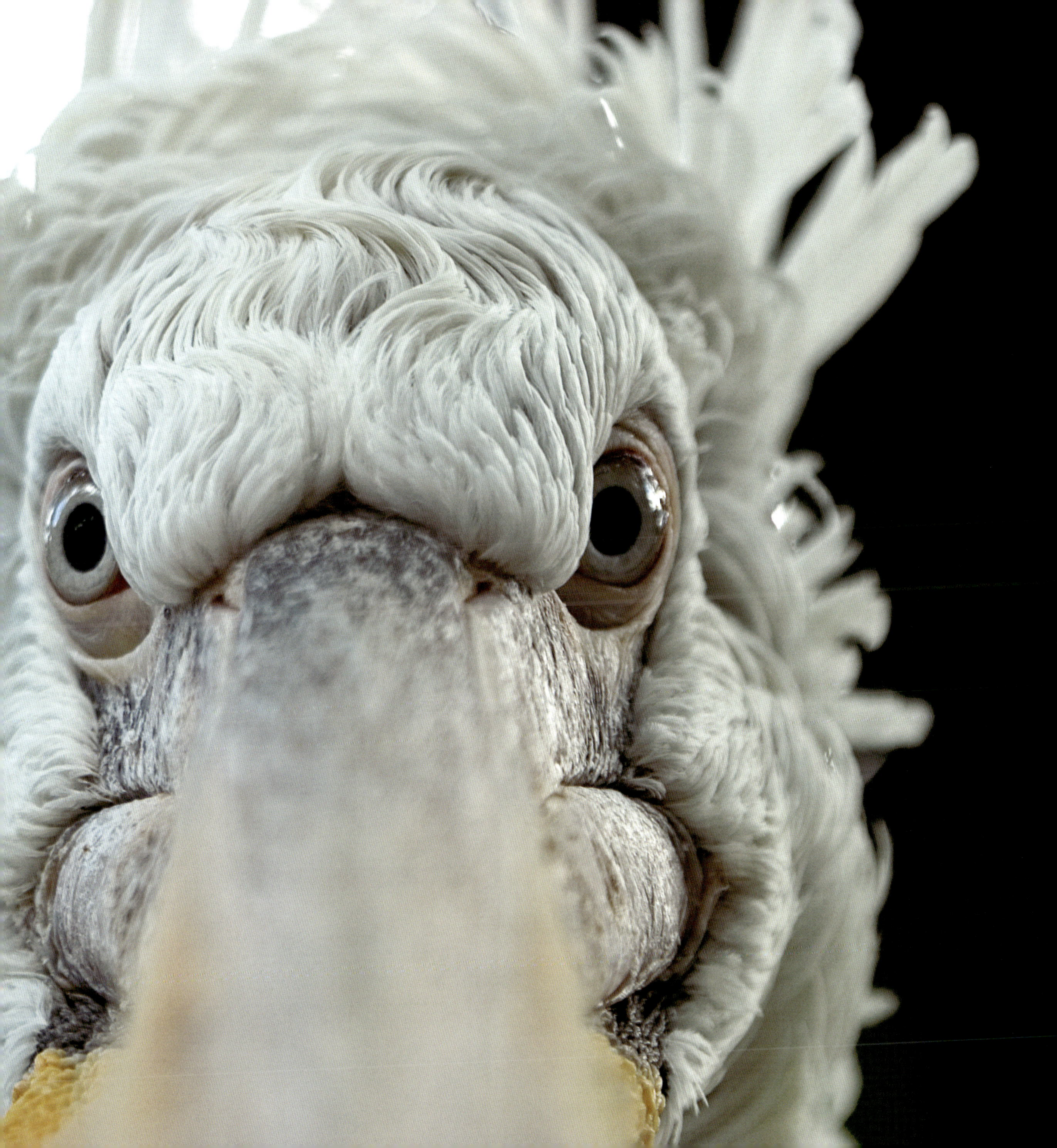

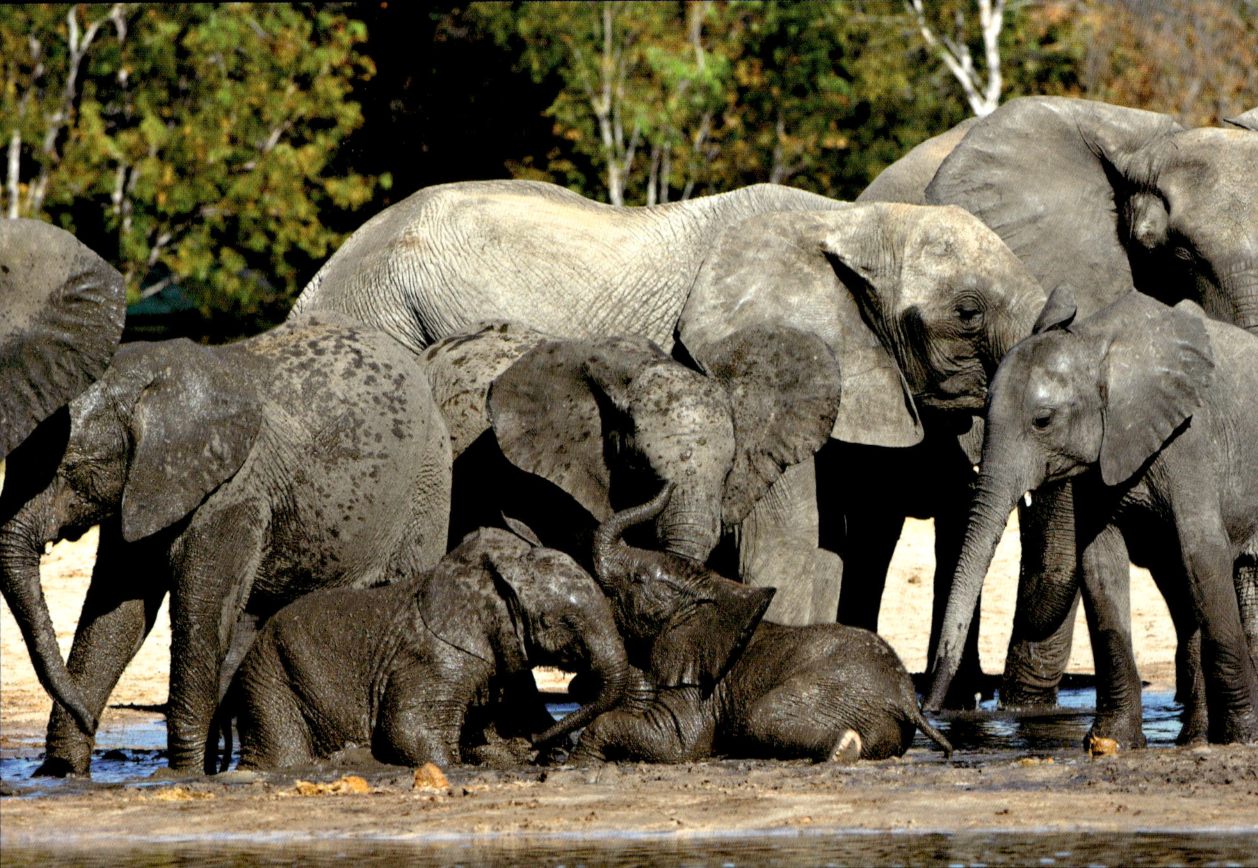

Elephant bathtime

Anais Nussaume

THAILAND

Babies, children, teenagers, mothers, even grandma (back right), all pile into the bath after a hot morning on the savannah in Hwange National Park, Zimbabwe. 'We went to the hides around this water-hole at midday,' says Anais, 'a great time to watch animals coming to drink at really close range.' The elephants drank, played with the mud, relaxed. 'On the second day, this big group of elephants with young ones ran to the water-hole. The two young ones at the front were really enjoying the water,' says Anais, 'and so I put them in the centre of the picture.'

Nikon D2x with 300mm f2.8 lens; 1/800 sec at f8.

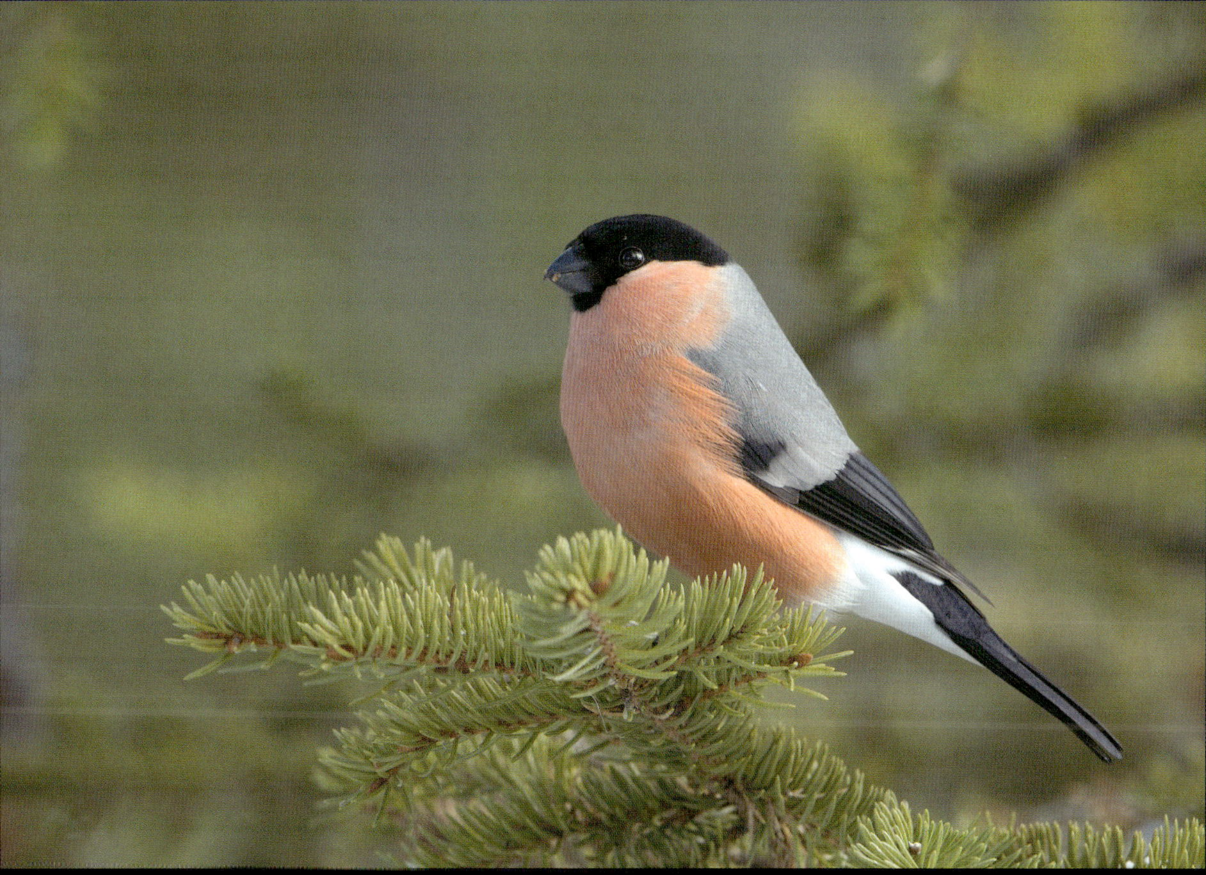

Bullfinch on display

RUNNER-UP

Ilkka Räsänen

FINLAND

Ilkka spent several days with his uncle in a hide in the forest in southern Finland watching the birds. 'My favourites were the bullfinches,' says Ilkka. 'They were not too shy.' He took this picture on a cloudy day when the light wasn't too strong, highlighting the colours of a male in his full breeding plumage.

Nikon D70s with Nikkor 300mm f4D lens; 1/250 sec at f6.3; 400 ISO; tripod.

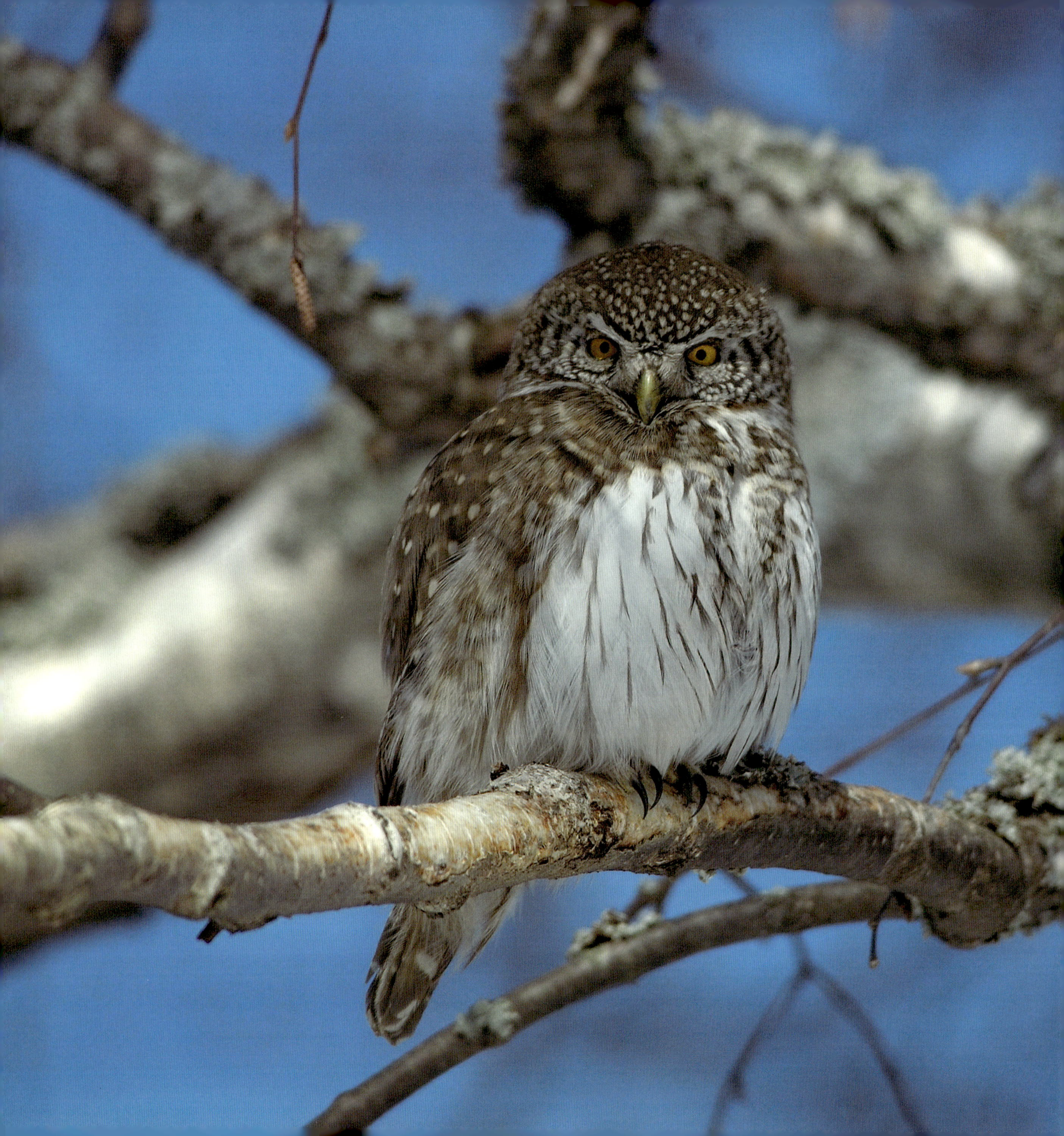

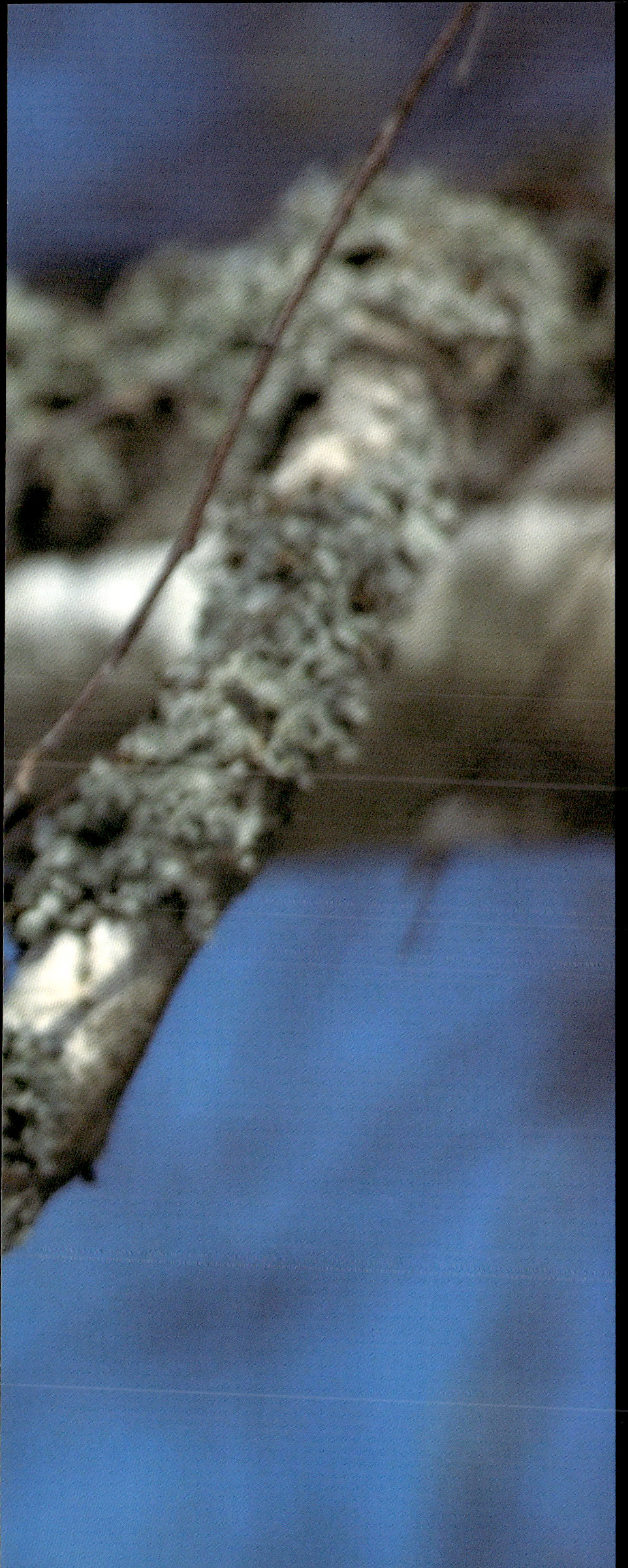

Pygmy owl stare

SPECIALLY COMMENDED

Ilkka Räsänen

FINLAND

'I had just got back from school', says Ilkka, 'when a friend phoned to say that a small owl had landed in his back garden. I grabbed my camera and my uncle – and we sped off.' The owl was waiting for them, perched on a branch complete with lichen and a blue backdrop – the perfect stage. 'I managed to creep very close,' says Ilkka, 'and was so excited to have eye contact.'

Nikon D70s with Nikkor 300mm f4D lens and 1.4x teleconverter; 1/600 sec at f6.3; 400 ISO; monopod.

Index of Photographers

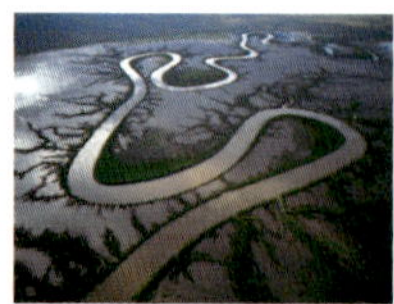
102
Theo Allofs (Germany)
allofsphoto@northwestel.net
www.theoallofs.com

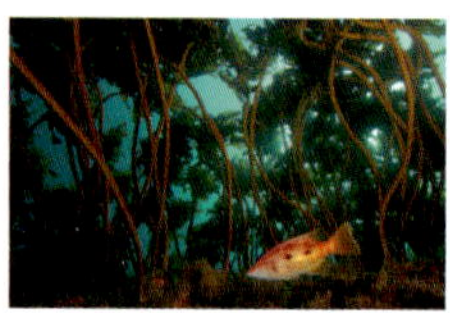
58
Ross Armstrong (New Zealand)
ross@oceanwildlife.com
www.oceanwildlife.com

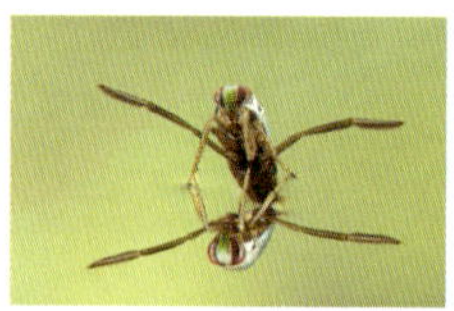
71
Ingo Arndt (Germany)
ingo@ingoarndt.com
www.arndt-photo.com
Agents
www.mindenpictures.com
www.naturepl.com

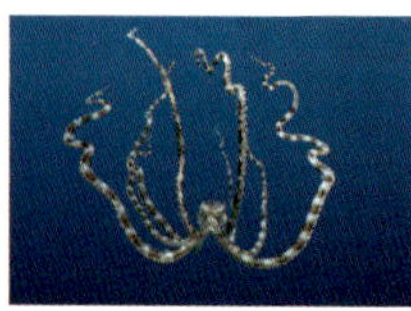
52
Michael AW (Singapore)
one@michaelaw.com
www.michaelaw.com

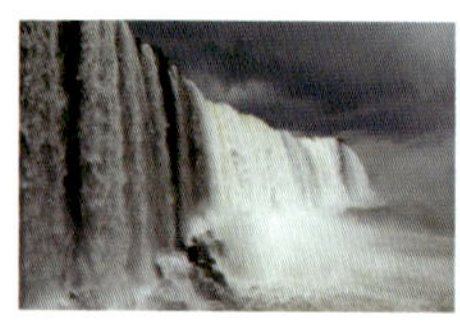
106
Jan Baks (The Netherlands)
janbaks@gmail.com
www.kopvangoeree.net
Agents
www.alamy.com
www.fotonatura.com

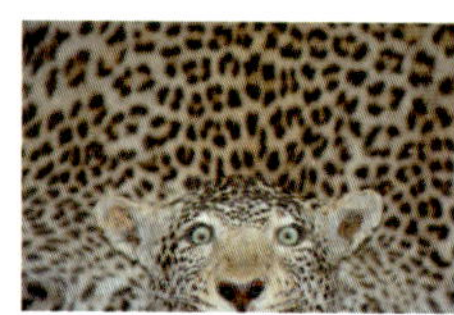
112
Alessandro Bee (Italy)
alessandrobee@hotmail.com
www.alessandrobee.it

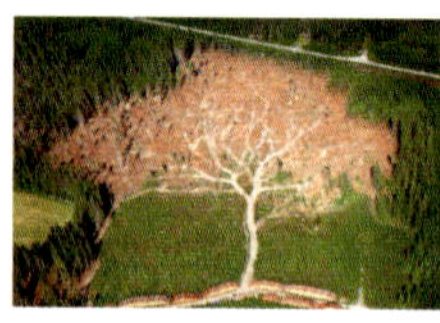
108
Jocke Berglund (Sweden)
flygbilder@telia.com
www.fotoflyget.se

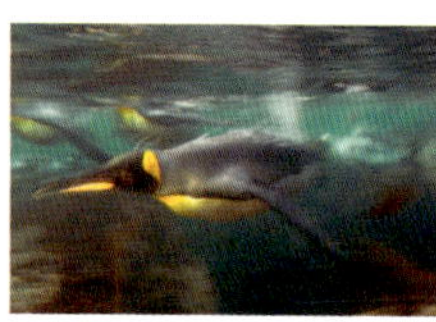
60
Tobias Bernhard (Germany)
wildimages@hotmail.com
www.tobibernhard.com
Agents
www.corbis.com
www.gettyimages.com
www.osf.co.uk
www.zefa.de

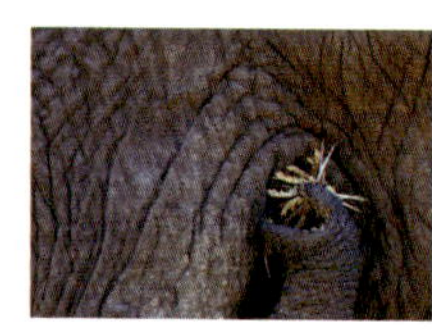
94
Andy Biggs (USA)
andybiggs@gmail.com
www.andybiggs.com

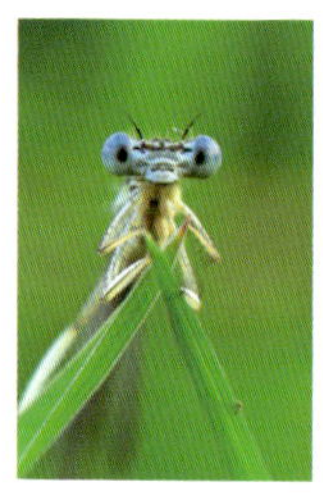
70
Theo Bosboom (The Netherlands)
bosboom@dirkzwager.nl
www.theobosboom.nl

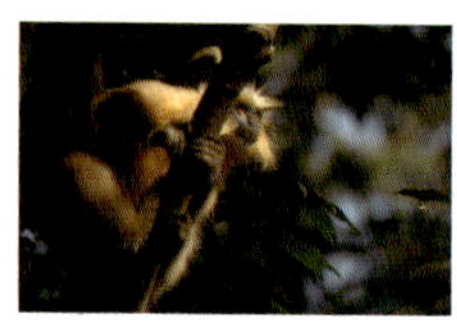
120
Bernard Castelein (Belgium)
bernard.castelein@skynet.be
Agent
www.naturepl.com

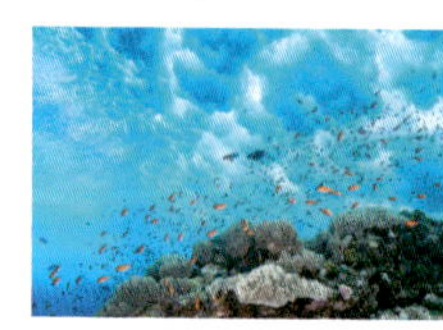
100
Jordi Chias (Spain)
jordi@uwaterphoto.com
www.uwaterphoto.com

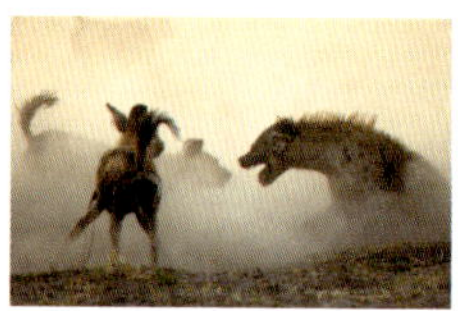
19
Christophe Courteau (France)
courteau.photo@wanadoo.fr
www.christophe-courteau.com
Agent
www.naturepl.com

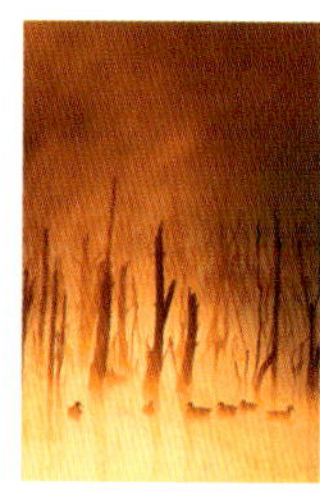
48
Arnaud Darondeau (France)
marie-noelle.darondeau@wanadoo.fr

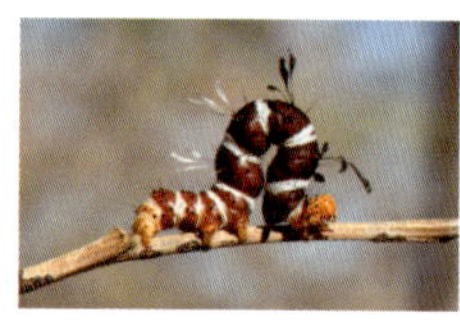

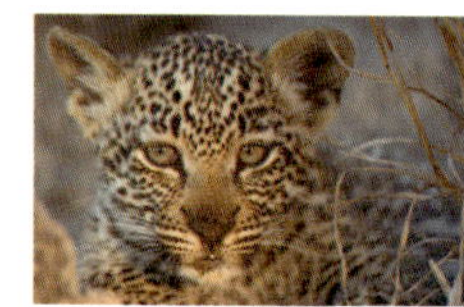
146, 147
Kyle Dickerson (South Africa)
jennette@nelspruitonline.co.za

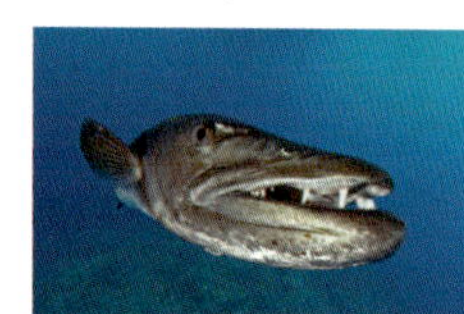
62
Tibor Dombovári (Hungary)
dombovari@chello.hu
www.dombovaritibor.hu

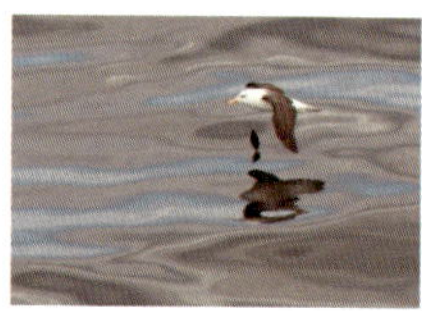
50
Pat Douglass (UK)
xpandinghorizons@btinternet.com
www.xpandinghorizons.co.uk

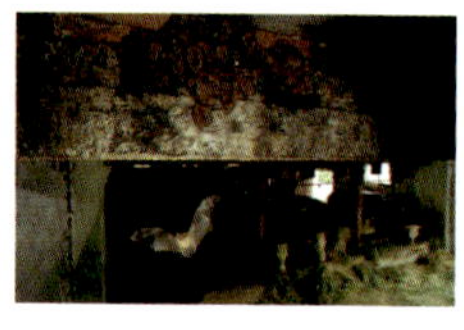
82
Klaus Echle (Germany)
echle.alpirsbach@t-online.de

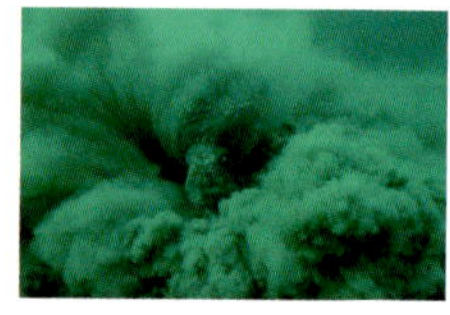
14, 16
Göran Ehlmé (Sweden)
goran@waterproof.se

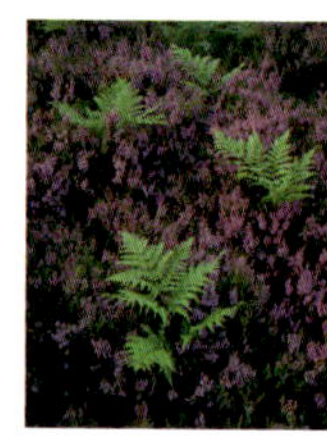
77
Per-Olov Eriksson (Sweden)
po.eriksson@mbox303.swipnet.se
Agent
www.woodfall.com

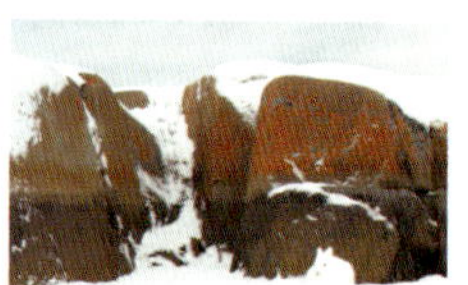
40
Cheryl A Ertelt (USA)
ndcheryl@aol.com
www.photosphrases.com

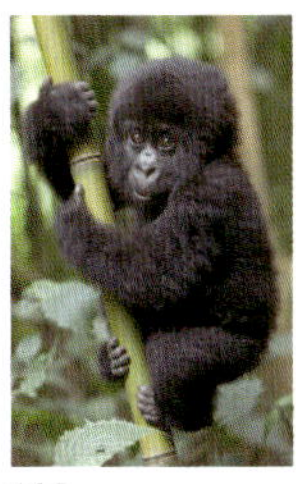

116
Suzi Eszterhas (USA)
suzi@eszterhasphotography.com
www.eszterhasphotography.com
Agents
www.animalsanimals.com
www.mindenpictures.com
www.naturepl.com

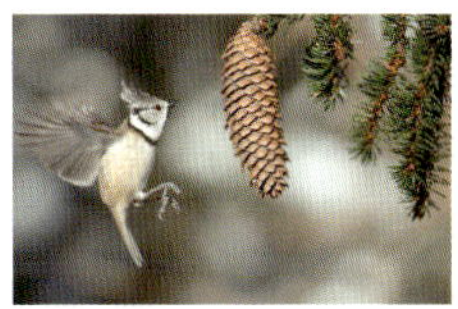

145
Alberto Fantoni (Italy)
fantoniluca4@virgilio.it

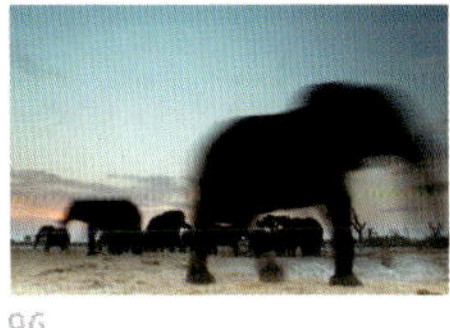

96
Lorenz Andreas Fischer (Switzerland)
lafischer@allvisions.ch
www.allvisions.ch
Agent
www.allvisions.ch

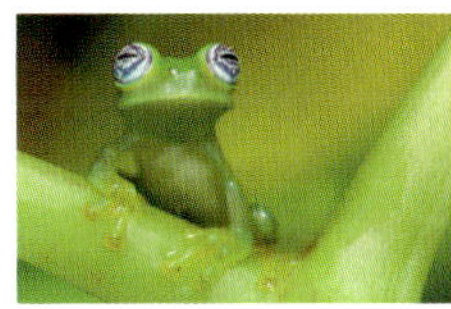

66
Edwin Giesbers (The Netherlands)
info@edwingiesbers.nl
www.edwingiesbers.nl

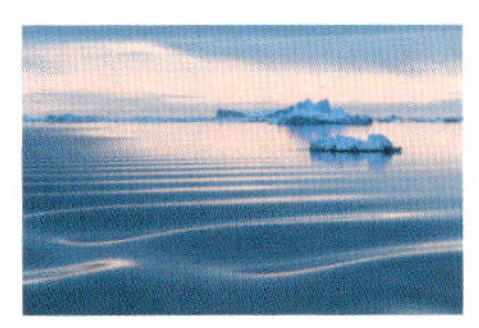

104
Daisy Gilardini (Switzerland)
dgilardini@bluewin.ch
www.daisygilardini.com

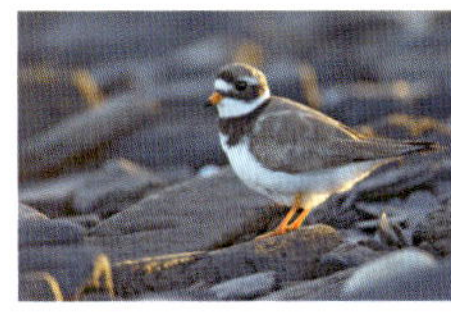

148
Fergus Gill (UK)
fergusgill@hotmail.co.uk

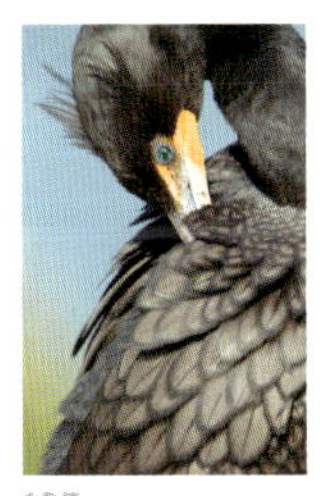

137
Evan Graff (USA)
egraff89@yahoo.com
www.philzworld.com/evanzworld/

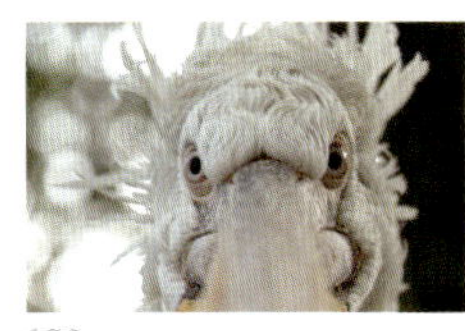

150
Nils Grundmann (Germany)
info@farben-koennen-zaubern.de

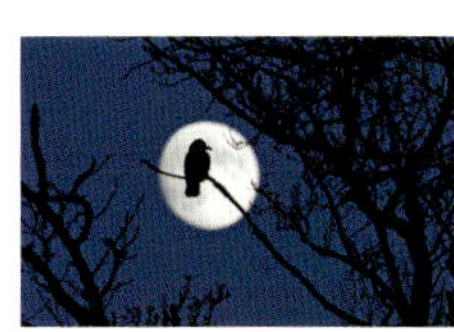

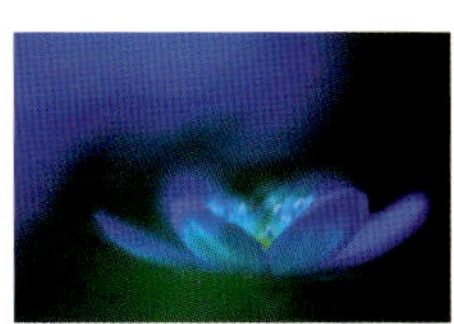

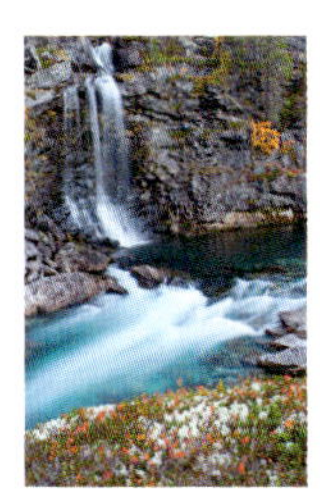

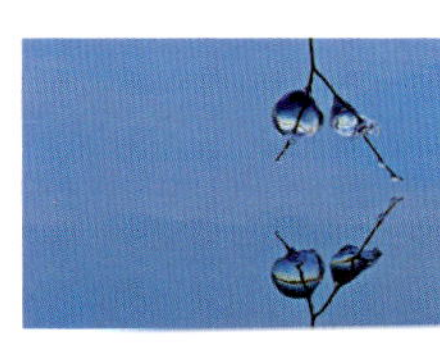

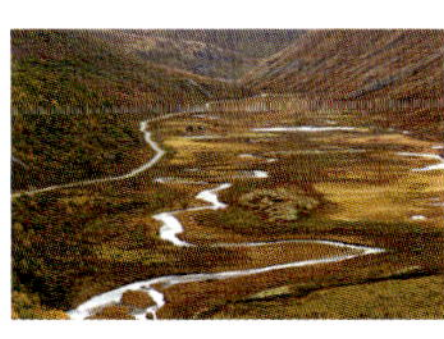

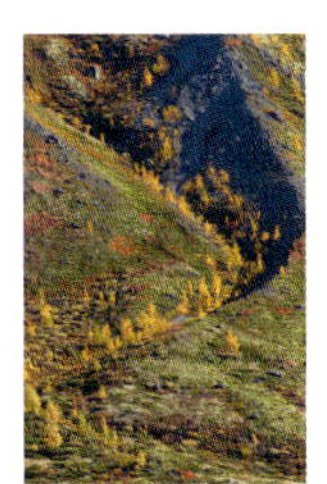

122 129
Serkan Günes (Turkey/Sweden)
info@serkangunes.com
www.serkangunes.com

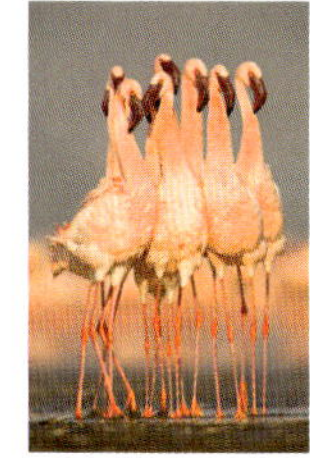

22
Todd Gustafson (USA)
gustaphoto@aol.com
www.gustafsonphotosafari.com

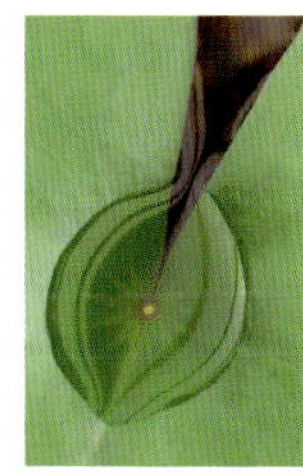

74
Dirk Heckmann (Germany)
dhfotografie@aol.com
www.farben-koennen-zaubern.de

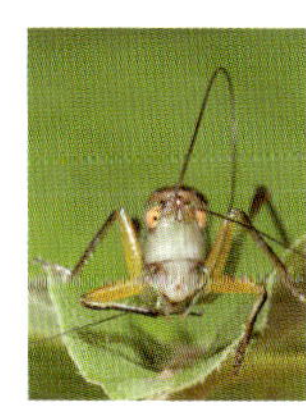

36
Wil Hershberger (USA)
woodsong_wv@earthlink.net
www.natureimagesandsounds.com

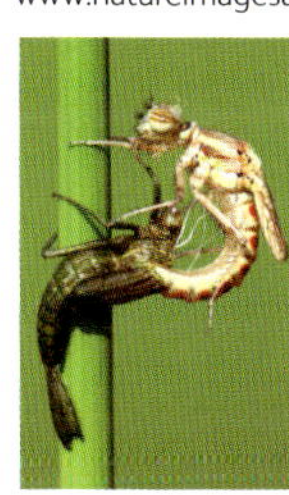

34
Ross Hoddinott (UK)
info@rosshoddinott.co.uk
www.rosshoddinott.co.uk
Agent
www.naturepl.com

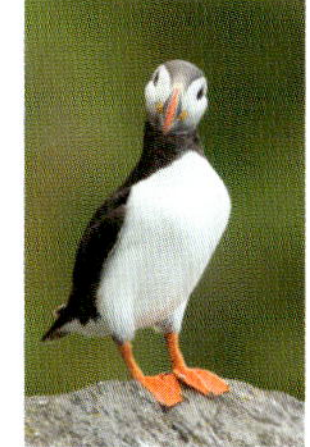

144
Adrien Imre (Hungary)
info@imre-photo.com
www.imre-photo.com

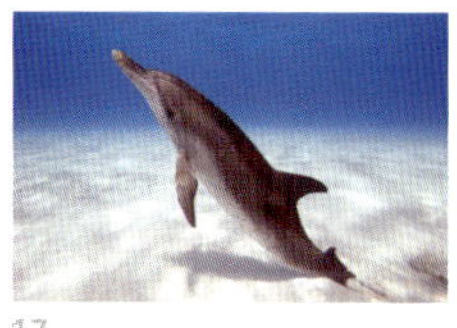

17
John Johnson (USA)
john@onebreathphoto.com
www.onebreathphoto.com

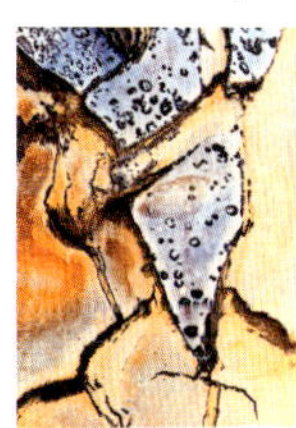

95
Katherine Keates (Canada)
k-keates@sympatico.ca
www.miragephotoart.com

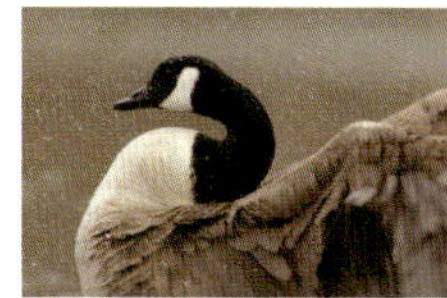

139
Avi Kenny (USA)
avi.kenny@gmail.com
www.avikennyphotography.com

Index of Photographers

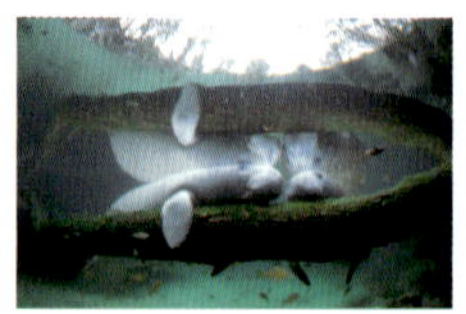

118
Jun Kezuka (Japan)
vzh02610@nifty.ne.jp

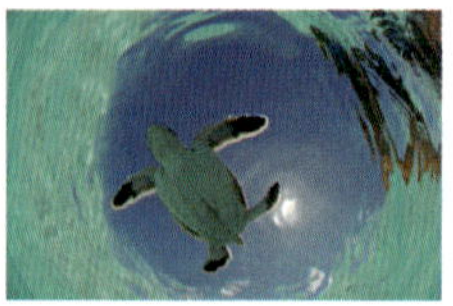

56
Willem Kolvoort (The Netherlands)
kolphot@hetnet.nl
www.kolvoortonderwaterfoto.nl
Agent
www.fotonatura.com

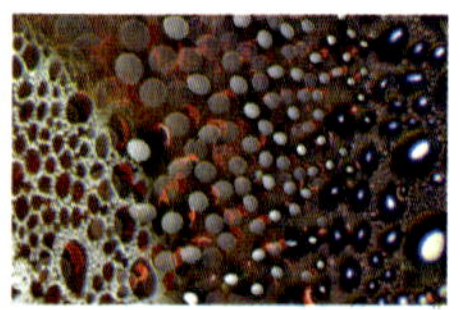

86
Juhani Kosonen (Finland)
juhani.kosonen@kymp.net

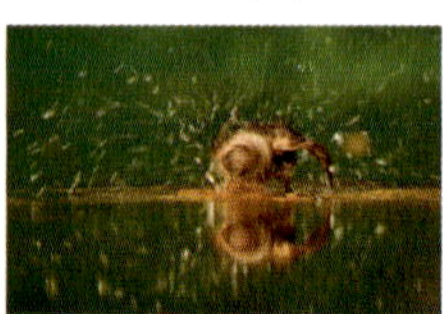

142
Péter Kovács (Hungary)
fox91@t-online.hu
www.kovacsfoto.com

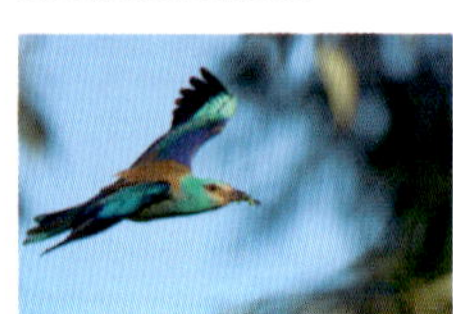

134
Mateusz Kowalski (Poland)
foto@mateuszkowalski.art.pl
www.mateuszkowalski.art.pl

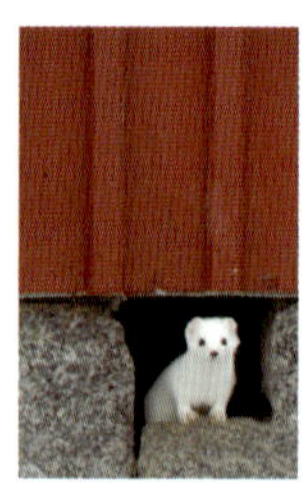

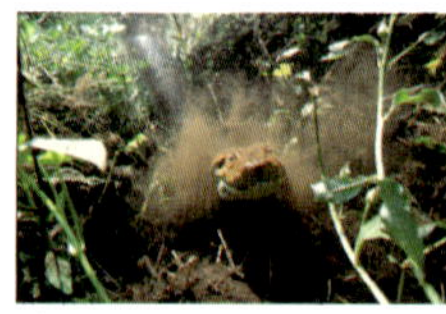

85,113
Peter Lilja (Sweden)
peter@peterlilja.com
www.peterlilja.com
Agent
www.gettyimages.com

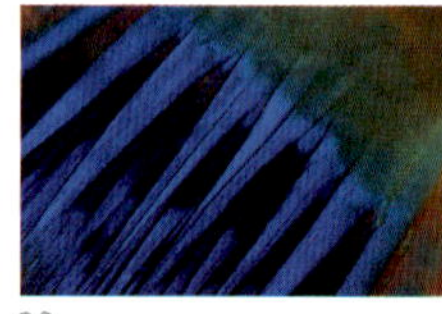

49
Michel Loup (France)
loupmichel@wanadoo.fr
www.michelloup.com

90
Magnus Lundgren (Sweden)
magnus@aquagraphics.se
www.aquagraphics.se

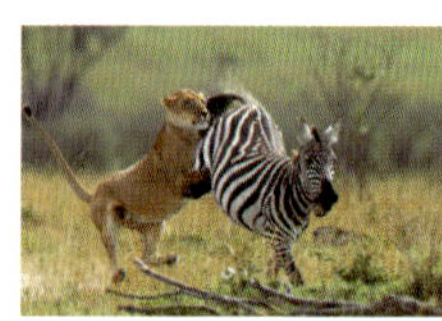

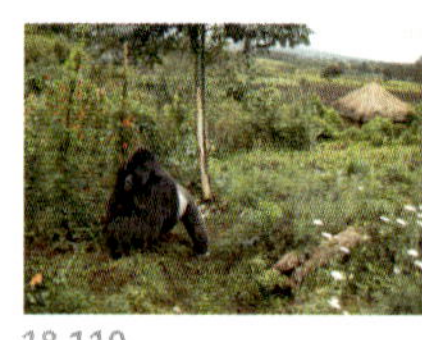

18,110
Joe McDonald (USA)
hoothollow@acsworld.com
www.hoothollow.com

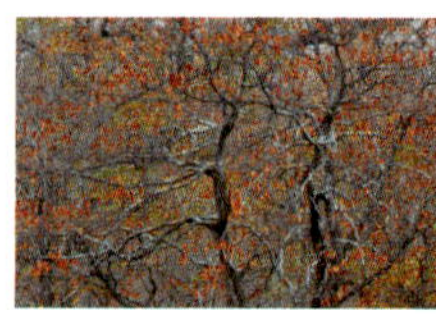

78
Johann C Mader (South Africa)
jcmader@mweb.co.za
www.afri-foto.co.za

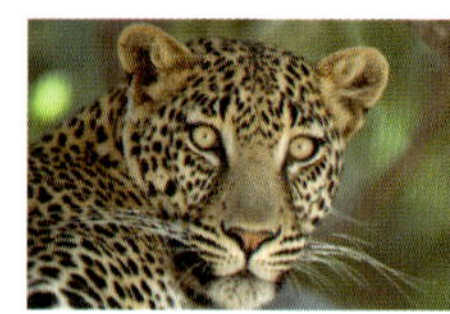

136
Luke Marazzi (UK)
marmaluke@gmail.com
Agent
www.papiliophotos.com

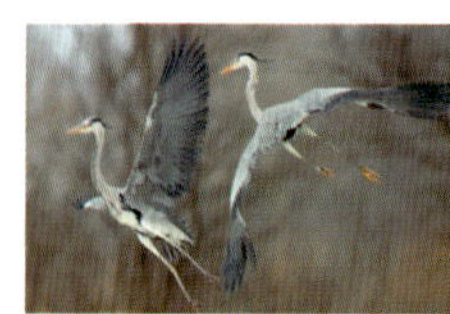

28
Bence Máté (Hungary)
bence@matebence.hu
www.matebence.hu
Agent
foto@matebence.hu

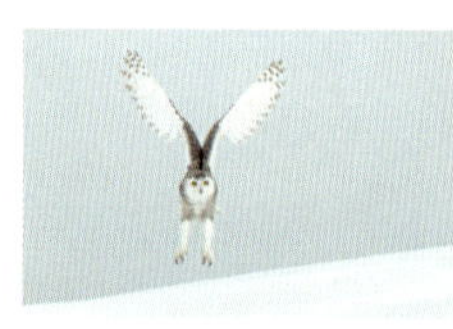

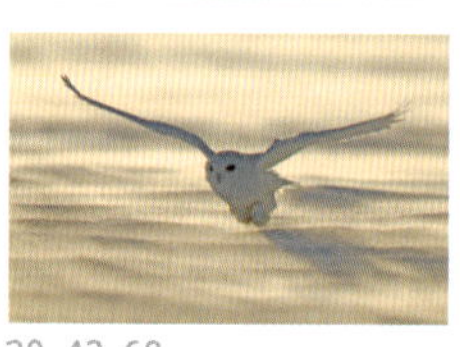

20, 42, 68
Vincent Munier (France)
photo@vincentmunier.com
www.vincentmunier.com
Agent
www.naturepl.com

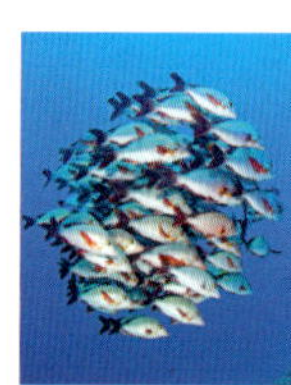

37
Alexander Mustard (UK)
alex@amustard.com
www.amustard.com

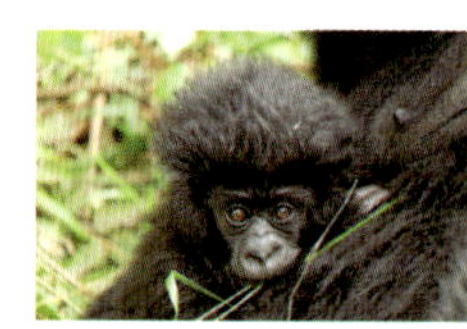

138
Cameron Amadeus Myhrvold (USA)
biagia98039@hotmail.com

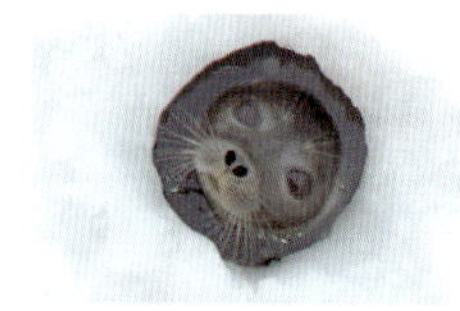

64
Baard Næss (Norway)
baar-na@online.no

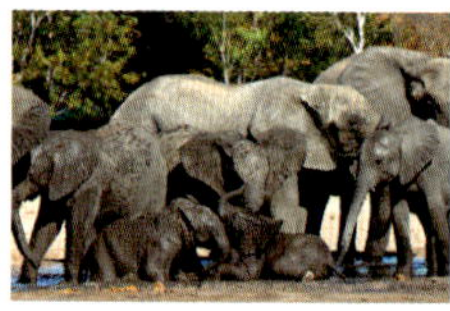

152
Anais Nussaume (Thailand)
marcnus@hotmail.com
www.marcnus-photography.com

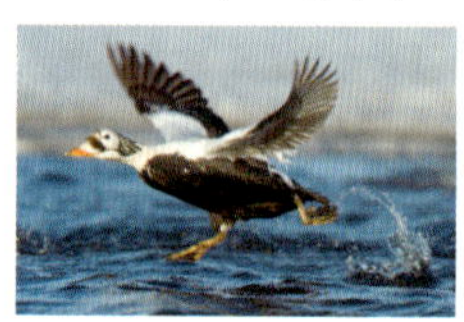

114
Stig Frode Olsen (Norway)
stigfolsen@c2i.net

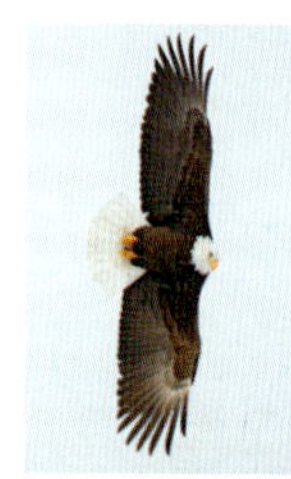

30
Robert O'Toole (USA)
rmotoole@gmail.com
www.robertotoole.com

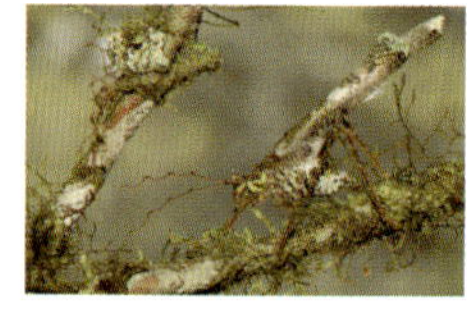

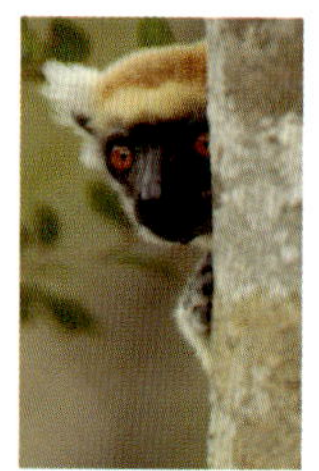

44, 117
Pete Oxford (UK)
pete@peteoxford.com
www.peteoxford.com
Agent
www.mindenpictures.com

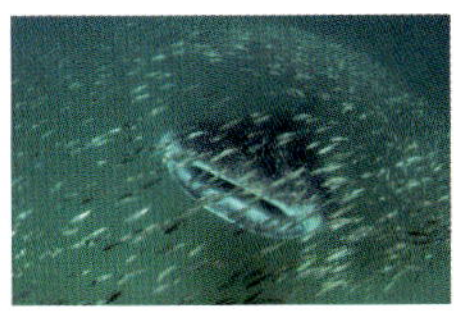

57
Gavin Parsons (UK)
gavin@h2o-images.co.uk
www.h2o-images.co.uk

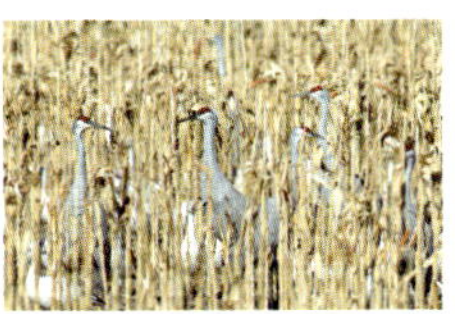

46
Laszlo Perlaky (USA)
naturalperl@houston.rr.com
www.naturalperl.com

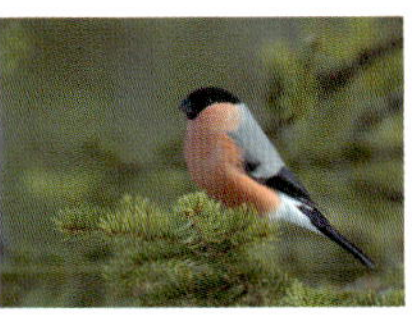

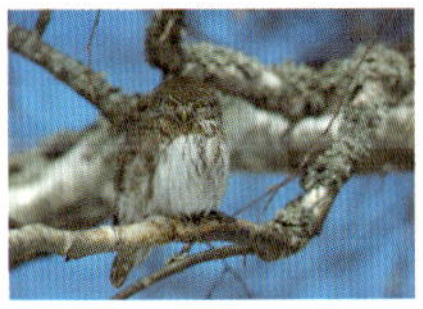

153, 154
Ilkka Räsänen (Finland)
ilkkao.rasanen@pp.inet.fi

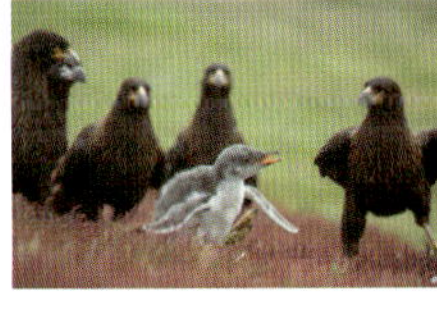

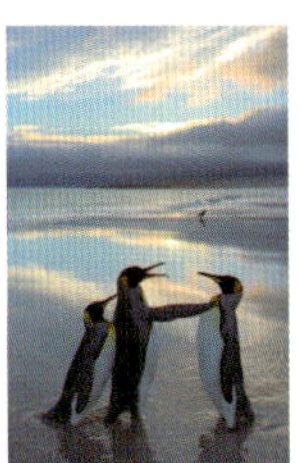

26, 29
Andy Rouse (UK)
sales@andyrouse.co.uk
www.andyrouse.co.uk

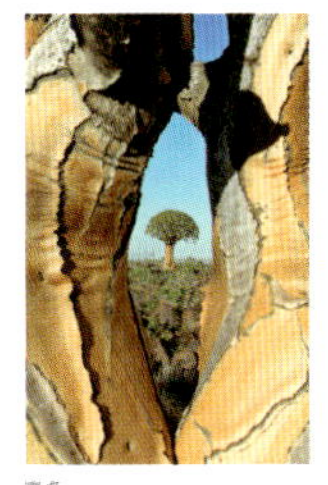

76
Steffen Sailer (Germany)
info@sailer-images.com
www.sailer-images.com

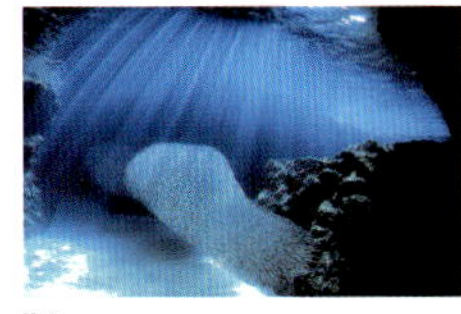

54
Manu San Félix (Spain)
manu@vellmari.com

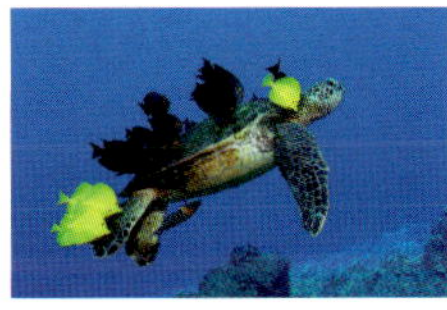

32
Andre Seale (Brazil/USA)
aseale@artesub.com
www.artesub.com

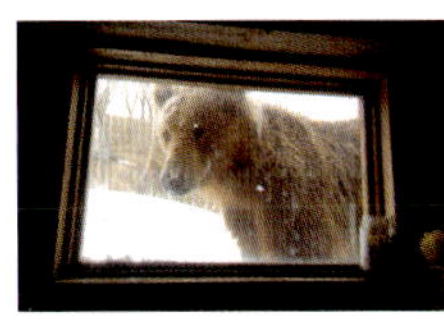

80
Igor Shpilenok (Russia)
shpilenok@mail.ru
www.shpilenok.com
Business manager: Laura Williams
as above

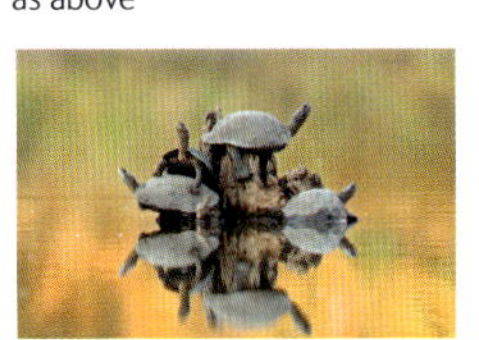

35
Manoj C Sindhgi (India)
mcsindhgi@gmail.com
www.manojcsindagi.in

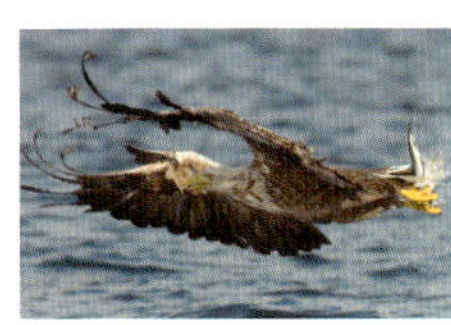

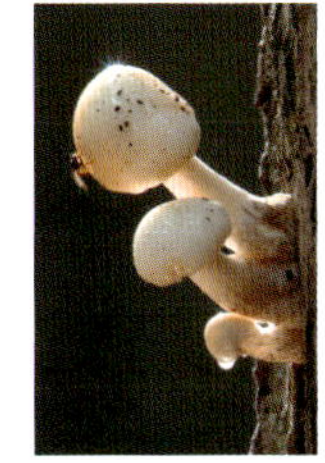

132, 140
Mart Smit (The Netherlands)
mart@martsmit.nl
www.martsmit.nl

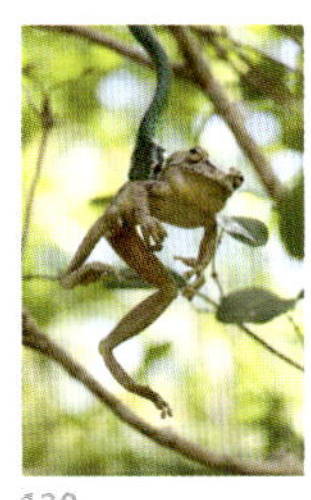

130
Rick Stanley (USA)
jkhs@msn.com

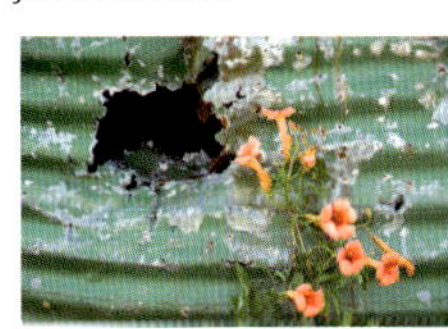

135
Daniel Tregeagle (Australia)
daniel@tregeagle.org

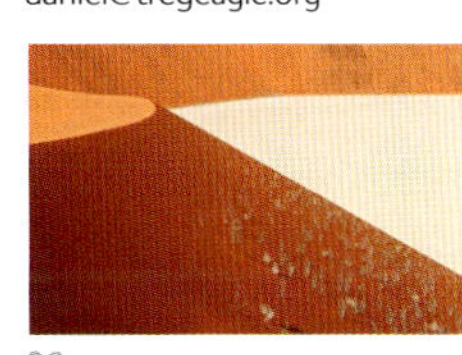

98
Bernard van Dierendonck
(The Netherlands)
bernivd@bluewin.ch
www.vandierendonck.ch
Agent
www.look-foto.de

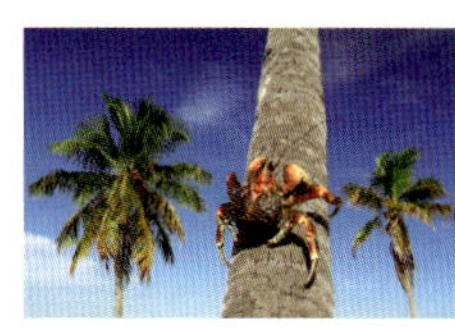

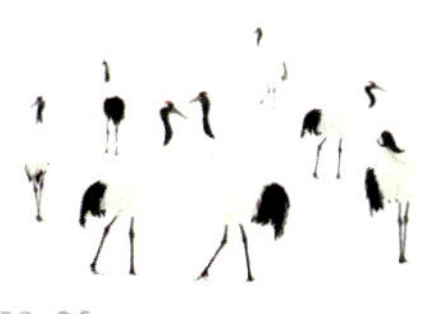

38, 88
Jan Vermeer (The Netherlands)
janvermeer.foto@planet.nl
www.janvermeer.nl
Agent
www.fotonatura.com

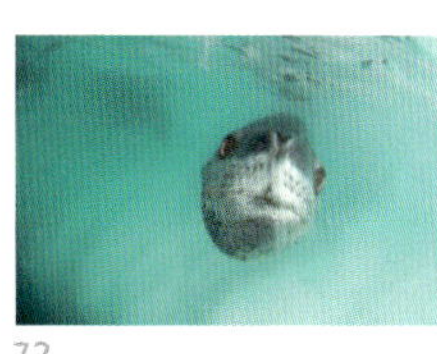

72
Carlos Villoch (Spain)
carlos@villoch.com
www.magicsea.com

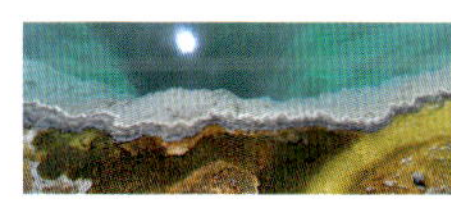

92
Benjamin D Walls (USA)
info@benjamindwalls.com
www.wallsphoto.com

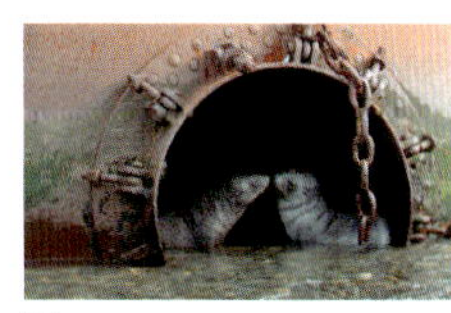

84
Fanus Weldhagen (South Africa)
fanus@afrifoto.co.za
www.afrifoto.co.za

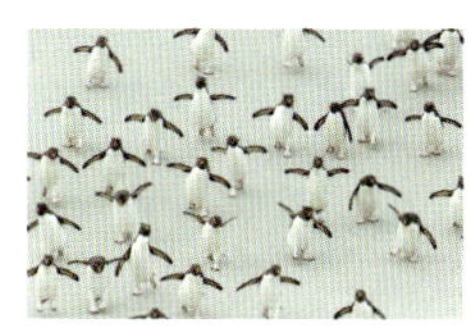

24
Solvin Zankl (Germany)
info@solvinzankl.com
www.solvinzankl.com
Agent
www.naturepl.com

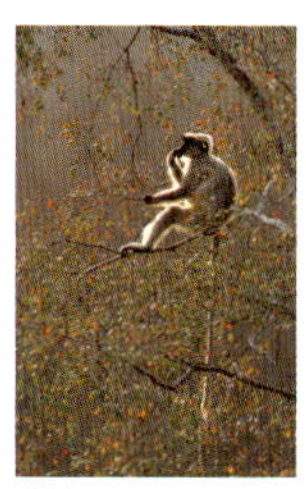

121
Jean-Pierre Zwaenepoel
(Belgium)
jp.zwaenepoel@telenet.be
Agent
www.naturepl.com